Reviewed by Ian Newboul...
Historical Review, 98 (December, ...,

D1002128

Catholic Emancipation

Catholic
Emancipation

A Shake to Men's Minds

WENDY HINDE

BLACKWELL
Oxford UK & Cambridge USA

Copyright © Wendy Hinde 1992

The right of Wendy Hinde to be identified as author of this work has
been asserted in accordance with the Copyright, Designs and
Patents Act 1988.

First published 1992

Blackwell Publishers
108 Cowley Road
Oxford OX4 1JF
UK

Three Cambridge Center
Cambridge, Massachusetts 02142
USA

All rights reserved. Except for the quotation of short passages for the
purposes of criticism and review, no part may be reproduced, stored in
a retrieval system, or transmitted, in any form or by any means,
electronic, mechanical, photocopying, recording or otherwise, without
the prior permission of the publisher.

Except in the United States of America, this book is sold subject to the
condition that it shall not, by way of trade or otherwise, be lent, resold,
hired out, or otherwise circulated without the publisher's prior consent
in any form of binding or cover other than that in which it is published
and without a similar condition including this condition being imposed
on the subsequent purchaser.

British Library Cataloguing in Publication Data
A CIP catalogue record for this book is available from the British
Library.

Library of Congress Cataloging-in-Publication Data
Hinde, Wendy.
Catholic emancipation: a shake to men's minds/Wendy Hinde.
p.   cm.
Includes bibliographical references and index.
ISBN 0-631-16783-8 (alk. paper)
1. Ireland—History—1800–1837.   2. Catholic emancipation.
I. Title.
DA950.3.H54   1992   91-29537
941.5081—dc20   CIP

Typeset in Baskerville on 10/12 pt
by Best-set Typesetter Ltd., Hong Kong
Printed in Great Britain by
TJ Press (Padstow) Ltd, Padstow, Cornwall

This book is printed on acid-free paper

Contents

Illustrations

Preface and Acknowledgements

The Catholic question – political equality for the Roman Catholics – was the most intractable and divisive issue in English domestic politics for the first thirty years of the nineteenth century. It aroused genuine fears for the constitutional stability of the state as well as deep religious prejudices, and it could not be ignored, or only intermittently, because of the imperative need to pacify Ireland and an increasingly more liberal climate of opinion in England. In this book I examine the train of circumstances and the interaction of events and personalities which brought the issue to a crisis – threatening civil war in Ireland – at this particular time, and how the British government, headed by the Duke of Wellington, managed to overcome the obstacles to a settlement. The historic significance of this settlement, apart from its significance for individual Catholics, can be disputed, but that does not detract from the intrinsic interest of how it was achieved.

I should like to express my warm thanks to Mrs Sue Dearden for reading an early draft, and to Professor Owen Chadwick and Dr Boyd Hilton for reading and commenting on the completed manuscript. Any deficiencies in judgement and fact are entirely my own.

I would like to thank the Marquess of Anglesey and the Deputy Keeper of the Records of Northern Ireland for their kind permission to quote from the Anglesey Papers deposited in the Public Record Office of Northern Ireland. I would also like to thank the Controller of Her Majesty's Stationery Office for permission to quote from Crown copyright material.

Introduction

'If every sect of religion be admitted to an equal share of government, the Protestant religion will cease to become what we have hitherto considered it – an essential portion of our glorious constitution . . .'

John Leslie Foster, MP for County Louth, to the House of Commons,
28 February 1825

For the first three decades of the nineteenth century Catholic emancipation was the most controversial and intractable issue in English politics. It could not be ignored – or only intermittently – because of its intimate connection with the endemic unrest in Ireland, and it could not be settled because it aroused such profound emotions and prejudices. To deny a man his full political rights – in other words, his right to sit in Parliament and to hold political office – simply because of his religious beliefs was increasingly coming to be seen as unjust, illiberal and altogether contrary to the 'spirit of the age'. It was also unwise and dangerously insensitive to refuse to remove a grievance which, to the predominantly Catholic Irish, was the chief symbol of English oppression. The opposition to these rational views was founded on ancestral memories of Protestant martyrs burnt at the stake in Mary's reign and a despotic Catholic king, James II, who himself owed allegiance to a foreign potentate – the Pope. It also sprang from a determination to preserve inviolate the constitutional settlement of 1689 which, it was assumed, had preserved Britain from the revolutionary turmoil recently witnessed in France and

Throughout this book, the terms 'Protestant' and 'pro-Catholic' refer to attitudes against or for Catholic emancipation, not to religious beliefs.

would continue to protect its citizens from arbitrary rule. It was reinforced by a chronic dislike and distrust of the Irish and a fear that what they were really after was not political equality alone but separation – if not complete separation, at least a separate Parliament.

When in 1801 William Pitt tried to bring peace and stability to Ireland through a union of the Westminster and Dublin Parliaments, he gave the Catholics the impression that they would soon be accorded their full political rights. But George III was convinced that if he gave political equality to the Roman Catholics he would be breaking his coronation oath to maintain the rights and privileges of the Church of England. The fact that the oath had been introduced in 1689 to meet a danger that no longer existed was to him irrelevant. Pitt failed to overcome the King's conscientious scruples and felt obliged to resign. When he resumed office three years later he promised the King not to raise the Catholic issue; however, the Whig Ministry of All the Talents, formed after Pitt's death in January 1806, was forced to do so by the unrest in Ireland. It quarrelled with the King over a measure of partial Catholic relief and was dismissed after less than fifteen months in office.

When the Prince of Wales became Regent five years later, his conscience – contrary to expectations – proved no more accommodating than his father's had been. In any case, the Tories, whom he had asked to remain in office, were so sharply divided on the Catholic issue that the Prime Minister, Lord Liverpool, found it expedient to make it an open question on which ministers could, in their individual capacity, speak and vote as they chose. Henceforward, throughout Liverpool's long fifteen-year premiership, there was not, and could not be, any official attempt by the government to use its authority to push through a settlement. In 1812 it looked as if one might be achieved without government help. George Canning, not at that time a member of the government, introduced a motion to consider the Catholic disabilities; the Commons accepted it by a majority of more than a hundred. But next year a Catholic relief bill was so vehemently denounced by the Irish Catholics because it included 'securities' designed to remove Protestant fears, and was so drastically watered down by Protestant diehards in the Commons, that its author, the famous Irish orator Henry Grattan, eventually abandoned it in despair. The issue continued to be raised and debated almost every year, but it was not until 1821 that a bill to emancipate the Catholics passed through the House of Commons, only to be thrown out by the Lords. Four years later a similar bill met a similar fate.

When in February 1825 Canning, now Foreign Secretary, spoke in favour of a motion to consider the whole Catholic issue, he told the Commons that he could hardly imagine on what grounds it could be opposed; 'he could not by any process of reasoning understand why all the subjects of the same kingdom . . . – those who lived in the same country, mingled in the daily offices of life, and professed a common Christianity – should be excluded from the common benefits of the constitution of their country.'[1] There was, however, as he well knew, much more to it than that. Under the constitutional settlement of 1689 the country had prospered greatly. It had been spared civil strife at home and had grown powerful and respected abroad. The Anglican Church was an integral part of this settlement; as the established Church it was believed to be linked indissolubly to the state. To give political power to the members of another religious denomination would, it was believed, undermine the Church's security and authority and consequently threaten the stability of the state. To Lord Eldon, the leader of the extreme reactionary Tories (known as ultras), the only safe course was to exclude every variety of non-Anglican – Dissenters as well as Catholics. 'The Church . . . was essentially and inseparably connected with part of the State. . . . The Constitution required that the Church of England should be supported; and the best way of affording that support to her was to admit only her own members to offices of trust and emolument.'[2]

Nobody advocated penalizing a man for his religious beliefs as such. (After all, Queen Elizabeth had given high office to Catholics whose loyalty she could trust.) But it was difficult to argue that religious beliefs had nothing to do with politics when the King's forebears had been brought to the throne precisely because they held certain religious beliefs and would protect the Protestant religious establishment of the country which a Catholic monarch was threatening to overthrow. On the whole, the Dissenters were accepted as loyal subjects and most people would not have objected to granting them the theoretical right to full equality which they already largely enjoyed in practice. The problem with the Roman Catholics was that their religion was believed to imply a degree of intolerance, disloyalty – or at least divided loyalty – and dissimulation that in the eyes of many honest Britons made them quite unfit to enjoy the privileges of full citizenship. Sir Edward Knatchbull, a well-known Tory back-bencher, told his Kentish constituents in 1826 that he would give religious toleration to everybody, but he 'would not give political power to those persons who would not tolerate the religions of others'.[3] A few years earlier one of Lord Sidmouth's correspondents declared that he was willing to give the Catholics 'all the civil and religious liberty that they can enjoy'; but he would not give them 'a *legislative authority* which their principles would oblige them to use for the suppression of *heresy*, that is in their language *Protestantism*, and the establishment of the Papal faith and influence over the British dominions . . .'.[4]

Roman Catholicism was seen as an intolerant, proselytizing and authoritarian creed that would never be content to co-exist with the Protestant Church, and which, moreover, could command the un-questioning obedience of those who professed it. The Roman Catholic Church's principles, declared Eldon, 'are founded in ecclesiastical tyranny, and ecclesiastical tyranny must produce civil despotism'.[5] Moreover, Catholics divided their allegiance between Pope and King, and since the Pope was a foreign potentate who might exercise his authority in ways inimical to the state their loyalty was suspect. So too was their good faith in political matters, for it was widely, if erroneously, believed, even by men of such distinction as Locke and John Wesley, that a priest could absolve a Catholic from any under-taking made to a heretic. (Yet Catholics were excluded from political life because they refused to take the oaths that they were alleged not to respect.) Most educated people (but not the mob) did not believe that the Pope himself represented much of a threat once he was no longer under Napoleon's thumb. But they were concerned about the influence of the Catholic bishops and clergy, above all in Ireland where they were associated with nationalist aspirations, and where the established Protestant Church was especially vulnerable to en-croachment by the Church to which the great majority of the popu-lation belonged.

Lord Liverpool, a moderate opponent of the Catholic claims, told the House of Lords in 1825 that he objected to the doctrines and dogmas of the Roman Catholic Church – '. . . not to the doctrine of transubstantiation or purgatory, but to the power, the temporal, the practical power of its priesthood over all the relations of private life'.[6] Even so rational and sensible a person as Robert Peel confessed to the Commons that although he never allowed religious differences to affect his private relations, he did have a distrust of the Roman Catholic religion.

> Could any man acquainted with the state of the world doubt for a
> moment that there was engrafted on the Catholic religion something
> more than a scheme for promoting mere religion? . . . Could he know
> what the doctrine of absolution, of confession, of indulgences was,
> without a suspicion that these doctrines were maintained for the pur-

pose of establishing the power of man over the hearts and minds of men?[7]

The advocates of Catholic relief argued that times had changed. 'When I hear', wrote Sydney Smith, the well-known Whig preacher, wit and polemicist, 'any man talk of an unalterable law, the only effect it produces on me is to convince me that he is an unalterable fool.'[8] But those with an instinctive fear of Catholicism were not impressed by the argument that the laws penalizing the Catholics had been introduced to meet specific dangers which no longer existed and had therefore lost their point. 'The very mention of his holiness, the Pope of Rome', remarked the radical aristocrat, Sir Francis Burdett, 'seems to raise, in the minds of some men, images of horror – half historical, half romantic – which have nothing to do with the world as it now exists.'[9] Mockery moved such men as little as common sense. What exactly would these 'dreaded Catholics' do if they were emancipated? How could a few – or even a hundred – Catholic members change the character of Parliament? It was never suggested that the presence of a few 'gallant members' gave the House of Commons a military character. But the instinctive fear of Catholicism felt by Peel and so many others was absorbed unquestioningly from childhood. It formed the basic inspiration of innumerable speeches and pamphlets, embellished and amplified with abstruse excursions into the political and constitutional history of past centuries, or highly polemical (and irrelevant) digressions on the theological and ecclesiastical attributes of the Roman Catholic religion.

By the 1820s many Protestants felt that the limits of concessions to Catholics had been reached. During the eighteenth century the formidable apparatus of penal repression imposed during Elizabeth's reign, and after James II's unsuccessful attempt to regain his throne with the help of the Irish, had seldom been enforced very methodically or rigorously, and during the last quarter of the century much of it had been legally dismantled. The Catholics' freedom of worship was restored and a variety of galling restrictions removed. Catholics were, for instance, no longer forbidden to inherit, buy or lease land; to own a horse worth more than £5; to have their own schools; or to have more than two apprentices. Catholic solicitors were no longer confined to conveyancing work, and Catholics were allowed to practise as barristers (but not to take silk). In 1793 Irish Catholics were given the vote in parliamentary elections and made eligible to hold minor civil posts and junior commissioned rank in the army and navy. They owed these concessions to Pitt's anxiety to make sure of their loyalty in the war with revolutionary France; their co-religionists in England, who could not be considered any sort of threat, were not similarly favoured. In effect, however, both Irish and English Catholics were still largely excluded from public life – from sitting in Parliament and from holding a wide variety of posts in government service, the administration of justice, municipal government and the armed services – by reason of religious tests, or declarations, or oaths, with which they could not conscientiously comply.

In England the Catholic community was much too small to possess any political clout. But by the early nineteenth century it was growing steadily in size. (The number of Catholics in the country was also swollen by a greatly increased influx of Irish immigrants.) The English Catholics, like the rest of the population, were gradually moving from the country to the towns. The aristocracy and gentry who, together with their dependants and tenants, had worshipped in their own private chapels, served by their resident chaplains, were gradually dying out, or in some cases conforming to the established Church. The Catholic middle classes, on the other hand, were increasing in numbers and prosperity. There were no economic constraints to prevent Catholics from making money, and the spectacular expansion of industrial and commercial activity that characterized the period gave them unprecedented opportunities to do so. Catholic manufacturers, entrepreneurs and businessmen may have been responsible for only a very modest share of the whole country's economic expansion, but in terms of their own community it was a significant achievement. Their numbers were increased by recruits from the younger sons of the gentry and from farming families as well as through mixed marriages and conversions.

The Catholic clergy had never allowed the penal laws to stop them from saying Mass, but the removal of legal constraints on Catholic worship in 1791 encouraged them to extend their activities, and the rapidly expanding towns and industrial districts, where the established clergy were often thin on the ground, gave them ideal opportunities for missionary endeavour among all classes, from poor factory workers to middle-class business and professional families. Their work was underpinned by prosperous merchants and manufacturers who often contributed generously to the building of chapels and the support of the clergy.

There was still plenty of popular prejudice against the papists. The Gordon riots of 1780 were the last manifestation of large-scale anti-Catholic mob violence, and they were largely confined to London. But anti-papist hostility continued to simmer below the surface, stimulated by fears of the consequences for jobs and wages of the increasing number of Irish immigrants. From time to time hostility erupted into violence. On election day in East Retford in 1826 a 'no-popery' mob assailed one of the candidates with such vigour that the military had to be sent for to restore order. According to an eye-witness, the mob, although not drunk, cried 'we are betrayed' and 'they are all Romans'.[10] Although such violent scenes of unthinking prejudice were becoming more rare, virulent verbal and printed no-popery propaganda continued to a greater or lesser extent. It was, in fact, particularly powerful in the decades after Catholic emancipation.

On the whole, however, the attitude of those members of the educated classes who were not tainted by religious bigotry did not give the English Catholics a great deal to complain about. There was still some disapproval, even suspicion, as indeed there was until well into the twentieth century. But as the Catholics gradually ceased to keep themselves to themselves they did not find social barriers erected against them, and individual contacts and friendships punctured the traditional stereotype of the bigoted, priest-ridden, potentially disloyal Catholic. John Skinner, rector of the Somerset parish of Camerton, was agreeably surprised when, through their common interest in antiquarian research, he made the acquaintance of the Catholic Lord Arundell of Wardour. 'I am decidedly against the Catholic claims taken as a political measure', he confided to his journal on 4 January 1824; 'still, when there are such liberal-minded men who are excluded from a participation of [*sic*] what the most worthless and irreligious actually do enjoy, it then assumes a rather injurious appearance.' And after visiting a school run by a Catholic priest, he could not help asking himself: 'Are not these as likely to become good citizens and subjects as the puritanical levelling Methodists and Presbyterians?'[11] The Catholics, usually quiet and inoffensive, were not infrequently compared favourably with the noisy and assertive Methodists. (But Skinner remained firmly opposed to Catholic emancipation.)

In general, individual Catholics were judged by what they were, not by what archaic legislation supposed them to be; and these laws were increasingly ignored or circumvented. A Catholic was twice made lord mayor of York, and Catholics held other civic offices in the city. Some Catholics were able to hold commissions in the army because the authorities dispensed with the usual oath. Others, like William Jerningham who had served in the Austrian army, obtained a commission through family influence. But Lord Clifford, a prominent Devon Catholic, was refused a commission in the yeomanry in 1798, when a French invasion was believed to be imminent, although he had been closely involved in organizing the local defences. He formed a private force at his own expense, put them into uniforms of his own design and made himself their captain. They joined in exercises with the Devonshire yeomanry, and when peace was signed in 1802 the yeomanry officers presented Clifford with a silver urn. When the war was resumed he re-formed his private army and it was not finally disbanded until 1827.[12]

No one could hope to get a commission if George III knew he was a Catholic. Yet the King's conscientious scruples did not make Catholics less acceptable to him socially. They were received without question at court, sometimes on the most friendly terms, and were themselves allowed to entertain the royal family. When the King went to Essex in 1778 to review his troops, he and the Queen stayed for two nights with the Catholic Lord Petre. He once arrived by frigate at Lulworth Castle, the home of a wealthy Catholic family. The royal tour of inspection included a new Catholic chapel built in the grounds, inside which the local children were assembled to sing 'God Save the King'. This was two years before the penal constraints on Catholic worship were lifted and, not surprisingly, the King's host, Mr Weld, was very glad to get what amounted to royal approval for his new chapel. Afterwards he wrote to a Catholic friend: 'I think the King's seeing the Chapel in that public manner must be a kind of sanction to it.'[13]

Many English Catholics were, it seems, satisfied with the religious toleration they were granted in 1791 and were disinclined to agitate for anything more. But some undoubtedly resented their continued exclusion from political and public life, from the judicial bench and from commissioned rank in the armed services, especially when, in social and economic terms, they were on an equal footing with their Protestant neighbours. Even those without ambition for themselves must have felt the stigma of second-class citizenship. Lady Jerningham, who enjoyed the friendship of the royal family and an active social life in London, Brighton and Norfolk, can herself have had little to complain about. But she clearly felt considerable bitterness about the future of her grandson whose parents were obliged to say to him: 'You must be satisfied with your own correctness and not intermeddle with what is passing, as drawing breath in your own country is all that is allowed of.'[14]

Some 'meddling' was possible for Catholic landowners who had a parliamentary borough in their gift or who could control their tenants' votes at election times. Sheridan, always a staunch supporter of

Catholic emancipation, was returned half a dozen times for Stafford, where the Jerninghams had considerable influence. In 1811 he referred to 'the Jerninghams who in the handsomest manner have ever given me their warmest support',[15] and in the election the following year Edward Jerningham, a barrister and a prominent advocate of the Catholic claims, thought that 'by great personal exertion' he could muster nearly a hundred votes for Sheridan.[16] (Unfortunately, on this occasion the opposition proved too strong.) For men like Edward Jerningham the barriers that impeded their full participation in public life must have been hard to bear.

In their efforts to remove those barriers the English Catholics were beset by internal disagreements over the extent to which they could distance themselves from papal authority. They were also distracted by a continuing battle with their bishops to secure some lay participation in ecclesiastical affairs, such as the choice of bishops and parish organization. The first Catholic Committee, set up in 1778 to work for Catholic relief, was deliberately composed only of lay members mostly from the South and Midlands. Its efforts helped to secure a relief act which repealed some of the penal laws affecting the clergy and the ownership of land, and allowed Catholics to serve as privates in the army. (Although the concessions were modest they led to the Gordon riots.) When the committee was re-formed in 1782 its claim to speak for the whole Catholic community was not well received either by most of the clergy or by the conservative northern Catholics; nor were its efforts to emphasize the undivided loyalty of the English Catholics and minimize their connection with Rome. In its negotiations with the government for full religious toleration the committee accepted a form of oath to be taken by Catholic priests which the bishops thought implied far too sweeping a repudiation of the Pope's authority. They lobbied successfully to get it amended in the 1791 Act. Afterwards a conservative Catholic gentleman from Derbyshire thanked one of the bishops for having 'rescued us from the oppression not only of ancient penal statutes but also from the new more galling ones forged for us by our own *false* brethren'.[17]

When the Catholic Committee was wound up in 1792 some of its members formed the Cisalpine Club. They were anti-clerical in feeling and anxious to reach an accommodation with the state which would allow them to play their full part in public life. However, they were shunned by the clergy and the northern Catholics and their club never became an effective pressure group. In 1808 a new body, the Board of British Catholics, was set up. It included some clerical members, in particular the four vicars apostolic, but was predominantly lay in composition. In spite of the conciliatory efforts of the board's secretary, Edward Jerningham, the two sides, lay and clerical, were soon at loggerheads over a scheme to make emancipation acceptable by conceding a measure of royal control over episcopal appointments. Some of the Catholic clergy were prepared to negotiate on some form of veto, but they were overborne by Bishop Milner, vicar apostolic of the Midland district and the agent and mouthpiece of the Irish bishops. Milner was uncompromising in his defence of papal authority and in his hostility to any interference by the English Catholic laity in the affairs of their Church. He had no use for the Catholic Board whose members, he felt, were prepared to sacrifice the interests of their Church in return for concessions that would benefit only the Catholic aristocracy and gentry. The hostility between the two sides grew so bitter that in 1813 some opprobrious comments by Milner about the leaders of the Catholic laity led to his expulsion from the Board's select committee. For the next ten years the English Catholics remained divided and ineffective.

In Ireland, where the Catholics formed six-sevenths of the population, their predicament had a national dimension which gave it an enormously increased bitterness. But efforts to organize an effective agitation were handicapped by legal pitfalls, disagreements over tactics and, above all, deep divisions over whether or not to accept 'securities', in particular some form of government veto over episcopal appointments. Legally, the Irish were better off than the English Catholics. In practice, however, they were worse off. In England the penal laws against the Catholics tended not to be enforced; in Ireland Catholics were often excluded even from those posts they were entitled to hold. The Protestant minority, which enjoyed a virtual monopoly of power in central and local government, had no intention of relinquishing more of it than it had to, and after the final defeat of Napoleon in 1815 the authorities in London no longer had an incentive to insist on observance of the law. Catholics, for example, occupied only a tiny proportion of the minor judicial posts for which they were eligible. No Catholics were appointed to directorships of the Bank of Ireland after they became entitled to hold these posts in 1793. On grand juries Protestants of modest means were often preferred to Catholics with substantial properties. For the Catholic gentry, no longer barred from acquiring land, and the small but increasingly prosperous professional and commercial classes, it was all the more frustrating to be denied political equality when their material stake in the country was steadily growing.

But the great majority of Irish Catholics, who lived on and by the land, had only a precarious stake in the country. (The exception was Ulster, where the growth of industry relieved the pressure on the land and where there was a more equitable system of land tenure.) Their circumstances, of course, varied, but very many lived in a state of poverty described by Sir Walter Scott after a visit to Ireland in 1825 as being 'on the extreme verge of human misery'.[18] The land was their only resource and means of employment and as the population relentlessly increased, each family had to make do with less and less of it; only by the repeated division and subdivision of holdings could grown-up sons and daughters be provided with the means of survival for themselves and their offspring. The intense competition for land forced up rents. Absentee landlords spent their rental outside Ireland and in return contributed nothing, either material or moral, to the welfare of their tenants. Rapacious middlemen extorted so much in rent, produce and services that however hard their victims worked to improve their lot, they were left with only a bare subsistence. If threatened with eviction for rent arrears or for any other reason, a peasant had little other defence than to appeal to his landlord's compassion or to resort to violence.

Moreover, all Catholics who earned their living by cultivating the land were forced to pay tithes to the clergy of an alien and – as they believed – heretical Church. The Church of Ireland had been made one with the Church of England by the 1801 Act of Union and it was extremely resistant to change or reform. Its establishment consisted of four archbishops, eighteen bishops and about 2,000 other clergy. Its members numbered about 800,000 scattered among more than six million Catholics. In 1828 Thomas Creevey, the diarist, visited a large, well-populated parish in County Kilkenny where there was not a single Protestant except for the family at the 'big house' (but not their servants) and one other 'Ascendancy' family. The Protestant incumbent received £500 a year, and the Catholic priest £70.[19] The gross annual income of the Irish Church was more than £800,000 (very unequally distributed), of which well over half was obtained from tithes extracted from the members of another religion. To add injury to insult, the claims of the tithe-owner had precedence over those of the landlord, with the result that tithe payments could lead to rent arrears and possible eviction. In spite of attempts to improve the method of calculating the tithe, no other grievance aroused so much bitterness and violence.

A few landlords, both resident and absentee, did take their responsibilities seriously and did care about the welfare of their tenants.

Not all middlemen were hard-hearted despots. By the 1820s experienced observers (as opposed to transient visitors) felt that the peasants'
condition was improving by comparison with what it had been fifty
years earlier. But it was still very bad – as the endemic outbreaks of
violence by men made desperate by their plight made shockingly
clear. So did the witnesses brought to London to enlighten Parliament
about the state of Ireland. Between 1810 and 1833 Parliament appointed numerous royal commissions and select committees to try to
discover why Ireland was hardly ever free of violent unrest in one part
of the country or another. The great mass of factual information
collected clearly showed that Ireland could not be subjected to the full
rigours of *laissez-faire* economics, but it failed to stimulate persistent
and effective remedial action. In any case the English tended to
dismiss the Irish as turbulent savages. Even an educated man like
Robert Southey could write that nothing could redeem Ireland 'but a
system of Roman conquest and colonization – and shipping off the
refractory savages to the colonies'.[20] As Sydney Smith sadly noted,
'the moment the very name of Ireland is mentioned, the English seem
to bid adieu to common feeling, common prudence and common
sense, and to act with the barbarity of tyrants and the fatuity of
idiots.'[21]

Common sense might seem to indicate that Catholic emancipation
could contribute little or nothing towards improving the peasants' lot.
No peasant could aspire to the positions still barred to Catholics,
although a better-off tenant farmer might have ambitions for his son
or grandson which the existing law would frustrate. Opponents of
emancipation, especially those who lived in England, were never
tired of pointing out that the Irish peasant suffered from social and
economic ills, not political inequality, and moreover that a Catholic
landlord might treat him just as badly as a Protestant one. All this
was true, except in so far as emancipation might – it was hoped –
tranquillize the country and thereby encourage English investment in
a countryside starved of capital.

But most Irish peasants knew they were treated as second-class
citizens because of their religion; and although this might make little
or no practical difference, it made them feel that they belonged to a
conquered and degraded race, oppressed by alien rulers from whom
they could expect neither justice nor fair treatment. So they were
stung into relieving the frustrations of their hard and poverty-stricken
lives by taking the law into their own hands. They formed secret
societies; burned houses and property; maimed cattle; drove off constables trying to execute warrants; rescued men under arrest. A

magistrate from County Cork, giving evidence to a House of Lords committee in 1824, spoke of 'the total insignificance of the law'. He also said that the inequality of the Roman Catholics was 'an eternal source of discontent'.[22]

A prominent Irish Whig politician, Thomas Spring-Rice, spelled out to the House of Commons in March 1827 the consequences of failing to remove this gnawing discontent. Although, he said, the poorer classes might not expect to benefit directly from emancipation, 'its spirit, like the air, would influence them'. They knew that the law made an unjust distinction between Protestants and Catholics, and so long as they believed the law to be unjust,

> so long would life and property be without security; and so long would that unhappy country be the scene of discord and tumult. In England, the constable's staff was respected, by virtue of public opinion; but in Ireland the people had no confidence in the laws, and therefore, the usual and ordinary symbols of law excited other feelings than those of respect.[23]

The following year Daniel O'Connell was to demonstrate how effectively the Irish peasants could be mobilized, without breaking the law, in support of their political rights.

In the spring of 1823 O'Connell and another Catholic barrister, Richard Lalor Sheil, launched the Catholic Association. Sheil was the son of a Catholic merchant who had bought an estate in County Waterford. Called to the Irish Bar in 1814, he also made a name for himself as a dramatist and journalist and became deeply involved in Catholic politics. He had been in favour of conceding a veto over episcopal appointments in return for emancipation and in 1821 had quarrelled bitterly with O'Connell over this issue. In January 1823 the two men were reconciled and Sheil agreed to help O'Connell to reinvigorate the Catholic movement. At first it seemed unlikely that their initiative would be any more successful than previous attempts to persuade the Irish Catholics to campaign effectively for political equality. There was no agreement over the association's scope and aims. Some, including most of the aristocracy and gentry, wanted to concentrate entirely on emancipation. But O'Connell, alarmed by the rising tide of lawlessness in the countryside, was convinced that they could not control and lead the peasants unless they also campaigned against rack-renting, tithes, church rates, the burial laws and all the other grievances that directly affected the peasants.* Eventually he had his way, but at the cost of losing those who refused to venture beyond the traditional – and obviously futile – activity of petitioning Parliament for emancipation.

It was not until O'Connell launched his plan for a Catholic 'rent' that the Catholic Association really took off. Membership was thrown open to anyone who subscribed one penny a month, a sum small enough to be afforded by all but the very poorest peasant. The proceeds were to be used to pay for a variety of Catholic causes, such as legal aid for Catholics and the support of pro-Catholic newspapers, Catholic education and church building. In towns and rural parishes throughout Ireland committees were formed to organize the collection of the monthly subscriptions, sometimes by door-to-door collections, sometimes at the chapel door after Sunday Mass. The Catholic priests became energetic supporters of the scheme, and in the remoter parishes where it was not practicable to form committees, they took on the sole responsibility for organizing the collection. The local branches began to copy the Dublin association and hold regular meetings at which every conceivable Catholic grievance was discussed. Their enthusiasm provided the Catholic Association with a political organization, a network of committees, and individuals throughout the country who were in regular touch with the headquarters in Dublin and amenable to its influence and advice.

The successful launch of the Catholic 'rent' owed everything to the single-minded drive and determination of Daniel O'Connell and it made him for the first time the pre-eminent leader of the movement for emancipation. He came of a long-established Catholic family in the remote west of Ireland which had managed to hang on to much of its ancestral lands. He was an extremely hard-working and brilliant member of the Dublin Bar, prevented only by his religion from taking silk and aspiring to the judicial bench. As a politician he was supremely self-confident, sometimes to the extent of seeming insufferably arrogant and overbearing. He was seldom without impatient critics or challenges, more or less serious, to his leadership, but he never failed to maintain his authority in the end. He took the struggle for Catholic rights out of the clubs, counting-houses and drawing-rooms of Dublin into the Irish countryside, and the mass of poor Irish Catholics made him their uncrowned king. He could make himself heard in the largest hall and above the noisiest tumult. His

---

* Catholics had to pay church rates which were levied for the building and maintenance of Protestant churches. Catholic priests were forbidden to officiate at the funerals of their parishioners in Protestant (formerly Catholic) cemeteries.

speeches ranged from moving eulogies on the beauties of Ireland and stirring denunciations of its wrongs to coarse and scurrilous abuse of Tory politicians in London. He was a superb debater and he could curb the frenzy of his audience as easily as he could excite it.

His reputation as a successful demagogue among the wild Irish did not prevent O'Connell from being lionized by fashionable Whig society when he went to London early in 1825 as a member of a delegation from the Catholic Association. At dinner parties he appeared – according to a fellow guest – 'very pleasant, natural and easy'.[24] Another observer described him as having 'a very good-humoured countenance and manner' and as looking 'much more like a Kerry squire (which, in truth, he and his race are) than a Dublin lawyer'.[25] But in spite of the good impression he made, he and his delegation failed in the main object of their visit to London: to persuade Parliament not to pass a bill banning unlawful societies in Ireland and aimed primarily at the Catholic Association. The House of Commons refused even to grant them a hearing. Even Catholic sympathizers were alarmed by an organization that seemed bent on becoming a dangerous rival to government and Parliament in Ireland.

Both Houses of Parliament, however, were sufficiently alarmed about the state of Ireland to try yet again to investigate its problems. Throughout the spring of 1825 a stream of witnesses – landowners, politicians, magistrates, clergy, officials – crossed the Irish Sea to be painstakingly and courteously examined on the stark realities of life in their country. O'Connell himself was one of the most informative witnesses, all the more impressive for the clarity and moderation with which he gave his evidence. The tale of poverty, injustice, unrest and religious discrimination that emerged from the inquiries reinforced the alarm created by the Catholic Association and made the Commons feel that something really should be done for the Irish Catholics. On 10 May they gave a third reading to a Catholic relief bill which O'Connell had helped to draft. The bill's passage was eased by two 'securities' or 'wings': the disfranchisement of the 40s. freeholders (so that Catholic MPs would at least be elected by more substantial and, it was assumed, more responsible voters), and state salaries for the Catholic clergy. Victory for the Catholics was so widely believed to be imminent that Lord Liverpool, the Prime Minister, and Robert Peel, the Home Secretary, both staunch Protestants, contemplated res-ignation. But on 18 May the Lords threw out the bill. That morning O'Connell wrote sadly to his wife in Dublin: 'This day I have nothing to say or sing but defeat. Blessed be God. We must begin again.'[26]

On his return to Dublin O'Connell found his popularity among the masses undimmed, but he was furiously criticized by some of his rivals and associates for having agreed to disfranchise the 40s. free-holders. He admitted his mistake, successfully faced down his critics and set about organizing a new association that would take advantage of loopholes in the law banning the old one. The New Catholic Association, set up in July 1825 to devote itself to 'public and private charity and such other purposes' as the law did not prohibit, was a much more restrained affair than its predecessor. At first it made no attempt to collect a Catholic 'rent', and all political and petitioning activity was left to a countrywide series of aggregate meetings which culminated in a fourteen-day (the legal maximum) meeting in Dublin in January 1826.

There was, however, no grand appeal from Dublin to Westminster. England had gone through one of its periodic 'no-popery' convulsions during Parliament's debates on Ireland and the Catholics; there were public rejoicings and the ringing of church bells when the Catholic relief bill was defeated. Canning, bitterly disappointed by the loss of the bill, realized that it would be foolish to exacerbate anti-Catholic feeling when a general election was due the following summer at the latest. Before the end of 1825 he promised Liverpool that he would not let the Catholic issue be raised again in the House of Commons before the election, and he strongly advised the Irish to lie low for the time being. O'Connell, preoccupied by the sniping at his leadership and the urgent need to increase his own income, was content to tread water in the rather forlorn hope that the new Parliament would prove more sympathetic to the Catholic cause.

He did not foresee that the general election itself could be turned into a popular demonstration of the Irish Catholics' dissatisfaction and potential strength. In each of the thirty-two Irish counties the choice of two parliamentary representatives was usually fixed by the local landowners without recourse to an actual poll. If an election was held, the biggest contingent of voters was made up of 40s. freeholders, who were almost invariably regarded by those above them in the social scale with pity and contempt. Their freeholds often consisted of little more than a quarter-acre potato patch and a cabin, and since their rent was usually in arrears (it was in fact usually the custom to pay it in arrears) they faced being distrained or evicted if they would not perjure themselves by swearing that their miserable freehold was worth 40s. and then casting the vote thus acquired as and when their landlord demanded. In the words of one witness before a Commons committee in 1824, they were 'driven by the landlord into the hustings, as a salesman drives his flock into the market'.[27] The enfranchisement of the 40s. freeholders was widely deplored as having encouraged the repeated subdivision of the land, lowered the moral standards of the peasants by condoning perjury, and facilitated the concentration of political power in the hands of local oligarchies. Even O'Connell dismissed the 40s. freeholders as voting fodder for the landlords and in 1825 was prepared to agree to their disfranchisement.[28]

Yet in three contested elections in 1818 and in a by-election in 1823 the 40s. freeholders, spurred on by their priests (and in 1823 by O'Connell himself), had rejected their landlords' choice in favour of pro-emancipation candidates. The significance of these portents was not altogether lost. In particular, in County Waterford a number of landed, professional and commercial men, mostly Catholics but including some liberal Protestants, began to prepare a challenge to the leading local family, the Beresfords, known throughout Ireland as pillars of the Protestant Ascendancy and implacable opponents of the Catholic claims. In 1826 a young Protestant landowner, Henry Villiers Stuart, who was committed to emancipation and had actually joined the Catholic Association, was put up to fight Lord George Beresford for the county seat which the Beresfords took for granted was theirs by proprietorial right. Another young local landowner, the Catholic Thomas Wyse, emerged as the highly efficient leader of a campaign aimed at persuading every individual freeholder that it was both his right and his duty to vote as his conscience, not his landlord, dictated. The campaign, waged with the greatest energy and enthusiasm, was based on a network of committees, local agents and peripatetic speakers, powerfully reinforced by the parish clergy. The outcome was a stunning defeat for Beresford; even his own tenants rejected him.

Fired by Waterford's example, four other counties successfully mounted last-minute revolts by the Catholic freeholders, and there seemed no reason to suppose that similar revolts could not be organized throughout Ireland at the next general election. The belief that landlords could automatically command the votes of their 40s. freeholders had been shattered. Acknowledging that he had maligned them, O'Connell declared that emancipation must not be accepted if the price was the disfranchisement of the 40s. freeholders, and he proposed the collection of a new Catholic 'rent' to compensate those who were evicted by angry landlords. But the next general election could be as much as seven years away, and in the new House of Commons elected in the summer of 1826 the balance had shifted slightly against the Catholics. It looked as if they would have to hammer on a closed door for a good many years yet.

That the door began to open less than two years later was due in the first place to the unforeseeable vicissitudes of English politics. In February 1827 Lord Liverpool was incapacitated by a stroke. Two months later Canning was asked to form a new administration. When he was deserted by the Protestant Tories, including Wellington and Peel, partly, in some cases entirely, because of his pro-Catholic views, a group of moderate Whigs, led by the Marquess of Lansdowne, came to his rescue. Their support made it possible for him to form a government that from the point of view of the Irish Catholics was a great improvement on its predecessor. But although the will might be greater, the way was still obscure. Early in March the Commons had rejected a Catholic relief motion for the first time since 1819. The majority was only four votes, but it forced Canning to stick for the time being to the policy of government neutrality on the Catholic issue, and to acquiesce in George IV's determination to keep the regime in Dublin as ultra-Protestant as possible.

O'Connell was prepared to bide his time, realizing that renewed agitation in Ireland would make it impossible for Canning and his Whig partners to overcome the opposition to emancipation. Canning's death on 8 August 1827 was an unexpected disaster – 'another blow to wretched Ireland', as O'Connell put it.[29] By the end of the year it was clear that Canning's successor, Lord Goderich, was incapable of holding together the coalition of Whigs and liberal Tories, and that the only likely alternative was a Protestant Tory government uncompromisingly hostile to emancipation. When Goderich finally resigned early in January 1828, O'Connell and Sheil were already organizing meetings to be held simultaneously throughout Ireland to petition for Catholic relief. The news that the Duke of Wellington was to form a new government confirmed their worst fears. They did not realize that he was probably the only man who recognized that emancipation could no longer be refused and possessed the prestige and determination to carry it through. How he brought it about less than eighteen months later is the subject of this book.

1

Trials of a Soldier turned Politician

(January–May 1828)

'If people think I like this station, they are mistaken ... My line is to command the army, but if I think I can do any good by being Minister, I am willing to sacrifice my time and habits to do what I can.'

Duke of Wellington to Sir Colin Campbell, March 1828

Early on 9 January 1828, the Duke of Wellington was summoned to Windsor to receive George IV's command to form a new government. On the same morning Lord Anglesey wrote to William Huskisson, a fellow member of the outgoing Cabinet: 'We have now not to bewail the past, but to consider what is best for the future.'[1] It was a sentiment with which the duke would have thoroughly agreed. Although he had cautiously told the King that he must first consult his friends, he immediately set about trying to carry out the royal command. The King had stipulated that the new Cabinet was to be neutral on the Catholic issue and that the Lord Lieutenant of Ireland and the Irish Lord Chancellor were to be Protestants. He had indicated that he wanted the English Lord Chancellor, Lord Lyndhurst, a Protestant and a royal favourite, to remain in his post, but he had excluded nobody except Earl Grey to whom he had an insuperable objection. 'The King', Wellington felt, 'has been very fair, and has left me as unshackled as a person so employed has, I believe, ever been left.'[2]

His first step was to send for Peel who, after seventeen years in office, was enjoying the pleasures of family and country life unburdened by official cares. The summons reached Peel at Drayton Manor in Staffordshire about midnight; a few hours later he was on his way. After a 'melancholy' journey he reached his London house in Whitehall before eight o'clock on the morning of the 10th, and two hours later was with the duke at Apsley House. He found him 'most reasonable and friendly and satisfactory in every way'.[3]

In the unaccustomed task of Cabinet-making Wellington's reasonableness and friendliness were to be severely tried. He was not at all anxious to keep the Whigs who had come to Canning's rescue when he was deserted by most of the leading Tories. Nor were the Whigs keen to be kept on. Only the King minded. On purely personal grounds he wanted to keep Lord Carlisle, who had joined Canning's Cabinet as a personal friend rather than as a Whig, and the Duke of Devonshire who had exerted himself energetically to bring the Whigs into Canning's government and had himself accepted the post of Lord Chamberlain in the royal Household. But Devonshire refused to keep his post under Canning's enemies, although the King assured him that his departure 'would break his heart and drive him out of his senses'.[4] Carlisle, for his part, declared that he could not remain in a Cabinet that did not include his leader, Lord Lansdowne, and other Whigs.[5] But Lansdowne would not serve under an anti-Catholic Prime Minister; and Wellington in any case was reluctant to make him an offer which he would almost certainly refuse. Sir James Scarlett, the Whig lawyer who had served as Canning's Attorney-General, also preferred to remain aloof. Among the Whigs, only Lord Ellenborough, the future Governor-General of India, unburdened by any past Canning connection and yearning to spread his political wings, accepted the duke's invitation and joined the Cabinet as Lord Privy Seal.

To get rid of the Whigs was much easier and less painful than constructing a Tory ministry. Peel, who could not help hankering after his pleasant peaceful life at Drayton Manor, insisted that it should include only the 'efficient' members of the party. He was very reluctant to undertake the demanding office of Home Secretary (which included responsibility for Ireland) as well as the leadership of the House of Commons without the support of good speakers beside him on the Treasury bench.[6] In particular he was anxious that his front-bench colleagues should include William Huskisson, who was acknowledged to be the chief expert in the House of Commons on financial and commercial matters. As President of the Board of Trade between 1822 and 1827 Huskisson had begun the process of financial and commercial reform which Peel was to complete twenty years later. In the House of Commons his intellectual distinction gained him an attentive audience whenever he chose to speak, although his delivery was poor and his manner ungraceful. In private society he was agreeable, cheerful, amusing, unassuming, with a fund of information and anecdote. He had entered Parliament a couple of years after Canning, and had ever since loyally followed his fortunes through good times and bad, sometimes probably to the detriment of his own career. More than most of the Canningites he was bound to hesitate before joining those who had deserted Canning in his hour of need. Indeed, a few weeks after Canning's death (when he was perhaps still suffering from the shock of that tragedy) he had privately declared that he 'could not be in a Cabinet with those who had worried Canning to his doom'.[7]

On the evening of 10 January Wellington summoned Huskisson to Apsley House and told him that he wished to form a strong administration and bury the past in oblivion. Was Huskisson inclined to help? This military incisiveness was all very well, but after the violent upheavals of the past year it simply was not possible for men who set great store by personal considerations of honour, 'character' (reputation), loyalty and hurt pride to bury the past without further ado. For Canning's former friends and colleagues the past was still very much alive, and when Wellington went on to say that nothing was yet decided, not even who would head the new administration, Huskisson at once replied that he was willing to serve with Peel but not under him because 'that was the rule he [Peel] had laid down with respect to Mr Canning'. Next morning he said the same thing to Peel himself, and although his objection was governed more by emotion than by logic, he claimed that Peel accepted it as perfectly fair.[8] That left the duke as the only man capable of rallying the scattered Tory troops and acceptable to all of them. It was only nine months since he had assured the House of Lords, when explaining his refusal to join Canning's government, that it was totally out of the question for him to become Prime Minister and he would have been worse than mad to think of such a thing.[9]

Huskisson, who was suffering from a bad feverish cold and sore throat, left Apsley House without feeling able to commit himself. Next morning, even after talking to Peel, he was still inclined to think that the chances were ten to one against his joining the government. But he had at least made up his mind that if he did join it must be on the understanding that Canning's foreign and domestic policies would not be jettisoned and that his three Canningite colleagues, Lord Dudley, Lord Palmerston and Charles Grant, should continue to sit in the Cabinet with him.

Dudley had also been a personal friend of Canning's. An only child, he had been educated by a succession of private tutors, deprived of playmates or sports and made to work extremely hard. He emerged from this regime an excellent scholar but an eccentric man whose occasional oddities tended to make him the butt of contemporary wits. He sat in the House of Commons (as J. W. Ward) before succeeding to his father's title in 1823. The previous year he had had a severe depressive illness, and on his recovery refused, after much dithering, Canning's offer to make him Under-Secretary at the Foreign Office. When Canning persuaded him to become Foreign Secretary in April 1827, Dudley thought that even a temporary stint would be 'monstrously' above his strength.[10] But with Canning still the powerful guiding force at the Foreign Office Dudley settled down more or less happily in his subordinate role. After Canning's death his self-doubt returned, but Goderich persuaded him to stay on, and his brief experience of managing on his own seems to have boosted his self-confidence.

Palmerston, now in his forty-fourth year, had never lacked self-confidence. He had served as Secretary at War for nearly twenty years, and although the outside world was more impressed by his active social life, he had proved himself a competent and conscientious administrator. He had not been a personal friend of Canning's, nor a member of his inner circle, but he had always admired him and had increasingly come to sympathize with his struggle with the reactionary elements in what by 1826 Palmerston was calling 'the stupid old Tory party'. When Canning became Prime Minister Palmerston did not desert him. But like many other people Canning underestimated Palmerston. After offering him the Chancellorship of the Exchequer and then withdrawing the offer (partly to please the King), he suggested that he should go to Jamaica as governor. When Palmerston simply laughed at such an offer, he suggested the much more prestigious prize of India. But Palmerston refused to be shunted abroad and in the end Canning, desperate to gain recruits, let him keep the War Office and in addition gave him, for the first time, a seat in the Cabinet.

At Oxford Charles Grant had acquired something of a reputation as a poet. He entered Parliament in 1811 and in 1819 was made Chief Secretary for Ireland. The Protestant establishment in Dublin was outraged by his pro-Catholic sympathies and irritated by his supposed indecisiveness and his dilatory and unbusinesslike ways. In 1823 he was made Huskisson's deputy at the Board of Trade and remained there during Canning's brief ministry. Goderich promoted him to be President of the Board of Trade and brought him into his Cabinet. Like Palmerston he had become a Canningite through intellectual conviction rather than personal ties.

It took Huskisson and his colleagues a week to make up their minds to join the new government. For Huskisson there was a particular stumbling block in the shape of the outgoing Chancellor of the Exchequer, John Herries. After falling out with him over the chairmanship of the Commons finance committee – the quarrel had precipitated the fall of the Goderich ministry – Huskisson was convinced he could not honourably serve in a Cabinet in which Herries was Chancellor. Indeed, he doubted whether he could serve with him again in any circumstances. On 14 January he wrote to Peel explaining his doubts. Peel was alarmed, and also surprised since no offer had yet been made to Herries. He called on Huskisson to try to dispel his doubts and was so far successful that Huskisson decided to consult Dudley, Palmerston and Grant and abide by their advice. Peel professed to think this an excellent idea. The duke, less well endowed with patience, descended on Huskisson on the afternoon of the 16th, told him he had never intended to make Herries Chancellor of the Exchequer and pointed out that he was still waiting for an answer from the Canningites. He had to wait another twenty-four hours before Huskisson, with his friends' agreement, decided he could honourably join the Cabinet provided Herries was not Chancellor of the Exchequer.[11] So Henry Goulburn went to the Exchequer and Herries reluctantly agreed to be demoted to Master of the Mint.

The Canningites might not have made such a paper tiger out of Herries if they had not been filled with painful misgivings about joining a government led by Canning's enemies who might later see fit to overturn his policies. When Palmerston was first summoned to Apsley House on 13 January, he told Wellington that before agreeing to join him he must have assurances on the Catholic question – 'the most important which would probably occur during my life'. The duke assured him that the government would be neutral on the issue. Palmerston was not satisfied, and when he saw Wellington again a few days later he boldly spelled out the guarantees on the Catholic question which he required. With barely concealed irritation the duke made a rather dismissive reply which Palmerston found far from satisfactory.[12] Charles Grant was also uneasy about the Catholic question, and on the 17th he told Huskisson that he saw 'much difficulty and great ground of doubt and inquiry' in it.[13] Huskisson thereupon asked Charles Arbuthnot, Wellington's friend and confidant, for a copy of the memorandum in which Canning had carefully explained to the Whig leader, Lord Lansdowne, the position of his government with regard to the Catholic question. Arbuthnot sent it at once with an assurance that 'it contains precisely the wishes of the

Duke of Wellington and Peel'. He also added some conciliatory
comments on Palmerston's stipulations.[14] The issue was eventually sorted out in an interview between Wellington and the four
Canningites which Palmerston found 'perfectly satisfactory'.[15] It
may be doubted whether the duke was equally satisfied with such
independent colleagues whose hesitations had obliged him to postpone the opening of Parliament for a week.

There was a fifth Canningite, William Lamb, whom Canning had
made Chief Secretary for Ireland – in effect, the Lord Lieutenant's
right-hand man who went over to London to answer for Irish affairs
when Parliament was sitting. Lamb had had time to make his Catholic
sympathies plain to the Irish Catholics but not enough to do anything
tangible for them. He was in Dublin when Wellington took over the
government and reacted doubtfully to a letter from the duke which
asked him to stay on and assured him that there would be no sudden
change of policy towards Ireland. He confided to his brother that
Wellington and Peel had got 'such a damned character for intolerance
in this country that their accession to office would encourage the
violent Protestants and depress the Roman Catholics to such a degree
as would make it impossible for me to pursue my course ... with
credit and the appearance of consistency.'[16] However, when he went
over to London, Wellington satisfied him that he intended to govern
Ireland 'upon the most rational, sensible and liberal footing', and he
felt no further doubt about staying on as Chief Secretary.[17]

The other Canningites also kept the posts they had held under
Goderich. So, with their doubts over the Catholic question allayed,
with Dudley still at the Foreign Office and with Huskisson and Grant
in charge of colonial and commercial matters, they professed to feel
confident that Canning's principles of policy would be preserved and
that they would not be accused of deserting his memory.*

'We are in Huskey's boat', wrote Lady Granville from Paris where
her husband, a close friend of Canning's, was ambassador. 'We have
the greatest reliance on his integrity and honour.' But ten days later
she was lamenting Huskisson's 'most comfortless' position. Whilst she
thought it his duty to remain, 'I wonder every moment he does.'[18]
Some of Canning's friends and supporters were declaring angrily that
Huskisson had disgraced himself by joining a government led by
Wellington and Peel. In particular, Canning's widow, described by

---

* Lord Goderich, who had been Secretary of State for War and the Colonies in
Canning's ministry, gave this post to Huskisson when he himself became Prime
Minister.

Huskisson as being 'in a state of great excitement', heaped reproaches on him in London drawing-rooms and began to bombard him with angry letters. He wrote to Lord Seaford, another of Canning's close friends, begging him to come over from Paris for the opening of Parliament for he feared he was going to be violently attacked for allegedly deserting Canning's memory.[19]

If some Canningites were outraged by the new ministry, so too were some other Tories. Few were as sensible as Sir Henry Hardinge who, while deploring the inclusion of 'sad rogues and intriguers' (Canningites), fully recognized 'the absolute *necessity* in the lower H[ou]se of sacrificing honest indignation to the expediency of more talking strength'.[20] This, Peel felt, was also needed in the Lords, and he insisted on bringing in Lord Aberdeen (as Chancellor of the Duchy of Lancaster) as well as Ellenborough to improve the government's debating strength there. Lords Westmorland and Eldon were the most prominent ultra Tories who – in Croker's vivid phrase – were 'put into the dirty clothes basket . . . and *thrown overboard* – thrown overboard for Lord Ellenborough'.[21] Westmorland had served, without distinction, as Lord Privy Seal for nearly thirty years, but in 1827 had refused to go on serving under Canning who, twenty years earlier, had privately dismissed him as 'useless lumber'. Eldon had served nearly as long as Lord Chancellor. An immensely learned lawyer, his addiction to the time-consuming balancing of legal niceties had led to the accumulation over the years of a huge backlog of legal business. His political views were thoroughly reactionary and anti-Catholic. He was now nearly 77 and had let it be known that he did not wish to return to the Woolsack. But when Wellington not only took him at his word, but did not offer him a less onerous post, he was mortified and his friends were furious.

To other disappointed Tories the duke sent routine apologies. They were seldom well received. He blandly informed Lord Londonderry that he realized the new arrangements were perhaps not exactly what he might have wished, but Cabinet-making was not like arranging a dinner or a party in the country. Londonderry was not mollified. 'Some affectionate personal communication', he complained to Mrs Arbuthnot, 'as to the expediency and necessity of the present tableau might have been soothing to a devoted friend.'[22] Much more important was the attitude of the fanatically anti-Catholic Duke of Newcastle, and to him Wellington twice appealed for support. Newcastle flatly refused to give it. He had, he wrote, opposed Mr Canning's government and so he must oppose Wellington's, seeing that it 'is formed on the same principle and of mainly the same ingredients, those ingredients, too, being the most noxious in the whole *materia politica*.[23] One of the few leading Tories who did not complain was Goderich who, a few days after sloughing off the cares of office, was reported to be 'quite another man', cured of his insomnia and laughing and talking as usual.[24]

Beset by the importunities of both the greater and the lesser lights of the Tory party, Wellington confided to John Croker that he felt like a dog with a canister tied to his tail. Instead of getting on with the business of the country – and he pointed to 'a formidable heap of green bags and red boxes' – he was obliged to spend all his time 'in assuaging what gentlemen call their *feelings*'.[25] Peel also received his share of bitterly reproachful missives from disgruntled Tories; Huskisson, still wrestling with his conscience, was greatly cheered by their 'extreme fury' which made him feel that he had done the right thing.[26] Peel, for his part, was unmoved. He had no use for the ultra Tories. 'Every blockhead', he complained, 'is for the complete predominance of his own opinions, and generally with a vehemence proportionate to their impracticability.'[27] He had got what he believed was needed: a moderate government, with a ministerial team carefully balanced between pro-Catholics and Protestants that was administratively competent and capable of defending government policies in Parliament. But perhaps he had underestimated the difficulties, at an emotional level, of those who had separated – as he had put it – 'on no other account than a question about Canning's claim to be Prime Minister'.[28] At the first Cabinet dinner at Apsley House on 22 January, the courtesy shown by the guests – so Ellenborough maliciously recorded – 'was that of men who had just fought a duel'.[29]

Three days later, however, all except one were able to agree without difficulty that the same man could not be head both of the government and of the army. Wellington had hoped he could. He was greatly chagrined, but at least his successor at the Horse Guards was his old comrade, General Rowland Hill, and his sacrifice of his army post reconciled some Tories to the new government.

But the difficulty of maintaining relations of genuine trust and cordiality within the Cabinet was soon demonstrated. Like the other newly appointed ministers Huskisson had to seek re-election. In a speech to his Liverpool constituents he claimed – according to some press reports – that Wellington had given him guarantees that Canning's policies would be continued. The duke and the Tories were furious, and six days later, on 11 February, Wellington categorically denied in the House of Lords that he had given any guarantees to any members of his government or struck any 'corrupt bargain' with any of them.[30] Immediately after making his speech Huskisson had confided to his wife that he had not prepared it and had no idea afterwards what he had said.[31] But when he read the press reports, he was certain that they grossly and maliciously misrepresented him.[32] He had merely, he vehemently assured the Commons, said that the presence of Dudley, Palmerston, Grant and Lamb in the new government was the most satisfactory guarantee that its policies would not be changed. His recollection was confirmed in letters from those who had stood near him on the hustings and had read the garbled press reports.[33]

It was a storm in a teacup, blown up by Wellington's dissatisfaction, verging on contempt, for the Cabinet Peel had obliged him to preside over, and Huskisson's unhappy compulsion to justify his own presence in it. His colleague, the Foreign Secretary, was forced to do the same in the House of Lords when Canning's son-in-law, Clanricarde, demanded an explanation of his motives for joining the government. Would they, Dudley asked his fellow peers, accept 'such a plea as the sacred duty of immortalizing hatred'?; and he pointed out that Canning and Castlereagh had been able to bury the hatchet and work cordially together in the same Cabinet.[34] When Clanricarde found an excuse to return to the charge a fortnight later, Seaford, who had come over from Paris in response to Huskisson's plea, delivered a stout defence of both Dudley and Huskisson. It was, Wellington declared, an entirely uncalled-for discussion.[35] He might have added that it did nothing to strengthen the cohesion of his government.

At least, however, the government did not face a united Opposition. Some Whigs thoroughly distrusted and openly opposed the new government. Some, encouraged by the exclusion of ultra Tories like Eldon, were inclined to support it, while a third group preferred to suspend judgement for the time being. It was unfortunate for the government that its first serious test arose over an issue on which the Whigs did not disagree. On 26 February Lord John Russell introduced a motion for the repeal of those parts of legislation dating from Charles II's reign and originally directed against the Roman Catholics, which debarred Dissenters from holding public office. Although opposed by the government, the motion was carried by a majority of forty-four votes.

The blow came from an unexpected quarter. The Dissenters, who claimed to number two and a quarter million in England and Wales, including Wesleyans and Quakers, did not appear to have much to complain about and their situation did not arouse much public

concern. In theory they were excluded from public office by the Test
and Corporation Acts which required office-holders to take the
sacrament according to the rite of the Church of England. (They had
no difficulty with a further provision which required them to make a
declaration against transubstantiation and other Roman Catholic
doctrines.) Some Dissenters did take the Anglican sacrament once
in order to qualify for office, but many more relied on an annual
Indemnity Act, which granted exemption from the legal penalties
for breaking the laws. During the previous ten years three lord
mayors of London had been Dissenters. A Dissenter was free to enter
Parliament (although few did) because they were willing to take the
oath of supremacy.[36] Three members of Wellington's Cabinet were
Presbyterians. The legal discrimination against Dissenters, it was
argued, was a symbolic affirmation of the Church of England's
supremacy, but they could not claim that it was a practical grievance.

Many Dissenters disagreed. The terms of the Indemnity Act did
not in fact completely prevent the ill-disposed from blocking the
admission of Dissenters to office. Moreover, it gave indemnity on
grounds of ignorance, absence or unavoidable accident, but not on
grounds of conscience. Many Dissenters felt it would be unprincipled
and degrading to take office on such terms and refused to do so.
Above all, they strongly objected to being – as they saw it – stigmat-
ized as second-class citizens. 'Is the *stigma* nothing?', asked Brougham
during the debate on Russell's motion. 'Is it nothing that a Dissenter,
wherever he goes, is looked on and treated as an inferior person to a
Churchman?'[37] To Dissenters, this was not an exaggeration. Many of
them belonged to what today are called the upwardly mobile classes,
and they feared that their progress was being impeded by prejudices
fostered by their legal disabilities. 'They feel', a statement by their
official representatives declared, 'that these laws lie, and are persisted
in because they *do* lie, at the foundation of all the distinctions and
preferences which meet them at every hour, in town and in country,
in public and in private life, and mark them out as an isolated part of
the community.'[38]

It would have been much easier to satisfy the Dissenters if their
case could have been isolated from that of the Catholics. But it could
not. To those who clung to the belief that church and state were, and
must remain, indissolubly linked, it followed that only those who
belonged to the established church could in principle qualify for
public office. If the Dissenters were granted full citizenship, without
any obligation to take any religious test, the theory that church and
state were co-extensive would, it was argued, be fatally flawed. And if

it could no longer be maintained that religious belief must be a qualfication for public office, why should not the Catholics benefit as much as the Dissenters? The case against Catholic emancipation would have to be argued, not on the solid and respectable grounds of constitutional principle, but on grounds of expediency and alleged dangers which were coming to seem increasingly illusory. Thus repeal of the Test and Corporation Acts might well undermine, and eventually destroy, the chief bulwark against Catholic emancipation. And in the prevailing climate of greater liberalism – the 'spirit of the age', as contemporaries liked to call it – the practical impetus that repeal would give to the Catholic cause would make emancipation inevitable.

Not everybody, even among the supporters of the Catholic cause, argued like this. Some, including Huskisson (and Canning when he was alive) believed that repeal would so seriously reduce the pressure for the removal of religious disabilities generally that it was essential to obtain emancipation first. It was indeed doubtful whether many Dissenters would give wholehearted (or any) support to the Catholic cause once their own demands had been met. Their efforts to secure their own relief had frequently been hampered by divided views on whether they should campaign for the removal of all religious tests or only for their own.

Their divisions were reflected in their two representative bodies. The Dissenting Deputies were founded in 1732 for the special object of protecting the civil rights of Dissenters. Although they represented only the Dissenting congregations – Presbyterian, Independent and Baptist – within a twelve-mile radius of London, their committee of twenty-four was in touch with Dissenters throughout the country and was widely accepted as speaking for them. The Protestant Society for the Protection of Religious Liberty, founded in 1811, represented Dissenters all over the country, including Methodists, and was openly supported by prominent Whig politicians like Lord John Russell and Lord Holland. It was strongly evangelical and criticized the Dissenting Deputies for being insufficiently aggressive in pushing their claims. It also had a much more pronounced anti-Catholic bias. In November 1824, Dr John Pye Smith, one of the Society's founders, reported 'repeated and painful defeats at our meetings' for any petition in favour of relief for both Protestants and Catholics.[39]

In 1827 the chairman of the Dissenting Deputies was, and had been for more than twenty years, the MP for Norwich, William Smith, then in his early seventies. Smith had been born into a wealthy Dissenting merchant family in London. As a businessman he had failed lamentably, but as a dedicated, although moderate, reformer and champion of good causes he was greatly respected. He entered Parliament in 1782 as a supporter of Pitt, but switched to the Whigs when Pitt abandoned parliamentary reform and went to war with revolutionary France. Smith was a friend of Wilberforce and worked with him for the abolition of the slave trade. He served on the special committee set up by the Dissenting Deputies in 1786 to persuade the House of Commons to vote for the repeal of the Test and Corporation Acts. Three attempts were made between 1787 and 1790, all of them unsuccessful. In spite of these early setbacks, however, Smith never lost his belief in a cautious and moderate approach that would educate Parliament and the public without antagonizing them. Although he did not despise agitation outside Parliament, he put more faith in co-operation with influential Whig politicians, even though their primary aim was Catholic emancipation rather than repeal of the Test Act. He himself thought that emancipation must come first, but as there was an active anti-Catholic minority in the Deputies, he had to be careful not to provoke a split.

No sustained and vigorous campaign for repeal had been attempted since the failures of 1787–90, but during the 1820s the Dissenters found their inferior status increasingly intolerable. The state's assumption of authority to punish or tolerate the way someone chose to perform his religious duties was condemned in a petition drawn up in 1827 as 'a pretension to infallibility, an injustice towards individuals, an encouragement towards insincerity and a source of weakness in the state.'[40] In the spring of the same year the time seemed ripe for an assault on the obnoxious legislation. The unexpected defeat by the House of Commons of Burdett's Catholic relief motion seemed to dispose of the Catholic question for the time being. The Dissenters felt there was now a better chance of their own grievances being considered on their merits. Early in April 1827 the Dissenting Deputies formed a United Committee to agitate for repeal. It included the Unitarians and various smaller Dissenting congregations, but the Protestant Society still preferred to go its own more narrow way. In the event, the division did not matter because Canning, who succeeded Lord Liverpool as Prime Minister in the middle of April, soon made it clear that he would not support repeal until Catholic emancipation had been achieved. The Whigs agreed that emancipation must be the primary aim and at the end of May they managed to persuade the United Committee to agree, with the greatest reluctance, to the postponement of a motion for repeal that Lord John Russell was to have introduced in the Commons.

The United Committee had no intention of letting this setback be more than temporary. Preparations to renew the campaign for repeal were continued throughout the parliamentary recess. A publications subcommittee arranged for the widespread distribution of sermons, pamphlets, petitions and other propaganda material. Preparations were also made to bring out a monthly periodical that would publicize the activities of the repeal campaign and record all the relevant parliamentary debates, petitions and other documents. The first issue of the *Test Act Reporter* duly appeared on 1 January 1828.

By this time the United Committee was making sure that when Parliament reassembled towards the end of January it would be inundated with petitions in favour of repeal. Twelve hundred repeal petitions had flooded into the House of Commons during the previous session, but the work, it was felt, had to be done all over again; a stale year-old petition would not have the impact of a newly minted one even though the arguments were the same. Moreover, this time the House of Lords was to be petitioned as well as the Commons. A circular letter was sent to all Dissenting ministers, explaining the need for more petitions and giving detailed instructions on how to produce them, if possible with new signatures. Anglicans could be approached, but with tact, and the 'Committee again earnestly caution their more zealous friends against the use of any intemperate or offensive expressions'.[41] Altogether, the petitioning campaign was organized with an imaginative care, tact and attention to detail which a modern lobbyist would find hard to beat.

Petitions, however, would get the Dissenters nowhere without the active support of the Opposition. The United Committee took the initiative in renewing contacts with Whig politicians friendly to its cause and secured a promise from Russell to introduce his postponed motion early in the forthcoming session. In the new political situation it suited the Whigs to press hard for repeal. They no longer had to reckon with Canning's determination to make sure of emancipation first, and the appointment of a government led by Wellington and Peel would make it seem safer, to those opposed to Catholic relief, to concede legal toleration to the Dissenters. It was an issue on which the Whigs could sink their differences, and moreover it had a chance of securing enough liberal Tory support to be successful. But if the Catholics tried to join in with their own demand for political equality, they would probably upset the whole applecart. So when early in January 1828 Russell read in a newspaper that the Irish Roman Catholics were proposing to seek the co-operation of the Dissenters for their mutual objects, he immediately wrote to the United Committee to discourage it from accepting any Catholic overture. The committee thereupon formally resolved not to form any union with the Catholics.

Russell believed that his advice was in the best long-term interest of the Catholics. But paradoxically it had the effect of removing the objections which had prevented bigoted anti-Catholics in the Protestant Society from co-operating with the United Committee because they believed it to be soft on Catholicism. A few days after the committee had formally distanced itself from the Catholics, the Protestant Society resolved to join forces with it to work for repeal. Rather surprisingly, it was content to be represented on the committee by no more than six delegates. Moderate, conciliatory counsels were allowed to prevail, and the importance of this was to be shown in the days ahead.

The government decided to oppose Russell's motion on 26 February on the grounds that the Dissenters had only a theoretical grievance, that religious jealousies were gradually diminishing and that it was better to leave things as they were. To the House of Commons the argument against repeal must, as Peel privately admitted, seem 'threadbare in the extreme',[42] and no one on the government front bench distinguished himself during the debate. Huskisson began by agreeing that it was highly objectionable to impose a religious test as a civil disqualification, and then caused laughter and several minutes' uproar by regretting that the matter had been brought forward at the present time.[43] Lord Milton commented that Huskisson's speech was not at all like the clear statements he usually made on commercial questions, for his conclusion was 'wholly at variance' with the arguments with which he had started.[44] The same criticism could be made of Palmerston who set out all the arguments in favour of repeal and then announced he would vote against the motion because he thought the real grievances of the Catholics should be remedied before the largely theoretical ones of the Dissenters.[45] Peel contented himself with arguing that the Dissenters had no practical grievances and had remained quiet for the past forty years.[46] His arguments had already been demolished by a previous speaker, Lord Nugent, who declared that 'Insult is no theoretical grievance', and asked what the Catholic Association would think of the argument that those who had remained long-suffering and loyal for so long should continue to be ignored for that very reason?[47] Peel had no answer to this.

The outcome of the debate greatly annoyed the Duke of Wellington, not least because of the indiscipline shown by his rank and file in the Commons. 'Not less than 66 friends, many of them confirmed government men, voted against us; and 22 stayed away. This does not look well.'[48] Apparently the government whips had failed to make the Cabinet's attitude clear in time, so that many Tory members felt free to vote according to their conscience or the wishes of their Dissenting constituents.[49] On the other hand, persistent and energetic lobbying by delegates from the United Committee had made sure that the Dissenters' friends turned up in force.

On 27 February the ministers discussed their defeat after a Cabinet dinner at Lord Bathurst's, but failed to decide what to do about it. So when next day Russell proposed to follow up his success, Peel had to face the Commons without any firm guidance from his colleagues. He suggested an annual suspension of the Test and Corporation Acts instead of an annual indemnity, and when Russell turned this down he asked for a few days' delay. The ensuing discussion ended when Peel took umbrage at some remarks impugning – he felt – his motives for delay. He marched out of the Chamber after declaring that he would leave it to Russell to take whatever course he thought best. When told that Sir George Warrender, an independent back-bencher, had complained that such impatient conduct almost tempted him to withdraw his support from the government, Peel marched back again and claimed that he had merely gone out to get something to eat, having fasted since nine o'clock that morning. But although satisfying his hunger may have helped to restore Peel's equanimity, it did not remove his resentment, and his attitude towards repeal remained unclear.

What was increasingly clear was that the Dissenters would have to agree to make some sort of declaration instead of taking the sacramental Test. Their first reactions were uncompromisingly hostile and they were only gradually and with the greatest possible reluctance persuaded of the need to compromise. Lord Althorp claimed that many MPs who had voted for repeal would now be glad of an excuse to change their minds on the grounds that the Dissenters were completely impossible. Russell assured them that an unqualified repeal bill would certainly be thrown out by the House of Lords, and he hammered out a declaration that the Dissenters very reluctantly brought themselves to accept – 'for reasons of political expediency' – if their 'parliamentary friends' thought it was essential to save the bill.[50]

Meanwhile Peel had been privately coming round to the view that repeal was inevitable and he ought to make sure that it did not damage the Church. A majority of the Cabinet was in favour of accepting repeal; only Wellington and Bathurst were definitely against, and the duke soon realized that he would have to give way.

The bishops were bound to abhor the use of a sacramental test for civil office, and for that reason most of them favoured repeal if the interests of the Church could be safeguarded. On 15 March, the day after Russell's repeal bill had received its second reading, Peel went to Lambeth Palace to seek episcopal advice on how this could best be done. With the help of the two archbishops and the bishops of London, Durham, Chester and Llandaff he drew up a declaration that was little different from the text that Russell had already persuaded the Dissenters to accept. It would commit those making it never to use their office 'to injure or subvert the Protestant Church by law established in these realms, or to disturb it in the possession of those rights and privileges to which it is by law entitled'.[51] Three days later, during the committee stage of the bill, he proposed to add the declaration. Russell and William Smith felt obliged to oppose it in principle – Smith argued passionately that it was not necessary – but eventually they accepted it. At any rate the Dissenters would no longer have to take a religious test to qualify for a civil office.

Lord John Russell's goal was to abolish all religious tests – for Catholics as well as Protestants. On 31 March, after the repeal bill had been given its third reading in the Commons, he wrote: 'It is really a gratifying thing to force the enemy to give up his first line, that none but Churchmen are worthy to serve the state, and I trust we shall soon make him give up the second, that none but Protestants are.' And he added, 'Peel is a very pretty hand at hauling down his colours.'[52]

Peel, indeed, having made up his mind to support the repeal bill, did so wholeheartedly. He urged Russell and Smith not to give the Lords any excuse to 'meddle' with the declaration.[53] But they needed no excuse. Old Lord Eldon feared that repeal would open the way to Catholic emancipation; moreover, he believed that the Dissenters were actively hostile to the Church – as in fact they were to demonstrate during the coming decade. He cast his mind back forty years to the previous attempts to repeal the Test and Corporation Acts and claimed that the famous Dissenting minister, Dr Joseph Priestley, had boasted of laying a train of gunpowder under the Church which would blow it up, while another prominent Dissenter, Dr Price, had rejoiced that the revolution in France would destroy the union between church and state in England. 'The young men and lads in the House of Commons', he complained, 'are too young to remember these things.'[54] He realized that he could not get rid of the bill altogether. But he was determined to emasculate it as much as he could. Lord Holland, who had undertaken to steer the bill through the House of Lords, had a healthy respect for Eldon's legal expertise and his consequent ability to damage the bill. 'Eldon opposes tooth and nail', he told Russell on 3 April, and the bill's supporters must bestir themselves to secure votes and proxies.[55] He also sought the advice of legal experts on the United Committee on how best to resist the assaults of 'so able a guerilla chief as the ex-Chancellor'.[56] It was enthusiastically given.

On 17 April Holland moved the second reading of the repeal bill in the House of Lords. His wife reported that he was very nervous beforehand and could not sleep a wink afterwards.[57] But the bill, supported by Wellington, the Archbishop of York (speaking also on behalf of his colleague of Canterbury who was sick), and the bishops of Lincoln, Durham and Chester, was passed without a division. The real battle took place at the committee stage with the bill's opponents trying to turn the declaration into a religious test designed above all to exclude Catholics. Eldon was indefatigable and sometimes acrimonious, on one occasion ending a rather heated exchange with Bishop Blomfield by begging him to abstain from gratuitously tendering his advice. There was some arcane discussion of religious beliefs, and much argument as to whether the oath of supremacy and the declaration against transubstantiation really were adequate to exclude Catholics from corporations. Eldon insisted that they were not and wanted the bill's preamble to state that the 'true Protestant religion' should be 'effectually and unalterably secured'. Bishop Blomfield said this was not necessary. Lyndhurst, the Lord Chancellor, was not sure and suggested inserting 'Protestant' in the declaration to remove all ambiguity.[58] Eldon's motion was defeated all the same.

Undeterred, Eldon moved next day to insert 'I am a Protestant' in the declaration. Lyndhurst announced that after 'mature consideration' he had changed his mind and now believed that the existing laws were sufficient to exclude Catholics.[59] The amendment was duly defeated, but Eldon's eloquence had unnerved the bishops and all but three of those present supported him. Most of the members of the royal Household stayed away, although Wellington had written to the King to point out that they were expected to attend debates in the Lords. During a Cabinet meeting before this debate, Wellington received a letter from the King in which he emphatically declared his conviction that the word 'Protestant' must be inserted in the bill if the security of the established Church was to be preserved.[60] As the Cabinet had just decided that it need not, Wellington and Lyndhurst had to hurry round to Carlton House to calm the royal fears.[61] It was a foretaste of the struggles with the King's conscience, real or pretended, over the emancipation of the Catholics.

After further unsuccessful attempts by ultra peers to amend the repeal bill, it at last received its third reading in the Lords on 28 April.* On the same day the Lord Chamberlain, the Duke of Montrose, wrote to Wellington explaining his opposition to the bill in terms typical of the attitude of many independent and Tory peers.

> As to the measures on foreign politics, on corn, and bills of such nature, I think it right to give up my own opinions to a government in which I have full confidence; but on reform of Parliament, on the Catholic question, and the repeal of the Corporation and Test Acts, I consider them so materially affecting the constitution of the country, that till I am convinced of the propriety of changing the present system, I cannot agree to the bill now in the House, or to change the present state of things as relating to the two other points.[62]

Wellington replied with a reasoned defence of the government's action, emphasizing the danger of provoking a conflict between Lords and Commons, especially when the latter seemed to have the support of public opinion. Only at the end of his letter did he show his exasperation at the defection of those on whom he felt he ought to be able to rely. If 'the servants of the Crown' would not support him, either he or they must retire; he would much prefer the former, and he hoped the King would not find it difficult to select someone more to their liking.[63]

The duke's exasperation was not confined to recalcitrant Tory peers. He also found, rather to his surprise, that his Cabinet colleagues were often tiresomely reluctant to follow his lead. While the repeal of the Test and Corporation Acts was being fought over in the House of Commons, the Cabinet was waging a private battle over the terms of a new corn bill to replace the temporary bill passed the previous session. The corn laws had always aroused strong feelings and the history of the last attempt to regulate the import of corn (and hence the price of bread) did not make a fresh attempt any easier. In March

---

* The Dissenters still had five main grievances: (1) births could only be registered in parish churches; (2) only marriages in parish churches were legal, except for Quakers and Jews; (3) churchyards could only be used with Anglican rites or in silence; (4) Dissenters were liable for church rates for the repair of parish churches; (5) at Oxford and Cambridge degrees were only given to those who would subscribe to the Thirty-Nine Articles (O. Chadwick, *The Victorian Church*, vol. 1, pp. 80–1).

1827 a new, more liberal corn bill, largely drawn up by Huskisson, was introduced in the Commons by Canning and passed through all its stages. When the bill was debated in the Lords the following June, after Canning had become Prime Minister, Wellington successfully introduced an amendment in the mistaken belief that it would improve the bill and that it had Huskisson's approval. The government withdrew the bill and substituted a temporary measure. In the new Cabinet the Canningites wanted to retain the exact terms of the 1827 bill which had had their dead leader's blessing. Wellington, on the other hand, anxious to retain the support and respect of the great landed magnates, insisted on a more protectionist bill and in particular on keeping his amendment which forbade the release of stored corn from warehouses until the domestic price had risen to 66s. a quarter.

At the end of three Cabinet discussions, on 10, 11 and 12 March 1828, no decision had been reached and Wellington found himself in a minority of one. Even Peel, his right-hand man, came out firmly on Huskisson's side. Three days later a compromise seemed in sight: the duke agreed to give up his 'warehouse' amendment and Huskisson accepted higher rates of duty than in the 1827 bill. But Charles Grant, who as President of the Board of Trade would have to present the bill in the Commons, refused to accept any alteration to Canning's bill, although Huskisson and Peel pointed out that they had been equally responsible for it. And Huskisson, made doubly sensitive by the merciless attacks of Lady Canning and her friends for his alleged betrayal of her husband, made it clear in the Cabinet that he felt his own character and reputation would be ruined if he seemed to be clinging to office after his younger colleague had carried out his threat to resign. The collapse of the government seemed imminent.

For nearly a fortnight Grant stayed away from Cabinet meetings, harassed and distressed by the efforts of his colleagues to bring him round. On 24 March he had an interview with Wellington at which he handed him his resignation. The duke did not accept it but showed it to the Cabinet next day. On the 26th Peel saw Grant but could make nothing of him. (That evening, however, the Cabinet managed to eat a 'très recherché' dinner off 'very handsome plate' at Huskisson's without saying a word about corn.) On the same day the King learned from Dudley what was going on. He was extremely annoyed by the threatened Cabinet crisis, and the other ministers were annoyed with Dudley for revealing it. On the 27th Wellington decided he had better have a talk with the King. His main concern was to stop Huskisson from resigning if Grant – as now seemed highly likely – refused to introduce the corn bill in the Commons the following evening, Friday the 28th. The King was willing to help and commanded Huskisson to wait on him at three o'clock next day.

Huskisson himself was beginning to lose patience with Grant. 'For God's sake,' he wrote, 'weigh well the responsibility you are about to incur towards the King, as well as towards the public – how it must fall upon others as well as upon yourself.' He ended his appeal by offering to call upon Grant that evening (the 27th).[64] Grant hastily begged him not to. He had just spent two hours listening to Palmerston, who had argued that Wellington had made a great sacrifice in giving up his 'warehouse' amendment and ought to be given a decent bridge to retreat over. Palmerston had also pointed out that if Grant went all the rest of the Canningites would have to go too – since they had agreed to sink or swim together – and a purely Tory government would soon abandon all Canning's principles. This had seemed to shake Grant, but not enough to stop him from assuring Huskisson, in a letter written that same evening, that the proposed corn bill would be discreditable to the Cabinet. At this Huskisson's patience finally snapped and before going to bed he gave full vent to his exasperation.

> I shall not dissemble from the King my entire conviction that our retirement will be received in the first instance with shouts and throwing up of hats by all who are hostile to liberal politics; and afterwards when the ground of it is to be explained, with incredulous astonishment and ineffable ridicule by every other class of men in the State.[65]

Feeling as he did, Huskisson had some difficulty next day in explaining to the King why he himself must follow Grant's example. He compared himself to someone who felt obliged to fight a duel, although he knew he was in the wrong, simply in order to show that he was not a coward. In the same way, he himself was obliged to resign, although he did not want to, so that he could not be accused of corruptly clinging to office. The King admitted the force of this argument and suggested that he might resign temporarily. But Huskisson felt this would only be a 'juggle'.

Meanwhile, Wellington had despatched his Chancellor of the Exchequer, Henry Goulburn, to Grant to demand whether he would, or would not, introduce the corn bill in the House of Commons that evening. Grant suddenly gave way. He said he was too unwell to face the Commons that evening, but firmly promised to introduce the corn resolutions the following Monday. Huskisson was still resisting the King's persuasions when a brief note from Peel told him, to his own relief and the King's delight, that the crisis was over.[66]

Not everyone was delighted by Grant's sudden and surprising capitulation. Wellington, who was already sorry he had brought the Canningites into his Cabinet, had, it seems, found himself in the uncomfortably disingenuous position of trying to prevent something which privately he would have welcomed. According to Mrs Arbuthnot, to whom he was accustomed to unburden himself freely, he was vexed and disappointed at the outcome,[67] and Grant did not improve matters when he included an emotional panegyric on Canning in his speech on the new corn bill.

Foreign issues were another source of discord within the Cabinet, particularly the Greek struggle for independence. Canning had hoped to achieve this through the efforts of Britain, France and Russia. The Treaty of London, signed a month before he died, aimed at Greek autonomy under Turkish suzerainty and provided for an armistice to be followed by joint mediation by the three powers. The treaty also envisaged the use of force, if necessary, to end the fighting. The Sultan refused to sign an armistice, and in September 1827 reinforced his troops in the Morea. On 20 October an accidental incident in the bay of Navarino led to a general engagement in which Admiral Codrington very nearly wiped out the Turkish and Egyptian navies. It was a tremendous victory for the Greek cause, but in the King's Speech at the opening of Parliament in January 1828 it was referred to merely as 'an untoward event'. By then the Russians were pressing hard for the allies to overcome Turkish recalcitrance by force, and Wellington was far more concerned with restraining Russian expansion, which he greatly feared, than with freeing the Greeks, which he did not think important. His colleagues were united in their fear of Russia, especially after it was learned officially in March that the Tsar intended to declare war on Turkey. But they were not all equally committed to the Treaty of London as the best hope of liberating the Greeks without allowing the Ottoman empire to fall under Russian control. Nor did they agree on the objectives of the treaty. Palmerston, Dudley and Huskisson wanted to execute it in what they believed to be 'the fair spirit of those who made it', while Wellington wanted to impose drastic territorial limits on Greece and make it as dependent as possible on Turkey. 'The Duke,' wrote Palmerston, 'while he professes to maintain it [the treaty], would execute it in the spirit of one who condemns it.'[68] Throughout April and May repeated, increasingly fractious, debates in the Cabinet brought agreement no nearer.

Palmerston described the Cabinet as 'differing upon almost every question of any importance . . . meeting to debate and dispute, and separating without deciding'.[69] Lyndhurst thought Cabinet meetings might go better if they were not held after dinner: 'We all drink too much and are not civil to each other.'[70] Whatever their cause, the Cabinet's dissensions were not all the fault of the Canningites. During the corn crisis Wellington had at first been the odd man out, although Grant's obstinate refusal to compromise had prolonged the crisis. On Greece, Peel firmly supported the Canningites' arguments for the maximum possible independence for the Greeks. But Palmerston, who as head of the War Office had already annoyed Wellington over various military issues, was most prominent in arguing the Greeks' case. It was only too easy for the duke's irritation with his colleagues to focus sharply on the four Canningites. By the beginning of May he would not have been sorry to lose all of them except the invaluable Huskisson. A few weeks later he was anxious to get rid of him as well.

Ironically, the issue over which the Canningites finally came to grief was not one on which they would have chosen to make a stand. They were not, any more than Canning had been, genuine parliamentary reformers. They believed that on the whole the existing electoral system did produce a House of Commons that adequately represented all the great interests in the country. But they recognized that it was subject to abuse and that if it was to be preserved the worst abuses would have to be eradicated. In particular they were concerned about the lack of representation of the new industrial towns. As Palmerston mildly remarked after his resignation: 'When people saw such populous places as Leeds and Manchester unrepresented, whilst a green mound of earth returned two members, it naturally gave rise to complaint.'[71] So too did the wholesale bribery of voters. Bribery to a greater or lesser extent was common practice, and some MPs felt it was both hypocritical and inconsistent to condemn it in some cases and not in others. But most politicians felt the line had to be drawn somewhere. The problem was how to draw it so that the most glaring causes for complaint were removed without opening the way to what would be considered revolutionary change.

In 1821 Grampound had been disfranchised and the seats given to the West Riding of Yorkshire. Lord John Russell had then claimed that there were fifty to sixty other cases of equally gross corruption. But the Whigs were divided and diffident about parliamentary reform. Nothing was done until 1827 when the House of Commons decided that the boroughs of East Retford and Penryn had overstepped the mark and deserved to lose their franchise, in one case to Birmingham and in the other to Manchester. In East Retford there was a long-established custom for the freeholders (who were alleged to belong to the lowest class of society) to receive twenty guineas for their vote from each of the successful candidates. In 1826 there was a riotous contest for one of the seats and the unsuccessful candidate petitioned against the return. The subsequent investigation by a Commons committee established, with a wealth of vivid detail, that all the East Retford electors firmly believed that they were entitled to be paid for their votes. They also demanded to be lavishly 'treated' in certain public houses in the town all day and for several weeks before the election. They had even been known to turn up outside a public house at six o'clock in the morning and rattle the shutters to be let in so that they could make the most of a day's free drinks. The amount of liquor dispensed each day varied according to how well the rival candidates were reckoned to be doing.[72]

In the case of Penryn, three parliamentary inquiries, the latest in 1826, had established beyond doubt that no one could get elected to the borough without resorting to extensive bribery. Just before polling started in 1826 the town crier proclaimed that the practice of making voters 'comfortable' would be discontinued. But after one day's polling it was considered expedient to reintroduce it.[73]

In both Manchester and Birmingham the prospect of enfranchisement had stimulated petitions, public meetings and drafting committees. Soon after Parliament met in January 1828 their expectations looked like being realized. Two Whigs, Lord John Russell and Charles Tennyson, introduced bills to transfer Penryn's franchise to Manchester and East Retford's to Birmingham. Some MPs argued that it was unfair to punish Penryn, where not all the voters seemed to be corrupt, as severely as East Retford, where undoubtedly they all were. A lesser punishment would be to enlarge the constituency by extending the franchise to the neighbouring hundred, as indeed had already been done in a few cases. This arrangement appealed to those who were being pushed unwillingly towards reform because, although it diluted franchise rights, it did not abolish any; nor was it likely to alter the existing balance between agricultural and urban interests on which great store was set. On the other hand, opponents of reform sometimes argued that it would be better to enfranchise some new towns in order to stave off 'anything like violent innovation'.[74]

When the misdeeds of Penryn and East Retford came up for discussion in the Cabinet, Wellington and Bathurst opted for the lesser punishment of diluting the franchise. Huskisson and his friends favoured the more severe punishment, but only Dudley felt strongly that both Birmingham and Manchester should be enfranchised. Peel sympathized with the Canningites' attitude but was anxious – as

indeed were Huskisson and Palmerston – not to establish a precedent
that the franchise of corrupt boroughs should automatically go to new
towns. He therefore suggested as a compromise that one of the de-
linquent boroughs should lose its seats to a new town and the other
should be allowed to keep its franchise but with enlarged boundaries.
After some argument over which borough deserved the more severe
punishment, it was agreed that Penryn's franchise should be transferred to a new town and East Retford added to the neighbouring
hundred of Bassetlaw.

Peel's compromise was accepted by the House of Commons and by
the end of March the bill to transfer Penryn's franchise to Manchester
had passed through all its stages and been sent up to the Lords. But
when the representatives of Penryn were summoned to the bar of the
House of Lords to explain their election proceedings, they argued so
stoutly in their own defence that Lord Carnarvon, the Whig peer in
charge of the bill, let it be known that he could no longer support the
total disfranchisement of the borough, but would instead propose its
absorption into the neighbouring hundred. Peel's compromise had
been effectively sabotaged.

On 19 May the Cabinet met to decide what line to take in the light
of Carnarvon's decision. Peel declared that he would support the
extension of East Retford's franchise even though the other half of his
compromise had fallen through. But Huskisson pointed out that in
the House of Commons on 21 March he himself had categorically
accepted a commitment to the enfranchisement of at least one new
town. If the Lords would not let Penryn go to Manchester, then he
must support the transfer of East Retford to Birmingham. Bathurst
suggested that the issue should be treated as an open one, like
Catholic emancipation. In the ensuing discussion neither Wellington
nor Peel spoke, and Palmerston for one was left with the distinct
impression that they would not object if ministers voted according to
their own convictions.

In the debate that same evening Peel supported an amendment to
the East Retford bill extending its franchise to the neighbouring
hundred instead of transferring it to Birmingham. He angrily repudiated a charge of inconsistency, pointing out, quite correctly, that
he had never promised to support the enfranchisement of at least one
new town. Huskisson could make no such claim, and there were
mocking cheers from the Opposition when Lord Sandon pointedly
reminded him of his pledge. He at once acknowledged his commitment but then, in an effort to divert the debate and gain time,
suggested an adjournment. Peel refused to support this ploy and

Huskisson became increasingly uneasy and undecided. He was, Palmerston felt, 'in that state of anxious doubt that any strong advice would have led him either way'. Palmerston took it upon himself to give that strong advice, and both he and Huskisson opposed the amendment.[75] It was carried by a slender majority of eighteen.

Palmerston walked home after the debate without discussing it with anyone. His conscience was clear and he had no forebodings of trouble to come. Huskisson, on the other hand, had had to listen to some harsh criticism after the vote, and he arrived home at two o'clock in the morning in such a state of perturbation that he sat down there and then to make amends to Wellington. He felt, he wrote, that he should 'lose no time in affording you an opportunity of placing my office in other hands' in order to prevent any appearance of disunity in the government, 'however unfounded in reality, or unimportant in itself, the question which has given rise to that appearance'.[76]

Wellington received this letter at ten o'clock the next morning. He professed to be greatly surprised but lost no time in presenting it to the King. Huskisson, who in the cool light of day was inclined to make light of the previous night's vote, was horrified to receive a curt note from Wellington informing him that the letter which he had intended to be only an offer to resign, made as an act of courtesy, had been presented to the King as a positive resignation. Dudley happened to be in Huskisson's office when the duke's note was brought in; he realized that Wellington had misunderstood Huskisson's intentions and went off at once to explain them to him. The duke, however, coldly denied that he had made any mistake. Dudley then enlisted the help of Palmerston who brought Wellington out of a debate in the House of Lords and for half an hour exerted all his powers of persuasion on him as they walked up and down the long gallery together. It was all to no avail. Palmerston went back to Huskisson and suggested that he had better send an explanatory letter to the duke. Between them they composed the letter (which Wellington received that evening) and then decided to go to the House of Commons and behave as if nothing was amiss.

Next day, Wednesday the 21st, there was a further exchange of letters between Huskisson and Wellington, and on the morning of the 22nd Huskisson received a third unyielding letter from the duke which both he and Palmerston felt closed the door on any further explanations. Palmerston, who on his social round the previous evening had been busy contradicting reports of his resignation, went off to tell Peel that he would no longer be in a position to introduce

After his resignation has been accepted by Wellington, Huskisson, dressed as a schoolboy wearing a dunce's cap, pleads with his schoolmaster, Wellington, that 'It's a *mistake*, please let a poor boy in again' (*c.* May 1828). Reproduced by kind permission of the Trustees of the British Museum, London.

the army estimates on the 23rd. They shook hands, both regretting that they were obliged to part.[77]

Dudley, however, professed to believe that all was not yet lost. He went to Wellington and suggested that the whole correspondence should be withdrawn as 'non-avenue'. The duke replied that it was not for him to instruct Huskisson, but as a man of sense and of the world he must know what he ought to do. Huskisson described this pronouncement as very oracular. With some exasperation he told Dudley that he had 'given the Duke every explanation he could think of, and was he now to embark on a game of political blind-man's buff until he managed to catch what would do?'[78] What the duke seemed to want from Huskisson – or rather what he would feel obliged to accept – was not any more explanations, but a simple withdrawal of his resignation. This, however, Huskisson argued he could not provide because he had never resigned in the first place.

By Sunday, the 25th, Wellington's patience had run out. He told Dudley, the would-be mediator, that if he did not hear something satisfactory from Huskisson by two o'clock that afternoon, he would go to the King with the name of his successor. Dudley, however, did not choose to be the bearer of an ultimatum, and so the deadline came and went while Huskisson was composing yet another explanation of his conduct, this time for the benefit of the King, who had refused to receive him. About 7.30 that evening he received a note from Wellington informing him that a new Colonial Secretary had been appointed.

Before going to bed that night Palmerston wrote a formal letter of resignation to Wellington. William Lamb regretfully sent in his resignation next day, and Dudley even more reluctantly (and to Wellington's surprise) followed suit on the 27th. Charles Grant, who had taken no part in the crisis because of the illness and death of his sister, also resigned. So did two junior ministers. 'We joined as a party,' wrote Palmerston; 'as a party we retired.'

Huskisson claimed that he had been 'very uncourteously *turned out*'.[79] But he acknowledged that he was to blame for providing Wellington with an excuse in the shape of an ambiguously worded letter written in haste and agitation in the middle of the night and never reconsidered in the cool light of day.[80] But instead of retrieving his blunder by accepting the duke's interpretation of his letter and simply withdrawing it, he had persisted in trying to explain that he had not really meant to resign at all. The duke had simply ignored his explanations. As Lord Granville (who refused to stay in Paris under an undiluted Tory government) put it, the Duke of

Wellington 'adheres to any view of a subject once taken by him, with a tenacity which in his military capacity may be useful, but which is very inconvenient to those who act *with* him and not *under* him in politics'.[81]

Although Wellington took nearly a week to end the uncertainty by appointing Sir George Murray as Huskisson's successor, there seems little doubt that he seized on Huskisson's unfortunate letter to get rid of the Canningites. He had found his ministerial team unexpectedly difficult to manage, and he could not ignore hints – well-meaning or malicious – that he looked like being as weak and ineffective a Prime Minister as Goderich had been. Even the King was reported to have talked to him in this strain. By their votes on 19/20 May Huskisson and Palmerston had reinforced this impression of a thoroughly disunited government and had fanned the dissatisfaction of the ultra Tories in the House of Commons.

Moreover, Wellington was greatly irritated by the way the Canningites always stuck together and never lost an opportunity to proclaim their devotion to the principles of their dead leader. Only a few days before the East Retford debate Palmerston had infuriated Wellington by declaring, during a debate on a pension for Canning's family, that 'the government of this country would be entitled to parliamentary support in proportion as it adhered to the principles of Mr Canning'. Granville, who felt that Huskisson's letter had been a hasty and unnecessary gesture, thought it was a pity that 'the friends of Canning' were not separating from the Tories 'upon some broad political principle intelligible to the common sense of the world'. But by the end of the crisis Huskisson had become bitterly convinced that Wellington was determined to get rid of him somehow in order to keep control over the restive ultras in his party. 'Where there is a will there is always a way. A most unimportant occurrence on a most trifling question ... afforded the way.'[82] He could not foresee the momentous consequences that would flow from that 'most unimportant occurrence'.

2

The Turning Point

(January–July 1828)

'. . . I entertain a confident hope that, if you elect me, the most bigoted of our enemies will see the necessity of removing from the chosen representative of the people an obstacle which would prevent him from doing his duty to his King and Country.'

O'Connell's election address, 24 June 1828

While the Duke of Wellington was still in the throes of Cabinet-making, O'Connell and the Irish Catholics were declaring their un-compromising hostility to an administration that they firmly believed would be totally opposed to their claims for political equality. On Sunday, 13 January 1828, simultaneous meetings were held in nearly two thirds of the parishes of Ireland. The *Dublin Evening Post* estimated that there must have been about one and a half million people assembled at the same time for the same purpose: to approve petitions demanding unconditional and unqualified emancipation. In Dublin the New Catholic Association held a fourteen-day meeting at which speaker after speaker demanded unqualified emancipation and denounced Wellington, Peel and the Tories in general. On one occasion O'Connell went so far as to suggest that if the ultra 'boroughmongering faction' should prevail in the new administration, they might have to petition both for reform (parliamentary) and the repeal of the Union.[1] He was loudly cheered when he defied the government to prevent the Irish from discussing Catholic politics: 'if they prevent us from talking politics, why we will whistle or sing them.'[2] The meeting's defiance culminated in a resolution to consider 'every Irish member of Parliament an enemy to the freedom, peace

and happiness of Ireland, who will support, either directly or indirectly, any administration of which the Duke of Wellington, or any
individual professing his principles, is the head or contriver'.[3] In
future even a parliamentary candidate who was personally in favour
of emancipation would be opposed if he supported the Duke of
Wellington.

But meetings in Dublin, however enthusiastic, were of only limited
value unless the Association could extend and consolidate its influence
throughout Ireland. In 1824 O'Connell had successfully achieved this
through the Catholic 'rent'. Those who paid it and those who collected it felt involved in a common enterprise in which they all
had a personal stake. But when reintroduced by the New Catholic
Association after the 1826 general election, the Catholic 'rent' failed to
make much impact. O'Connell tried hard to reinvigorate it. 'There is
nothing', he wrote in April 1827, 'our enemies dread so much as the
extension and permanence of the Catholic Rent.'[4] At the end of the
year he hit on an improved method of collecting it which not only
greatly increased the amount subscribed, but also helped to emphasize the Association's concern with every kind of local grievance.
At his suggestion two churchwardens were appointed in each parish,
one chosen by the priest and the other by the church vestry. They
supervised the collection of the 'rent' and also acted as a kind of two-
way channel through which the Association's headquarters in Dublin
and local Catholic parishioners throughout Ireland could be kept fully
informed about each other's concerns and activities. The churchwardens were instructed how to prepare monthly reports on all kinds
of local matters, such as the progress of the 'rent' collection, the
amounts paid (principally as tithes) to the Protestant Church, the
progress of education, Protestant proselytizing, evictions and the
maintenance of the electoral registers. Every Saturday each church-
warden was sent a copy of a *Weekly Register* containing full reports
of the speeches made and resolutions passed at the twice-weekly
meetings of the Association in Dublin. The churchwardens lent it to
those parishioners who could read, and on Sunday read it aloud at the
chapel door. According to Thomas Wyse, admittedly a biased witness, passages from the speeches recorded in the *Register* could be
heard for weeks afterwards 'accompanied with the shrewdest comments from the mouth of the humblest peasant in the country'.[5]
Inevitably, not all the churchwardens were equal to the demands
made upon them. But they did improve the collection of the 'rent'.
Even in the first week of the new system, when it was only very
partially in operation, the total amount subscribed more than trebled.

At the end of February 1828 Field Marshal Henry William Paget, first Marquess of Anglesey, sailed into Dublin bay to take up his post as Lord Lieutenant. He had been one of the best cavalry officers in the British army. He had taken part in all four of the army's attempts to grapple with revolutionary and Napoleonic France between 1794 and 1809 and had greatly distinguished himself during Sir John Moore's retreat to Corunna. He took no further part in the Peninsular campaign, because he happened to be senior in rank to the commanding general, Arthur Wellesley, and also because he had caused a spectacular scandal by eloping with the wife of Wellesley's brother, Henry Wellesley. But he ended his military career with glory on the field of Waterloo where he commanded the allied cavalry and lost a leg during the closing stage of the battle. He returned home to a hero's welcome and the reward of a marquessate. But it was more than ten years before he was able to embark on a public career in civilian life. He was not unacquainted with politics; like other officers at that period, he had combined his army career with a seat in the House of Commons until his father's death in 1812 sent him up to the House of Lords as the Earl of Uxbridge. He attended the debates quite regularly, although his extreme aversion to public speaking prevented him from taking part in them. He felt, however, that he owed it to himself and to his family to play a dignified and useful role in public life if he could find one.

Anglesey was not a party man, and the post of Master General of the Ordnance, which was closely connected with the army, was, he felt, the only position in the government that would suit him. In April 1827 Canning offered him this post together with a seat in the Cabinet. Anglesey had hoped to be offered the first without the second, partly because he had doubts about some of Canning's policies and partly because as a member of the Cabinet he might be faced with the dreaded ordeal of speaking in the House of Lords. It took him a fortnight to make up his mind to join the Cabinet, and when he did he made it clear that he was obeying the King's command rather than the Prime Minister's wishes. He also indicated that he would much rather be the King's representative in Dublin. He had not long to wait. In July Canning agreed that he should succeed Lord Wellesley as Lord Lieutenant at the end of the year.

On the great issue that dominated the government of Ireland – Catholic emancipation – Anglesey's views were not at all clear. Although he had no sympathy at all for the ultra Tories, he was assumed to be a Protestant. This presumably was largely why Canning was anxious to include him in his Cabinet, which looked like being

too pro-Catholic to satisfy the King. But Anglesey sometimes gave
the impression that he was not really a convinced opponent of the
Catholic claims. According to Lady Cowper, in August 1827 he was
said to be 'very sincere for the Catholics'.[6] He certainly had been
once. Between 1817 and 1822 he had voted four times in the House of
Lords in favour of the removal of some Catholic disabilities. But
he had been greatly alarmed by the success of O'Connell and the
Catholic Association in stirring up the whole of Ireland to agitate
for Catholic relief, and in May 1825 he had seconded a successful
motion in the Lords to defeat the Catholic relief bill approved by the
Commons. He told the Lords that he had changed his mind because
the Catholics seemed to be aiming not just at emancipation but at a
complete Catholic ascendancy. He would still gladly relieve them of
all their disabilities, but not at the expense of the Protestants. Two
years later he told Lord Holland, a Whig and an unwavering supporter of emancipation, that to grant it under duress would be to put
a premium on violence, but if Holland could find some unequivocal
guarantee for the existing Protestant establishment, 'you shall have
me with you *tooth and nail*'.[7]

Whether or not Anglesey was right in supposing – as he probably
did – that this condition could be met, his attitude was certainly far
less extreme than that of the ultra Tories who simply ruled out
Catholic emancipation altogether. After Canning's death he was dis-
mayed by the possibility that the King might again fall under the
ultras' influence, but still insist, on grounds of personal friendship,
that Anglesey should stick by him and go to Dublin.[8] He realized
what a formidable task governing Ireland would be and was appalled
by the prospect of having to tackle it as the representative of an ultra-
Tory, anti-Catholic government. When he heard on 9 January that
Wellington had been asked to form a government, he happened to be
completely prostrated by one of the very severe attacks of facial
neuralgia which periodically afflicted him and which was causing
rumours that he would not in any case be fit enough to go to Dublin.
But he roused himself to write to Huskisson to urge him not to refuse
to serve in the new government. 'I fear Ultraism from whatever
quarter, and you appear to me to be the person who will take the true
view of affairs.'[9]

In the event, Anglesey's fears were only partly realized. A ministry
headed by Wellington and Peel was indeed sure to arouse Irish
hostility. But the Cabinet was almost equally divided into pro- and
anti-Catholics, and the Chief Secretary, William Lamb, sympathized
with the Catholics' case. In the previous September Anglesey had told

Lamb that he rejoiced to know he would have with him in Dublin a man whose views on the Catholic question appeared to be identical with his own.[10] He would also retain the politically neutral Sir Anthony Hart as Irish Lord Chancellor. Hart, an eminent English lawyer whom Canning had made Vice-Chancellor of England, had replaced the aggressively Protestant Lord Manners in Dublin a few months earlier.

Moreover, Wellington and Peel gave no sign of dissatisfaction at having inherited Anglesey as the next Lord Lieutenant in Dublin. On 21 January Wellington told him that it was the anxious wish of the King, Peel and himself that he should still go to Ireland.[11] Five days later Peel assured him that he had 'cordially rejoiced' in his appointment and hoped that he would not now change his mind because of the change of government.[12] Both Peel and Wellington apparently believed that Anglesey was 'safe', from their point of view, on the Catholic question (although London society seems to have had a different impression) and his consultations with them before his departure were satisfactory to all three. So Anglesey, who certainly would not have stooped to practise any sort of dissimulation, went to Dublin in the reasonably confident expectation that he would be able to get on with the government he represented.

It does not seem to have occurred to him that they might not be able to get on with him, although he might have been warned by an exchange at his farewell audience with the King. According to Anglesey's son-in-law, Lord Mount Charles, who was present, the King said: 'God bless you Anglesey! I know you are a true Protestant.' To which Anglesey replied: 'Sir, I will not be considered either Protestant or Catholic; I go to Ireland determined to act impartially between them and without the least bias either one way or the other.'[13]

This ringing declaration in favour of even-handedness would not have surprised O'Connell if he could have heard it. A few days before Anglesey's arrival in Dublin O'Connell told the Catholic Association that he did not anticipate evil from the new Lord Lieutenant's administration. 'I believe at least that he will come over with the intentions of discharging his functions for the benefit of all; but we ought to recollect that he will be surrounded by the worst men that ever poisoned the ear of authority.'[14] O'Connell tended to spoil a good case by exaggeration, but Dublin Castle, the seat of government, was undoubtedly a citadel of the Protestant Ascendancy. Most of the permanent officials who manned it could not possibly claim to be without 'the least bias one way or the other'. The most important and influential of them was the Under-Secretary. He was privy to all the most confidential official business and was the channel through which the Castle communicated with the local, military and ecclesiastical authorities. In practice he deputized for the Chief Secretary during the latter's lengthy absences in London.

The present Under-Secretary was William Gregory, son of a Galway landowner, who had been educated at Harrow, Cambridge and the Inner Temple, and had held several official posts in Ireland before being appointed Under-Secretary in 1812. He had married into one of the most powerful Ascendancy families and his own views were uncompromisingly and rigidly Protestant. In contrast to William Lamb, who believed 'that the distractions of Ireland could never be composed while the civil distinctions remained',[15] Gregory's remedy for Catholic unrest was always repression, never concession. When told that a new Catholic club in Dublin had ordered uniforms and twenty-five brace of pistols, he asked: 'Can the blockheads think to terrify by these manifestations? Or are their necks itching for the rope?'[16] When Canning, with his well-known Catholic sympathies, became Prime Minister, Gregory's first reaction was to resign; his second was to withdraw his resignation.[17] Anglesey, who had received the most virulently hostile reports about him, was anxious to get rid of him. In October 1827 Lansdowne had told Lamb that the Cabinet were looking for a way to do this 'that shall be both civil in manner and satisfactory in substance'.[18] No way was found. In any case, in spite of their different outlooks, Lamb got on well with Gregory, a man of polished and agreeable manners, and was not anxious to lose him.

It had been rumoured in Dublin, perhaps because of Anglesey's military reputation, that the new viceroy would make his state entrance into the city clad in a suit of armour borrowed from the Tower of London. Instead he wore a plain blue coat and a round hat, his only ornament being the ribbon of the Garter. He was rowed ashore through ships dressed overall to a pier lined with troops, while guns fired salutes and rockets soared skywards. The Dubliners had turned out in force and he responded to their enthusiastic cheers by bowing to all around him before getting into his carriage to be driven through the city to the Castle. 'Every window', wrote the correspondent of *The Times*, 'from the entrance to the city to the Castle, is crowded by thousands of elegantly-dressed women – the housetops are, as it were, living, so great is the density of persons who have taken their station upon them.' Inside the Castle Anglesey took the prescribed oath, made the statutory declaration, received the sword of state and was invested as grand master of the Order of St Patrick. When the lengthy ceremonial was over, the state trumpeters blew their trumpets, and the guns in Phoenix Park fired salutes. Anglesey, still in indifferent health, found it 'a very hard day's work', but he wrote cheerfully to Lamb next day: 'It all went off vastly well, and as there was nobody to give me dinner, I gave an impromptu of 30 covers to all the Bigwigs. I was a good deal fagged, and had much pain, but I was not interrupted in the proceedings.'[19]

Convinced that he could do nothing with or for the Irish people until he had earned their trust, Anglesey proceeded to build on the excellent first impression he had made. Every morning, when he was fit enough, he rode through the city, dressed in the plainest of clothes and accompanied by only a single equerry. He made a point of buying all he needed locally, choosing his tradesmen without reference to their religion. He entertained lavishly, both Catholics and Protestants, in the belief that it could only do good to oblige them to mix socially under his roof. Between 4 March and 19 April he gave fourteen dinner parties and attended three; he held three levées and two 'drawing-rooms', and gave four balls; he went four times to the theatre and once to a concert.[20] An aristocratic German visitor, who dined with Anglesey at the viceregal lodge in Phoenix Park, wrote that no man had 'a more graceful and polished address in society'. (He added that he had never seen 'a more perfect work of art than his false leg'.[21])

Outside Dublin, a world away from its drawing-rooms and ball-rooms, the peasants continued their sporadic warfare against grasping landlords or their agents. In the monthly police reports one or two murders and a few riots or other 'outrages' did not disqualify a county from being described as 'perfectly' or 'generally' quiet. But in parts of central Ireland, particularly in Tipperary where more than fifty persons were on trial for murder, rent increases and evictions had provoked the agrarian secret societies – Whiteboys, Ribbonmen, Rockites – into more than 'normal' activity. Anglesey took it all very coolly. 'Tipperary', he told Peel on 9 April, 'is not in so desperate a state as you seem to imagine.'[22] Three weeks later he assured the Home Secretary that the monthly police reports showed a reduction in crimes and misdemeanours and he thought the country was 'going on well'. The rest of his letter hardly bore this out. In County Louth a nest of Ribbonmen had been uncovered (presumably with the aid of an informer) and nearly 200 were believed to have fled the country. The Rockite system was abating in the western part of Wicklow 'where it had got to a great height'. In County Cork, 'where great

excesses had been committed', Mr Villiers Stuart's property had had
to be protected. 'The movement of some of the Constabulary forces to
the neighbourhood supported at some distance by a few dragoons,
appears to have restored order.' In part of Kildare the Duke of
Leinster's plans to enforce part of the highly unpopular Sub-Letting
Act had caused 'some commotion'.* After reading this catalogue of
dangers overcome, Peel may well have felt disinclined to accept the
breezy assurance with which Anglesey had begun his letter: 'You
must always suppose that no news is good news.'[23] By the end of
May, however, Anglesey's unobtrusive demonstrations of force had
snuffed out the disorders and what passed for normality in the Irish
countryside had been restored.

Like other temporary residents of Dublin Castle before him,
Anglesey was well aware that repression was not the answer to the
endemic unrest of the Irish peasants. He realized that the plight
of many of them was desperate and that they resorted to violent
remedies because no peaceful ones seemed to be available to them.
'The people of Ireland', he told William Lamb, 'want proof that their
interests are attended to and that they are to be improved by other
means than mere acts of Parliament!'[24] He set himself to study what
those other means might be, and in the middle of May he began to
bombard Peel with appeals and suggestions. 'I feel, as you will already
have observed, very anxious (too sanguine you will probably think in
the expectations I entertain) that something should be done to call
forth the energy of this people and to direct it from its present idle and
dissolute habits.' He suggested, among other things, that the import
duty on coal should be repealed so that Irish manufacturers could
compete on more equal terms with their English competitors, and that
public money should be provided for road-building which would both
provide employment and open up the more inaccessible parts of the
country. He sent Peel a long list of proposals drawn up by the Society
for the Improvement of Ireland, annotated in the margin with his own
shrewd comments. Public works, such as building roads and police
barracks, provided only temporary employment and Anglesey gave
a cautious welcome to the Society's proposal for a commission to
dispense a parliamentary grant in loans to be used for creating
permanent employment and then gradually repaid. It was, he felt,
'very captivating upon paper' and if it could be proved that the

---

* The Sub-Letting Act, passed in 1826, was designed to strengthen the law against
the subdivision of land without the landlord's permission. It was bitterly opposed by
O'Connell and the Catholic Association.

money would be repaid 'surely the government might be prevailed upon to advance a little?'[25]

Peel had been over this ground many times before during his stint as Chief Secretary between 1812 and 1818. When the potato harvest partially failed in 1817 he energetically organized the expenditure of large sums of money on famine relief measures. But in more normal times his thinking did not stray far beyond the boundaries set by the *laissez-faire* doctrines that were the received economic wisdom of the day. He assured Anglesey that his report would be fully considered, but pointed out that there were 'real and solid objections' to any government interference in the establishment of manufactures. 'The effect of such interference upon pre-existing establishments founded by the unaided efforts of individuals must of course be considered.' But he acknowledged that Ireland was a special case. 'Still I am willing to admit that general principles must not be pushed too far in their application to a country wherein the necessity of an immediate remedy is so urgent as it is in Ireland'.[26]

Anglesey was sufficiently encouraged to send Peel more details of his plans. 'I beg you not to consider me as a visionary', he wrote, apparently still afraid that the experienced politician in London would not take him sufficiently seriously. 'I have taken great pains to inform myself upon these subjects, and I feel quite confident that I am not misleading you. You will observe that for the roads, a most *material object*, not more than £10,000 will be wanted and the advantages to be expected from them are very great indeed.'[27] But just as Peel was going to consult his colleagues about Anglesey's proposals, the four Canningites resigned and the problems of Ireland had to give way to the more pressing preoccupations of a government reshuffle.

When Peel's carefully considered reply finally came towards the end of July, it was not encouraging. He refused outright any government help towards setting up new industries, agreed to consider the removal of the duty on coal imports, and promised £10,000 towards road-building if a similar sum was raised locally.[28] When Anglesey renewed his appeals, Peel set out in detail what had been spent in recent years on trying to develop the Irish economy.[29] It was a time-honoured expedient, still much favoured by governments today, for fending off requests for money. But then, as now, it was no help at all to those whose needs were still so great.

Agrarian unrest was such an accepted fact of life in Ireland that the authorities were not inclined to blame the Catholic Association for its

resurgence in the spring of 1828. But Peel, whose familiarity with the
problems of law and order in Ireland had not made him treat them
with contempt, was seriously worried about the trouble-making
potentialities of the Association itself. The orators at its weekly meetings in Dublin were uncompromisingly hostile to the Wellington
government. When O'Connell, acting on a suggestion of Lord John
Russell's, proposed that the Association should withdraw its opposition
to all parliamentary candidates who supported the present government, as a conciliatory response to the repeal of the Test and Corporation Acts, he was so violently opposed that he had to drop the
idea. Moreover, the plan to establish churchwardens in each parish,
acting in effect as the agents of the Association's headquarters in
Dublin, looked suspiciously like an attempt to set up a subversive
organization throughout the country. The 1825 Act banning unlawful
societies was due to expire at the end of the current parliamentary
session, and both Wellington and Peel were far from happy at
relinquishing any legal weapon against the Association, however
ineffective it had been. When Lamb told the duke that in his opinion
to renew the Act would only produce 'useless and unnecessary
exasperation', Wellington 'looked staggered and with that air, which
he always has, of a man very little accustomed to be differed from or
contradicted, and changed the subject'.[30]

When the New Catholic Association was first formed in 1825, the
law officers of the Crown, in both Dublin and London, were so
uncertain whether a jury would agree that it was illegal that no action
was taken. In April 1828, the Irish Attorney-General, Henry Joy, a
man with pronounced Orange sympathies, produced a lengthy legal
opinion in which he argued that although individual Catholic meetings were not illegal, the Association had acted in such a way as to
make it an illegal assembly under the 1825 Act. But whether it should
in fact be suppressed was a matter of expediency which the government must decide. Anglesey had no difficulty in making up his mind.
He was strongly of the opinion that it would be inexpedient to
suppress the Association and useless to renew an Act which Catholic
lawyers were so much better at evading than the Crown lawyers were
at enforcing. He felt that a really watertight law would have to
infringe so much on the subjects' rights of petitioning and assembly
that Parliament would never accept it. With his usual optimism, he
believed that the Association, at least the extremist element in it,
was running out of steam and support and that this process would
continue as long as nothing was done to stir things up. 'If, however,
we have a mind to have a *good blaze* again, we may at once command

it by re-enacting the expiring bill.'[31] He strongly advised that the
1825 Act should be allowed to lapse without any publicity or fuss and
that the activities of the Catholic Association – and of the Orange
lodges* – should be firmly controlled by 'the strong arm of the
common law'.[32]

When the Cabinet met on 2 May to decide whether to renew
the 1825 Act, Anglesey's advice carried the day. Both Peel and
Wellington had doubts about the decision. On the same day Peel
wrote to Lamb urging him to watch the activities of the Association
with 'increased vigilance' and to find out from the law officers
whether the churchwardens were acting within the law in setting up
a system of communications throughout the country.[33] Henry Joy
decided that they were, so long as the association which appointed
them was legal. But he believed that their activities were 'pregnant
with danger to the country' and provided an additional reason for
suppressing the Association itself. 'Sooner or later', he added, 'that
must be done.'[34]

While the Irish Attorney-General was privately disposing of the
Catholic Association, the Irish Catholics were eagerly waiting for
news of yet another debate on Catholic emancipation in the House of
Commons. On 8 May Sir Francis Burdett tabled a motion to consider
the laws affecting the Roman Catholics 'with a view to a final and
conciliatory adjustment'. The motion was debated for three days.
There was nothing new to say on the subject, but it was said all over
again all the same. John Croker thought that Peel made a good
argument on the controversial Treaty of Limerick imposed on the
defeated Irish in 1691; 'but really one might as well, at this time of
day, talk of Noah's flood as of the Treaty of Limerick'.[35] In the early
hours of 13 May, in a crowded House, Burdett's motion was carried
by a majority of six. It was only a small majority, but to both the
friends and the opponents of emancipation it was a significant victory
for the Catholics. 'The turn of the debate,' wrote Lord Holland, 'the
tone of the government and a variety of other symptoms have convinced all rational men, if not that the question ought to be passed, at
least that it will and must be passed ere long.'[36]

Peel was one of these rational men. He had always been a dedicated, even bigoted, opponent of emancipation, and he remained

---

* The Orange Order was founded in 1795 by northern Protestants in response to
Catholic agitation. It was dissolved in 1825 under the law banning unlawful societies in
Ireland and reformed in the autumn of 1828 with the Duke of Cumberland at its head.

intellectually and emotionally unconvinced by all the arguments in its favour. But he realized that it could not be resisted any longer; the cost in terms of a divided government and an unsettled Ireland was too high. The consequence for himself, he felt, was plain: he could not continue as leader of the House of Commons when he was in the minority on the most important domestic issue of the day. He told Wellington he must resign from the government; he was too committed to opposing emancipation to play a leading part in carrying it now. But the duke was not similarly committed, and Peel urged him not to say anything in the forthcoming debate in the House of Lords on 10 June that would prevent him from making plans during the summer recess to settle the Catholic issue.

Wellington had always taken a cool pragmatic view of Catholic emancipation. He was anxious for a settlement, provided it included adequate protection for the Protestants and their Church against Catholic domination. When a crisis over emancipation threatened to topple the government in 1825, he had proposed to settle it by means of a concordat with Rome which would allow the government enough supervision of the Roman Catholic Church to protect Protestant interests. His suggestion was not taken up at the time, but he remained – as Palmerston found when discussing the Catholic issue with him in January – '*not* a bigot on that question. He considers it as a political and not at all as a religious question, and therefore perfectly open to consideration according to times and circumstances.'[37] Palmerston's impression was not mistaken. Wellington went so far as to investigate, very privately, the views of an Anglican cleric, Henry Phillpotts, on the securities that would be necessary if concessions were made to the Catholics. Phillpotts had published two pamphlets strongly arguing the case against admitting Catholics to Parliament. But he welcomed with enthusiasm the chance to influence a compromise settlement and Wellington received a steady stream of lengthy and learned letters on every aspect of the state's relations with the Roman Catholic Church. Phillpotts's efforts did not go unrewarded; in May he was made Dean of Chester.

The crisis caused by the Canningites' departure at the end of May stopped Peel for the time being from abandoning his post as well. The 'break-up' took him completely by surprise and he found himself heavily involved in helping the Prime Minister to repair the gaps in his administration. Lord Aberdeen, whom Wellington had brought into the Cabinet (for the first time) as Chancellor of the Duchy of Lancaster, replaced Dudley as Foreign Secretary. Sir George Murray, a veteran of the Peninsular war, was brought over from Ireland where he was commanding the army, to succeed Huskisson as Secretary of State for war and the colonies. Another old soldier, Sir Henry Hardinge, who had lost an arm at the battle of Ligny, took over from Palmerston as Secretary at War (but without a seat in the Cabinet). Finally, Vesey Fitzgerald, a Protestant Irishman, succeeded Grant at the Board of Trade. Palmerston, who after nearly twenty years in office found it 'quite comical' to be able to do what he liked every day, thought that the new government was 'somewhat too military to be very pleasing to the country'.[38]

That aspect of the political changes was not likely to bother Anglesey. But the departure of the Canningites upset and unsettled him to the point of contemplating resignation. He feared, he told Peel on 2 June, that he was holding on in Dublin by 'a very feeble tenure'; and after referring to a man suspected of conspiring against the government, he added with good-humoured resignation: 'I think you are all safe at this moment, for if the murdering of Ministers is the main object of the plot, he will be a clever fellow in these times to determine upon whom to strike the blow.'[39]

Although Anglesey was assured there would be no changes of policy, the new Cabinet certainly seemed less friendly towards the Catholics than the old one, and there was a general impression that the ultra Tories were in the ascendant. They themselves certainly thought so. At the Pitt Club dinner on 28 May they toasted the 'Protestant Ascendancy' with unrestrained jubilation, and Wellington by his presence seemed to give the proceedings his blessing. A few days later Anglesey complained to his brother that he was in a distressing dilemma. 'All *my* friends are walking off, I hardly know why. Yet all are requiring *me* to stay behind. To have a rear guard is very well, if you can count upon support, but when quite abandoned it alters the case.'[40] He had a horror of being associated with a Cabinet which, in his agitation, he feared would be ultra-Tory and anti-Catholic just when he himself was daily becoming more firmly convinced that the Catholic question must be settled. On the other hand, he did not want to embarrass the government by resigning. Nor did he want to abandon the task of tranquillizing Ireland, or risk making the situation there worse. 'It is certain', he told Lord Holland,

that I stand well with all parties, and that somehow or other, I have obtained a sort of influence with the Catholics, that at this moment actually keeps them quiet; now, if I withdraw, they will instantly suppose that I do so from a persuasion that their cause is hopeless

under the newly constructed government; and I should fear very unpleasant results from such an impression. I wish to God I knew how I
could serve the state – that course I would pursue. To serve it at all, I
must serve it consistently.[41]

Anglesey's distress was greatly increased by the government's failure
to pay attention to his wishes with regard to Lamb's successor. On 2
June he told Peel he was in no hurry to have the vacancy filled and he
hoped he would be consulted before a decision was reached.[42] Three
days later Peel assured him that he wanted to make an appointment
'in every way unobjectionable to you'.[43] In fact Wellington had
already made two unsuccessful attempts to fill the post. His first offer
was to Frankland Lewis, who had just resigned as Charles Grant's
deputy at the Board of Trade and understandably felt it would be
embarrassing to rejoin the government so soon. His second offer was
made to Wilmot Horton, a pro-Catholic of indeterminate party
allegiance, who refused after reading reports of the Pitt Club dinner.
Finally, Lord Francis Leveson-Gower, the younger son of one of
Canning's earliest friends, the Marquess of Stafford, was prevailed on
to accept the post. A young man of twenty-eight, he had entered
Parliament in 1822 and been given junior office by Canning five years
later. His political career was complicated by his feeling obliged to
defer to the wishes of his elderly and rather difficult father while
finding it impossible always to agree with him. In January 1828, after
some initial parental opposition, he accepted office as Huskisson's
Under-Secretary. At the end of May he resigned with the other
Canningites. According to Palmerston, he agreed to become Chief
Secretary because his father told him it was too good a post to turn
down.[44]

Of Leveson-Gower's Catholic sympathies there was no doubt. In
the Commons debate on 8 May he had robustly ridiculed Protestant
fears and insisted that emancipation was inevitable, and the sooner
the better. Peel assured Anglesey he knew no one better calculated 'to
act cordially with you. And from temper, manners and coolness of
judgment to give general satisfaction in Ireland.' Anglesey was not
convinced. He told Peel bluntly that Leveson-Gower would not do in
Ireland; indeed he would be a great embarrassment.[45] He was not
being altogether unreasonable. Leveson-Gower, besides being young
and inexperienced, had more of a reputation as a poet than as a
politician: his work had been commended by no less an authority
than Sir Walter Scott. To Anglesey such attainments were only an
additional source of annoyance. 'His scholarship,' he complained, 'his

taste, his literary acquirements are thrown away upon me. I can turn them to no account.'[46] Moreover, Lord Francis, whom one observer described as having 'a melancholy cast of countenance' (as befitted a poet presumably), lacked the cheerful extrovert kind of disposition that appealed to Anglesey. Although he told Peel that he did not object personally to Leveson-Gower, to his brother he described him as 'a man whose manner is so cold, so rebuffing, so distant that it will be impossible to establish free and familiar intercourse.'[47]

Finding, however, that he had no choice in the matter, Anglesey decided to make the best of it. With characteristic frankness he told Leveson-Gower that he had not wanted him: 'Being myself young in official life, altho' old in years, I felt that I wanted a practical man of business – one of more experience than either you or I possess, but I beg you to believe that as we are thus thrown together, I will act with you with as much cordiality and goodwill, as if the appointment had originated with me.'[48] His refusal to bear a grudge was well rewarded. Leveson-Gower was intelligent, able, good-tempered and kind-hearted. Three months later Anglesey was assuring Peel that he found in him 'a very able and zealous assistant, and I have no doubt that everything will go on most satisfactorily between us.'[49]

After only a few months in the country, Anglesey had lost whatever doubts he may have had about Catholic emancipation and felt an almost missionary zeal for the task of restoring peace and prosperity to Ireland. He believed that it was 'capable of great things – of immense improvement. With encouragement, with care, with firmness, with moderation, I am quite persuaded that it would make rapid strides in prosperity from the moment that the great question is satisfactorily adjusted.' He was, of course, referring to the Catholic question. But even before it was settled, he believed that 'much good may be effected', always provided that the Catholics were not deprived of a reasonable hope that the door to emancipation would not be finally closed.[50] Anglesey set out to keep that hope alive by a policy of friendly conciliation that would calm the extremists and strengthen the moderates. He adopted the same policy towards the leaders of the Orange party whose acquiescence, however unwilling, was essential to a peaceful settlement.

Anglesey, the man on the spot, believed that both Catholics and Orangists, however violent they might seem to be, would, with a little gentle persuasion, behave in a moderate and reasonable way. Wellington in London, on the other hand, felt that the Catholics, or at any rate the leading members of the Catholic Association, were

already behaving in a way that could not be allowed to pass un-
challenged. He would have liked the Association to be prosecuted as
well as the churchwardens who were having such 'odious' duties
imposed on them.[51] Although he was coming round to the view that
emancipation would have to be granted, he could not bear that it
should appear to be at the behest of the Catholic Association.

Wellington's dilemma was reflected in the speech he made on 10
June in the House of Lords opposing Lansdowne's motion to accept
the Commons' vote of 11 May on the Catholic issue. He acknowledged
that he would like to see the disabilities of the Roman Catholics
removed, but first he must be satisfied that 'our institutions' would be
properly protected, and he discussed in very general terms how this
might be done. He ended with the statement: 'If the public mind was
suffered to be thus tranquil – if the agitators of Ireland would only
leave the public mind at rest – the people would become more
satisfied, and I certainly think that it would then be possible to do
something.'[52] It could be interpreted either as an appeal or as a threat
to the Catholic Association.

The Lords threw out Lansdowne's motion by forty-four votes.
Wellington voted with the majority, but the moderation of his speech
caused a great deal of discussion about exactly how far he had
intended to go. Palmerston privately felt that whatever Wellington's
exact meaning, the question had been 'immensely' advanced because
the duke had abandoned all objections of principle and made his
opposition entirely a matter of expediency.[53] Lansdowne went further
and claimed that the duke had in effect pledged himself to take up the
Catholic question.[54] Bets were laid that there would be Catholics
sitting in Parliament next year. And on 18 June, a great public dinner
held to celebrate the repeal of the Test Act turned into a celebration
of an imminent Catholic victory. 'The whole proceeding', wrote one of
the diners, 'was a Catholic rather than a dissenting effort. There was
a great crowd and a handsome dinner, and very long graces and a
great deal of hypocrisy.'[55] Henry Grattan, the son of the great Irish
orator and patriot, described the dinner as 'a grand triumph' for the
Catholic cause. 'Nothing could be better', he told O'Connell. 'Their
[the Dissenters'] support of emancipation bordered on the spirit of
chivalry.'[56]

Some people, on the other hand, doubted whether Wellington
would do anything for the Catholics if he could avoid it, although few
probably went as far as Lord Lowther, who assured his Westmorland
constituents that the Prime Minister was leading the country back

into the 'ancient ways' of the constitution. Charles Greville perhaps analysed the situation most perceptively. He did not believe that Catholic emancipation depended either on the Whigs, who lacked the power to carry it, or the Tories, who lacked the inclination. 'The march of time and the state of Ireland will effect it in spite of everything, and its slow but continual advance can neither be retarded by its enemies not accelerated by its friends.'[57]

In Ireland the Catholics were doing their best to accelerate emancipation. At the meetings of the Catholic Association and in its inner counsels the wild men were becoming harder to control. To maintain his own pre-eminence in the movement O'Connell had to make it crystal clear that he would have nothing to do with any compromise settlement. At the end of May he publicly repudiated a suggestion in the English *Catholic Journal* that emancipation should be accompanied by securities; and he sent an urgent message to Edward Blount, the leader of the English Catholics, that if the *Catholic Journal* was not 'muzzled' on the subject of securities, there would be 'open war' between English and Irish Catholics.[58]

In Dublin, Anglesey's private interpretation of the Cabinet reshuffle caused by the Canningites' resignation was openly shared by Catholic and Protestant alike. The more moderate and peaceful atmosphere which Anglesey had felt he was having some success in creating, disappeared. 'The Orange party', he wrote on 20 June, 'is elated with what they call a triumph; the agitators [the Catholics] are furious and are using very unmeasured language.'[59] The hopes for the Catholic cause which Wellington's speech on 10 June had aroused in London were not echoed in Dublin. It was too vague either to alarm the Protestants or to appease the Catholics. Indeed, the duke's insistence that the Catholics could expect no relief until they refrained from asking for it, was hardly likely to be well received by men who were rapidly becoming convinced that only by ceaseless agitation would they ever get anything. Four days later, at a meeting of the Association in Dublin, O'Connell commented with furious sarcasm on Wellington's speech: '. . . they advise us to be quiet and good boys – and they hold forth the possibility of a probability depending on a remote contingency of taking the question into consideration if we cease to agitate.' To enthusiastic cheers he declared that he refused such terms. 'There is no reciprocity in them, or it is an Irish kind of reciprocity, all the one way . . . Agitation, by all constitutional means, is the proper course for us to follow.' Aggregate meetings in every county, simultaneous meetings in every parish, petitions to Parlia-

ment, the Catholic 'rent', the establishment of Liberal clubs – he went
through them all, and ended with a rousing call to 'all pull together
for old Ireland'.[60]

The opportunity to agitate – or, more accurately, to demonstrate the
strength of Catholic feeling – with an unprecedented dramatic impact,
was unwittingly provided by those most anxious to avoid it. Vesey
Fitzgerald was legally obliged to stand for re-election as a Member of
Parliament for County Clare when he took office as President of the
Board of Trade. He was one of the quite small band of Irish politicians
who, after the Union, had made their way with some success in
British politics. His father, a landowner in County Clare, had sat in
the Irish Parliament, and in spite of stoutly opposing the Union (for
which he lost his post as Prime Sergeant at the Irish Bar), sat for
several years at Westminster. In 1808, when he was about twenty-
five, William Vesey Fitzgerald succeeded his father as member for
Ennis, and since 1818 he had held one of the seats for County Clare.
He was appointed a Lord of the Treasury in Dublin in 1809 and
served as Irish Chancellor of the Exchequer from 1812 until the
separate Irish Treasury was abolished in 1816. Having refused two
minor offices, he had to wait until 1826 before being offered a post –
that of Paymaster-General – that he was willing to accept. He was a
clever, able man and an effective speaker; but he had a difficult
temperament and was not popular in the House of Commons. His
promotion to be President of the Board of Trade with a seat in the
Cabinet was not well thought of and was supposed to be Peel's doing.
It almost certainly was. They had been friends since their early days
at Westminster and close colleagues in Dublin after Peel became
Chief Secretary in 1812. Peel had always done his best to advance his
friend's career, and he wrote with genuine satisfaction to tell him
of his promotion to the Cabinet. 'I need not say how truly happy
I am to see you in your proper station – a member of the King's
Government.'[61] (Wellington, on the other hand, found Fitzgerald a
tiresome colleague and came to dislike him thoroughly.)
  Whatever might be thought of him in London, on his home ground
in County Clare Vesey Fitzgerald was in a strong position. His father
was a popular and liberal landlord whose vote against the Union had
not been forgotten. He himself had always been staunchly pro-Catholic
and he had distributed, among Catholics as well as Protestants, as
much local patronage as he could lay hands on. He was also well
thought of by the Catholic clergy, both locally and by the Catholic
hierarchy who were grateful to him for negotiating an increased grant

for Maynooth, the training college for Irish priests, while he was Chancellor of the Irish Exchequer. Altogether, it seemed unlikely that his re-election would be more than a formality.

The Catholic Association had pledged itself to oppose the election of any supporter, let alone member, of Wellington's government. It was well aware how difficult it would be to unseat Fitzgerald. If it tried and failed, it would lose prestige and credibility; if it shirked the challenge altogether the effect would be equally damaging. At the Association's meeting on 14 June O'Connell went no further than hoping that the freeholders of County Clare would see through Fitzgerald's 'miserable pretence' that he was a friend of the Catholics. This cautious approach was not nearly good enough for the more radical members of the Association, who had always found the moderation of O'Connell's leadership (as opposed to his rhetoric) hard to accept. One of the most prominent firebrands was James Patrick O'Gorman Mahon – he liked to be known as 'The O'Gorman Mahon' – a flamboyant young Catholic landowner of twenty-five from County Clare, who was a frequent and effective speaker at local meetings of the Association and had played a leading part in establishing a Clare Liberal Club. He assured the meeting that Major William Nugent MacNamara, a popular Protestant landlord in County Clare and a friend of O'Connell's, would stand against Fitzgerald, and he read out a letter from MacNamara confirming his willingness to be a candidate.

Brushing aside his private doubts, O'Connell accepted the wishes of the enthusiastic majority. On 18 June he publicly gave his blessing to MacNamara's candidacy. Two days later, at yet another meeting of the Association, he read out a long address to the Liberal Club and freeholders of County Clare, urging them not to vote for Fitzgerald. The Association's secretary, Richard O'Gorman, pleaded with the meeting not to embark on an enterprise that was bound to fail. His fears were dismissed, he withdrew his objections and the address was passed unanimously.[62] An initial fighting fund of £5,000 was voted and O'Connell promised to support MacNamara in person during the actual election.

There must, however, have been a certain air of unreality about the proceedings because on Saturday 21 June O'Gorman Mahon felt obliged to assure a meeting of the Association that MacNamara had pledged himself over and over again to stand and there was not the smallest possible chance that he would withdraw. At the end of the meeting he stepped straight into a post-chaise that was waiting for him at the entrance to the Corn Exchange, and set off for Ennis to set the campaign alight. He took with him another local landowner from Clare, a Protestant, Thomas Steele, who five years earlier had gone to Spain to support the revolt against Ferdinand VII, and who had just assured the Association that he would consider himself 'a disgrace to the name of Irishman, unless I hold my blood as much at the service of the Irish Catholics . . . as for the Spanish Constitutionalists when I was one of the garrison of Cadiz.'[63]

They were two uninhibited rumbustious characters, well suited by their appearance and manner to stir up the voters of County Clare. Steele, an extremely excitable man, declared that he was ready to fight any landlord who considered himself aggrieved by an attempt to influence his tenants' votes. O'Gorman Mahon, with his striking appearance and eccentric dress, could establish a remarkable hold over his audience: '. . . when O'Gorman Mahon throws himself out before the people, and, touching his whiskers with one hand, brandishes the other, an enthusiasm is at once produced, to which the fair portion of the spectators lend their tender contribution.'[64]

They travelled on through the night and the next day, stopping only to urge the people not to vote for Fitzgerald. As they journeyed on, the news of their coming preceded them and they were met with ringing church bells and welcoming crowds who took out the horses from their carriage and themselves pulled it through the streets. They arrived at Ennis at five o'clock on the Sunday evening and found a large crowd waiting for them in the Catholic chapel. They did not, however, find their candidate. MacNamara had changed his mind and refused to stand after all; he and his family were, he felt, too beholden to the Fitzgeralds.

The meeting in the Ennis chapel was still held, but it was a case of Hamlet without the prince. Vesey Fitzgerald was roundly abused and a resolution was passed that recalled how the Catholic freeholders of Waterford, Louth, Monaghan and Westmeath had successfully defied their landlords. But the name of the candidate who would allow the voters of County Clare to emulate these victories was missing.

The emissaries from Dublin, who had been received with such enthusiasm on their way to Ennis, were desperate to find someone. O'Gorman Mahon even tried to persuade Steele to step into the breach. But Steele, reckless and foolhardy though he was, drew the line at mortally offending an influential landowner in his own county. In the end O'Gorman Mahon set off back to Dublin with nothing better than a crazy plan to appeal to Anglesey's second son, Lord William Paget, to stand against Fitzgerald. Paget was a naval officer whom his father had made commander of the viceregal yacht. He was also MP for Caernarvon and had endeared himself to the Irish Catholics by braving his constituents' wrath and supporting Burdett's motion on Catholic relief in the House of Commons. On 16 June the Catholic Association had passed a resolution congratulating him on his stand. But as might have been foreseen, Paget would have nothing to do with O'Gorman Mahon's proposal. 'The conduct of some of these people', commented Anglesey when he heard of it, 'really looks like imbecillity [*sic*].'[65]

O'Gorman Mahon might have spared himself this rebuff, because while he was hurrying to and from Ennis a solution was evolving in Dublin. In Nassau Street, on the morning of Sunday, 22 June, Patrick Fitzpatrick, a Catholic barrister, chanced to meet David Roose, a liberal Protestant who sympathized with the Catholics' yearning for emancipation. Roose suggested that O'Connell himself should stand for County Clare. The law, after all, did not prevent a Catholic from standing for Parliament, only from taking his seat if elected. Fitzpatrick was impressed. He remembered that John Keogh, the veteran fighter for Catholic rights who had died eleven years earlier, had maintained that they would not get emancipation until a Catholic had been elected to Parliament.[66] He immediately sought out O'Connell and put the idea to him. O'Connell turned it down. He thought of the heavy expenses of an election; he may have thought even more of his large family, his debts, his pressing need to earn money at the Bar.

Fitzpatrick was rebuffed but not discouraged. He went round Dublin spreading the idea that O'Connell ought to be persuaded to stand for County Clare, and by the time the Association met the following day O'Connell's resistance was crumbling. He told the meeting that if MacNamara had not agreed to become their candidate he would have offered to stand instead. He left himself no way out, and next day, the 24th, when O'Gorman Mahon brought the news of MacNamara's defection, O'Connell accepted the challenge. He went off at once to the office of the *Dublin Evening Post* and there and then wrote out his election address. He insisted that he was qualified to be elected and he confidently hoped that if he was chosen, their most bigoted enemies would realize that the oath at present prescribed to Members of Parliament, which he could not possibly take, must be changed. He pointed unerringly at what in the eyes of Catholic voters was Fitzgerald's great weakness.

The oath at present required by law is, 'That the sacrifice of the Mass and the Invocation of the blessed Virgin Mary and other Saints, as now

An Irish freeholder, threatened with disaster either in this world or the next, thinks he had better vote for both priest and landlord (c. July 1828). Reproduced by kind permission of the Trustees of the British Museum, London.

practised in the Church of Rome, are impious and idolatrous.' Of course, I will never stain my soul with such an oath; I leave that to my honourable opponent, Mr Vesey Fitzgerald. He has often taken that horrible oath; he is ready to take it again, and asks your votes to enable him so to swear. I would rather be torn limb from limb than take it.[67]

He pledged himself to vote for all radical reforms of the representative system and to bring up in Parliament as soon as possible the question of the repeal of the Union. (A shorter form of the address, distributed as a leaflet, did not mention repeal.)

O'Connell's election address arrived in Ennis on the Dublin mail-coach at 2.30 on 25 June. But O'Connell himself, unable to leave his legal business unfinished, arrived only just in time for the election preliminaries on 30 June. During the intervening days contributions to his election fund poured in and his supporters set to work canvassing on his behalf. O'Gorman Mahon, Steele and an even wilder character, Jack Lawless, hastened hither and thither throughout the county, summoning meetings and haranguing the people. Richard Sheil arrived in Ennis to act as O'Connell's counsel, and other prominent members of the Association turned up to support him. But what was of crucial importance was the active and almost unanimous support of the parish priests. Contrary to the expectations of the authorities in Dublin, the bishops, many of whom disapproved of the Association's increasingly violent rhetoric, made no attempt to restrain them. On the contrary, Bishop Doyle, recently dubbed by Sydney Smith 'the Pope of Ireland', publicly declared his support for O'Connell.

James Doyle, Bishop of Kildare and Leighlin, was an influential pamphleteer and an ardent advocate of the Catholic claims. In October 1823 he published an open letter to the Lord Lieutenant, 'A Vindication of the Civil and Religious Principles of the Irish Catholics', which became the manifesto of the recently formed Catholic Association. More than 8,000 copies were distributed and extracts were put up on walls in towns and villages. Although he admired the British constitution and supported the Union, he warned in another open letter that the Catholic hierarchy could not be depended on to prevent rebellion. This created controversy but did not prevent Doyle from rallying the Catholic bishops to support the Association. In 1825 he publicly denounced the 'securities' which O'Connell had agreed to support in the abortive Catholic relief bill, and two years later he privately criticized him for his conciliatory attitude towards Canning's government. O'Connell could not count on Doyle's approval, and he

was greatly relieved and encouraged when he got it in June 1828.
'The approbation of Doctor Doyle will bring in our cause the united
voice of Ireland – I trust it will be the vox populi – vox dei.'[68]

In Dublin Castle there were no illusions about the strength of the
voice of the people, with or without the help of the deity. Fitzgerald
was already anticipating 'a violent and exasperated contest' a week
before O'Connell even announced that he would stand.[69] Before the
polling began, both Anglesey and Gregory had assured Peel that
Fitzgerald would lose. Gregory saw the election as the fulfilment of
'the long-suspended threat of numerical strength against property',
and hoped that the gentry, who all supported Fitzgerald, would not
shirk from appearing on the hustings and casting their votes for him,
even if their tenants voted the other way.[70] Anglesey looked at the
situation from another angle – its effect on the Catholics' struggle for
emancipation. O'Connell would undoubtedly get elected, but what
would be said of a popular representative who dared not present
himself before the House of Commons? 'I do not think', Anglesey told
Peel on 30 June, 'O'Connell is doing himself any good. I am *sure* he is
doing the Catholic cause much injury.'[71]

But Anglesey – unlike Gregory, who feared the worst – believed
that O'Connell and his supporters would at any rate do their best to
prevent any rioting, if only to demonstrate the strength of their hold
over the people. He took no chances all the same. 'Every legal means',
he instructed Gregory on 27 June, 'must be taken, and without a
moment's loss of time, to preserve the peace and to protect the
tenantry in giving their voluntary votes.' Three hundred constables
were concentrated in Ennis on the pretext of an inspection by
Anglesey's aide-de-camp, Baron Tuyll, who was already in the area.
In addition, a substantial body of infantry and cavalry was assembled
in the neighbourhood of the town to be used as a last resource if the
constables could not cope. Their commander was instructed 'to
inculcate perfect patience and forbearance in the troops, . . . to avoid
collision to the last moment and on no account to allow the use of
blank cartridges.'[72] Peel found no cause for complaint. 'I think', he
told the Lord Lieutenant, 'nothing can be more judicious than the
precautionary measures which you have taken and the instruction
which you have given for the general conduct of the military.'[73]

The man who had caused all these precautions to be set in train
did not set out from Dublin for the scene of action until the afternoon
of Saturday, 28 June. It was a triumphal journey all the way, as if he
had already won the election. Travelling all through the night, he
arrived at Rosecrea in time for eight o'clock Mass. At a small village a

few miles short of Nenagh he was met by a great crowd waving branches of palm, laurel and sycamore and shouting for 'the Man of the People'. At Nenagh he was met by 3,000 horsemen, at Limerick by a procession of all the different trade societies, at the bridge over the Shannon, where he entered County Clare, by huge crowds and blazing bonfires. He finally arrived at Ennis at two o'clock in the morning of 30 June, nomination day. He found the place filled with thousands of men and women who, led by their priests, had marched into the town from all over the county. 'No army can be better disciplined than they are,' wrote Baron Tuyll to Anglesey. 'No drunkenness or any irregularity allowed. O'Connell is called the Irish Washington and Bolivar; and people, instead of saying "God be with you", say "O'Connell be with you". The children in the street sing "Green is my Livrey" and the "Liberty Tree".'[74]

At the nomination meeting in the court-house almost all the local gentry squeezed on to the platform to show their support for Fitzgerald. O'Connell, on the other side of the sheriff, stood almost alone. His support came from the multitude crowding the floor. After the two candidates had been nominated, Fitzgerald made such an effective and moving speech that O'Connell was obliged to reply with all the passion and vituperation at his command in order to destroy the sympathy his opponent had aroused. It was rough stuff with no holds barred – Fitzgerald was frequently heard to mutter 'Is this fair?' – but it worked. When the sheriff called for the customary show of hands, the overwhelming majority was raised for O'Connell. But the voters still had to show that they were willing to stand up and be counted in the polling booth under the furious gaze of their landlords.

The polling went on for five days, with O'Connell's lead over Fitzgerald growing wider every day. The O'Connell camp, in particular the activists of the local Liberal Club and the Catholic priests, threw a degree of energy and enthusiasm into their canvassing which their opponents were quite unable to match. About 150 priests converged on Ennis from all over Ireland as well as from the surrounding county. They played a major role in organizing the commissariat arrangements for feeding the large numbers of people who flocked into the town, occupied every available lodging and empty warehouse and bivouacked in the meadows by the river. It was estimated that at least 30,000 to 40,000 friends and relations accompanied the 3,000-odd freeholders entitled to vote.[75]

Outside O'Connell's lodgings in the market square a large wooden balcony was erected and copiously decorated with greenery. From this balcony O'Connell himself and his supporters, lay and clerical, held

forth throughout the day, entertaining or edifying the crowds throng-
ing the square below. Groups of freeholders, who had been marched
into Ennis behind their landlords to vote for Fitzgerald, found themselves surrounded by a milling crowd urging them to vote for their
country, for 'the old religion', for O'Connell. On one occasion, a
group of about a hundred, who were being led through the square by
their Protestant landlord, deserted him to a man when they saw
O'Connell rush out on to his balcony and raise his arm.[76]

Vesey Fitzgerald's tenants were marched into the square together,
headed by fiddlers and pipers. After they had listened in silence to a
speech by their landlord, Father Tom Maguire, a famous Catholic
polemicist from Leitrim, stepped forward and confronted them with a
stark choice: 'Let every renegade to his God and his country follow
Vesey Fitzgerald, and every true Catholic Irishman follow me.' All
but a handful did follow him.[77] When Father Coffey, the only priest to
support Fitzgerald, brought his parishioners in to vote, they were met
by Father John Murphy, a formidable Old Testament figure whose
fiery eloquence had already persuaded his own parishioners to dis-
obey their landlord. 'Men,' he demanded, 'are ye going to betray your
God and your country?' They raised their hats, cheered for O'Connell
and marched off to vote for him, leaving Coffey standing forlornly on
the pavement.[78]

Some priests did not scruple to make their appeals more directly
personal, and therefore more compelling, by brandishing their
spiritual authority and threatening to withhold all religious rites from
those who voted for Fitzgerald. On one dramatic occasion a priest
announced to the huge crowd in the market square that a man who
had voted for Fitzgerald, after pledging himself to O'Connell, had
suddenly died. The implication was obvious and, led by the priest, the
whole crowd immediately knelt down in silent prayer.[79] According to
a correspondent of a Dublin paper, writing from Ennis after the
election, the priests, including Father Maguire, admitted that their
interference had been improper, but asked what else could they do?[80]
They might have pointed out that many landlords who supported
Fitzgerald had not hesitated to threaten their tenants with eviction if
they voted the wrong way. O'Connell tried to neutralize the threat
by warning the landlords that many of them did not enjoy legally
watertight titles to their properties, and if they tried to 'grind' their
tenants, he would start to 'grind' them.[81] But to many voters it must
have seemed that retribution threatened, either in this world or the
next, however they voted. Some, it was reported, 'were actually seen
crying whilst voting.'[82]

Yet in this highly charged, extremely emotional atmosphere, in this dangerously overcrowded little market town, there was no violence, no drunkenness (drink was banned), no threat to public order. The troops which the authorities had assembled outside the town remained in their barracks. 'The absolute quietness of the place', wrote Tuyll, 'is quite frightening.'[83] A correspondent of the *Dublin Evening Post* wrote euphorically from Ennis on 3 July: 'Now notwithstanding that the strength of the Agitatorarchy [Catholic Association] be thus at this moment concentrated in Clare, so far is the country from exhibiting any symptoms of convulsion that the power, the stupendous power of that internal Government *is shown in its very intensity by the tranquillity of the people.*'

The result was declared on Saturday, 5 July: 2,082 votes for O'Connell, 982 for Fitzgerald. The defeated candidate's agent argued that the election should be declared invalid since O'Connell, as a Catholic, would not be able to take his seat. But the assessor ruled that this must be decided by the House of Commons when O'Connell appeared before it, and the sheriff was obliged to declare O'Connell the elected Member of Parliament for County Clare. O'Connell's acceptance speech was mild and moderate, apart from a warning in passing that the repeal of the Union was not impossible. He said that his great object was to secure the repeal of the law that excluded a man from Parliament because he worshipped according to his conscientious belief. He also spoke warmly about his defeated opponent and apologized for any offence he might have given him on nomination day. Fitzgerald proved a good loser and in a graceful speech accepted O'Connell's apology. But privately he was appalled by the week's events, not so much on his own behalf (another seat would soon be found for him) as on behalf of the country as a whole. The Catholic Association's demonstration of its hold over the people, which had moved the *Dublin Evening Post*'s correspondent to such jubilation, filled him with foreboding. On the night after the result was declared, he unburdened himself to Peel. 'All the great interests broke down, and the desertion has been universal. Such a scene as we have had! Such a tremendous prospect as it opens to us!' He did not enlarge on that prospect, but he told Peel that 'the organization exhibited is so complete and so formidable that no man can contemplate without alarm what is to follow in this wretched country'.[84]

Two days later, after the customary chairing of the newly elected Member of Parliament, O'Connell began his journey back to Dublin. The chair in which he was carried round the town was covered with a

DANIEL the GREAT entering CLARE preceeded by the AMATEUR BAND.

Published by Tregear & Son 123 Cheapside Street Dublin.

After his election for County Clare, O'Connell is portrayed on a donkey, holding aloft a furled umbrella and wearing two wings labelled 'Clerical wing' and '40s. freeholder wing'. He is preceded by cat musicians on asses representing the Catholic Association (? July 1828). Reproduced by kind permission of the Trustees of the British Museum, London.

splendid canopy on which was inscribed the lines by Byron which O'Connell had adopted as his motto: 'Hereditary bondsmen! know ye not, / Who would be free themselves must strike the blow?' He was followed by a procession about 20,000 strong, headed by clergy and freeholders. The windows overlooking the route of the chairing were filled with 'a delightful display of the female fashion and beauty of Clare – waving flowers [and] handkerchiefs, many of these presenting the likeness of the patriot himself'.[85] Outside the town, the troops which the authorities had seen fit to station along the road were removed at the request of O'Gorman Mahon, leaving only the commanding general, Sir Charles Doyle, and his staff. When the procession reached them it halted while O'Connell stood up, took off his hat and exchanged compliments with the general. A few miles further on he changed into his own carriage and proceeded on his victorious way, stopping to address the crowds in the towns through which he passed.

Three days later O'Connell was welcomed back to Dublin at the end of his triumphant journey. He had let it be known that he wanted the rejoicings over his victory to be as restrained and decorous as the contest had been. But when he addressed the Catholic Association in the Corn Exchange on the day of his return, he was far from minimizing the significance of his election. 'I ask, what is to be done with Ireland? What is to be done with the Catholics? One of two things. They must either crush us or conciliate us. There is no going on as we are.' And in highly emotional language he went on to spell out his terms.

> I could forgive England for oppressing this country, for crushing our ancient chieftains and making them . . . breakers of stones and drawers of water. I could forgive her violation of the Treaty of Limerick; I could pardon her broken promises at the Union, and I say now, all, all shall be pardoned, forgiven, forgotten, upon giving us Emancipation, unconditional, unqualified, free and unshackled.[86]

The demand for emancipation had been made many times before. But could the British government afford any longer to ignore it? It knew how to deal with seditious speeches, rioting, armed revolt. But O'Connell and the Catholic Association had, almost by chance, certainly without much premeditation, stumbled upon the key which would open the door to emancipation and which could not be taken from them because it was perfectly legal and constitutional. O'Connell might not be able to take his seat in Parliament. But neither would the government be able to prevent a Catholic from being elected in every other Irish county by-election. The further consequences at the next general election were set out in London by *The Times* (which was strongly pro-Catholic) on the day on which O'Connell's victory was declared in Ennis.

> There rests no shadow of doubt upon our minds that at the very next general election, should emancipation not yet be carried, the policy of the Catholics thus driven to extreme courses will be, to obtain a return of members of their own communion throughout the whole of Ireland – that, being refused admittance to the Imperial Parliament, they will constitute a native Parliament in Dublin sitting, voting, practically legislating, for their country, and leaving the connexion between the two countries dependent on a thread, which the slightest movement in the politics of Europe will suffice to snap asunder.

If this threat to the Union, looming in the not very distant future, was to be averted, the oaths which Catholics could not conscientiously take would have to be administered before a poll was held, so that those who could not take their seat at Westminster could not stand for election either. But a House of Commons with a majority in favour of emancipation was hardly likely to agree to such a change in the law.

Looking back twenty years later, Peel saw that the Clare election was the turning point in the Catholic question.[87] It was the point at which the government was forced to abandon its passive, neutral attitude, defy the opposition of the King, the House of Lords and much of the general public, and make up its mind to settle the Catholic issue in the only way that would satisfy the Irish Catholics and – so it was vainly hoped – bring peace to Ireland.

3

Search for a Solution

(July–September 1828)

'The Duke of Wellington has hitherto thought that a touch of his would make all the world go right . . . but I suspect he has now found a task that makes his cheek pale, and his nights uneasy.'

Lord John Russell to Thomas Moore, 29 July 1828

'Nothing is talked of now', wrote Lord Eldon from London on 9 July 1828, 'which interests anybody the least in the world, except the return of Mr O'Connell.'[1] The Cabinet were greatly puzzled how to react to this startling event. There was a good deal to be said for avoiding any public discussion of it before Parliament rose for the long summer recess at the end of July. O'Connell himself decided not to provoke an immediate confrontation with the government, but to bide his time in Ireland while the full significance and consequences of his election sank into the minds of the English ministers. (He merely allowed himself the satisfaction of using his privilege as an MP to frank his own letters.) On the other hand, the Cabinet were tempted to try to dispose of the issue before Ireland boiled over. They considered making O'Connell appear before the House of Commons at once, if necessary by force, so that he could disqualify himself from taking his seat by refusing to take the prescribed oath. Even before his election was officially declared in Ennis, Peel had consulted the law officers and had agreed with the Speaker that if O'Connell appeared and refused to take the oath, the Speaker would order him to withdraw and if necessary call on the Sergeant-at-Arms to enforce the order.[2] But O'Connell could not be prevented from standing again unless the law was changed so that parliamentary candidates were obliged to take the oath before the poll was held. The House of

Commons would very probably refuse to change the law, and if it did
refuse, the Irish reaction might well be violent.

On 12 July the Cabinet decided that the least risky course would
be to allow O'Connell to enjoy his triumph until Parliament reassembled in the new year. Next day Vesey Fitzgerald arrived in
London and gave Peel such an alarming account of the situation in
Ireland – the despair of the Protestants, the jubilation of the Catholics
– that he felt his colleagues should have a chance to reconsider their
decision. On the 15th the Cabinet listened to Fitzgerald's extremely
gloomy account of the state of Ireland and his demand for immediate
action to exclude Roman Catholics from Parliament. But they preferred the chance of a quiet summer to the certainty of a convulsion in
Ireland if O'Connell were denied his seat.[3]

Even without any further stimulation it seemed doubtful whether
a convulsion in Ireland could be avoided. Lord Anglesey was no
alarmist but he could not help being deeply impressed by the strength
of popular feeling at the Clare election, and even more by the extraordinary discipline imposed there by the Catholic Association. 'I am
sorry to say', he wrote to his brother, Arthur Paget, on 11 July, 'that
bad as appearances were, previously to the Clare election, they are
now a great deal worse. The agitators have displayed a power over
the priests and, through them, over the people, that even themselves
were not aware of.'[4] He sent Major Warburton, who had commanded
the police during the election and was known to Peel as intelligent
and trustworthy, to London to brief the Cabinet in case they were
tempted to assume that Fitzgerald was too distraught and disappointed
to give an objective report.

The reaction of the Orangemen was also to be feared. For them the
triumphant jubilation of the Catholics was an almost unbearable
provocation, and the extent to which they might relieve their feelings
during their traditional march on 12 July greatly alarmed the
authorities. 'Whatever fears', wrote that unbending Protestant,
William Gregory, on 7 July, 'may be entertained from the excited
feelings of the Catholics, I apprehend greater danger from the sullen
indignation of the Protestants.'[5] Anglesey found them 'terrible people
to deal with' and reported that they were 'threatening all sorts of
mischief for the 12th of July'.[6] The Catholic leaders also anticipated
trouble on that day and feared that Orange demonstrations might
provoke the Catholics to violence. On 5 July the Association issued an
'Appeal to the Roman Catholics of the North', urging calm in the face
of Orange provocations, and O'Connell issued a similar personal
appeal from Ennis.

In the event there was comparatively little violence on the 'twelfth'. Presumably the appeals of O'Connell and the Association helped to restrain the Catholics. But would they be able to keep the mounting popular excitement under control? Since the Clare election, speeches at the Association's meetings had become more inflammatory and popular support was being demonstrated by a sharp increase in the amount of Catholic 'rent' collected each week; for the week ending 12 July it rose to £2,705, the highest ever weekly sum. When O'Connell attended a dinner at Dundalk on 14 July, his road on the last stages of his journey was lined with people waving olive branches or some other green emblem. Every cottage and carriage was decorated with greenery, there was a triumphal arch every few miles, a carriage procession at least a mile long, a thousand horsemen and 30,000 marching on foot. Several times O'Connell's barouche stopped and he addressed the crowd from the front seat. He urged obedience to the law and the observance of religion and stressed his determination to seek redress by constitutional means.

This high level of respectability was not maintained at the dinner in Dundalk where the first toast was to 'The people, the source of all political power', and O'Connell declared that he was, and ever would be, 'a Radical reformer'. This was not just an oratorical flourish. During the Clare election he had promised, if elected, to support efforts to make the House of Commons more truly representative of the people, and the Catholic Association had recently agreed to his proposal that in future parliamentary candidates should be required to pledge themselves to parliamentary reform. Irish liberal peers, like Rossmore and Duncannon, pointed out to him that this open commitment to parliamentary reform was bound to exacerbate the Tory government's fears and suspicions about his campaign for emancipation.[7] He himself was committed to reform by peaceful means only, but not all his supporters shared his genuine aversion to violence, and in order to retain his influence over them he sometimes had to present himself as more extreme than he really was.

On the whole, however, once the euphoria of the Clare election had died down, O'Connell gave more satisfaction to his moderate Irish advisers than to English radicals like Henry Hunt and the Friends of Civil and Religious Liberty, a society of Irish Catholics living in London with a comprehensive radical programme ranging from religious liberty to parliamentary and economic reform. 'Orator' Hunt, the irrepressible flamboyant demagogue who had spent two and a half years in Ilchester gaol for his part in causing the assembly that led to the Peterloo 'massacre' in Manchester in 1819, was loathed

by moderate reformers as much as he was idolized by the mob.
Everything was grist to his radical mill. Assuming that O'Connell
would come over at once to claim his seat at Westminster, he planned
to use the occasion to organize a mammoth procession and demonstration, and at a public meeting called by the Friends of Civil and
Religious Liberty, he tried to appropriate O'Connell irrevocably to
the extreme radical cause. He insisted that 'a *Radical Reform*' was the
essential prerequisite for emancipation or the redress of any other
grievance. 'We will not now suspect him [O'Connell] of shifting or
shuffling or deserting the cause of Radical Reform, because he is now
nailed, (*applause*), solemnly pledged, nailed to the cause of Radical
Reform. (*three rounds of applause*)'.[8]

O'Connell's failure to demand immediate entrance to the House of
Commons, and the increasing moderation of his public utterances –
he spoke of 'constitutional' rather than 'radical' reform – were a bitter
disappointment to Hunt. He was not mollified by O'Connell's private
assurances of his commitment to radical reforms or his occasional
reversion to radical rhetoric. He denounced him as an apostate and
even opposed a vote of thanks to him at a meeting of the Friends,
thereby dividing that contentious society into two hostile camps. But
emancipation came first in O'Connell's order of priorities, and he
knew that any close association with the wild men of radical reform in
England would only scare off liberal Protestants in Ireland from
openly supporting him.

Organization was the key to peaceful political change, and the Clare
election gave a great boost to the establishment of Liberal Clubs.
They were primarily the brainchild of Thomas Wyse who began to
draw up detailed plans in 1826 after the Association's spectacular
success in the Waterford election. In many places the foundations had
already been laid by the Association's arrangements for collecting the
Catholic 'rent', spreading propaganda and pursuing all the other
activities connected with the emancipation campaign. In addition to
carrying on this campaign, the new clubs were to form permanent
political and electoral organizations for tackling local grievances,
providing political education and, above all, ensuring that only pro-
Catholic candidates were returned to Parliament. At first some people
were put off by the supposedly Jacobinical associations of the word
'club'. But during 1827 the idea slowly caught on. The Clare Liberal
Club, founded in March 1827, played an important part in
O'Connell's election victory fifteen months later. What had been
achieved in County Clare could be achieved elsewhere in Ireland,

and by the end of 1828 the local political organization for securing the victory of the Association's candidates in future elections was becoming widely established.

Recollecting the crisis of 1828 in tranquillity twenty years later, Peel saw clearly that this was the real significance of the Clare election. It was not force or violence – 'not any act of which the law could take cognizance' – that was to be feared. 'The real danger was in the peaceable and legitimate exercise of a franchise according to the will and conscience of the holder.'[9] Presumably he realized this at the time, but the threat of violence must also then have seemed very real. Every day Lord Anglesey received alarmist reports and demands for reinforcements from all over the country. Lord Forbes, who usually found priests and people willing to talk freely with him when he attended the assizes at Longford, found this year that nobody at all would speak to him; they all seemed to be waiting for some great event to happen. This sense of expectancy had also apparently affected the Irish labourers who usually flocked over to England to earn some money by helping with the harvest. Peel heard from a clergyman in Grantham that not one fifth as many of them as usual had passed through the town, and from Staffordshire Lord Talbot (admittedly a scaremongering ultra-Protestant) reported that scarcely any had turned up in his neighbourhood. The implication was that they were staying at home in anticipation of a fight.

On his side of the Irish Sea Anglesey ordered an inquiry into the numbers of labourers embarking for England. He found it hard to believe that there was any immediate danger of violence, but suspected that preparations for armed revolt were being made – any number of pikes could be quickly and easily manufactured – and admitted that a sudden insurrection would not surprise him. To make matters worse, the authorities felt unable to rely completely on the loyalty of the army. It contained a large number of Irish Catholic soldiers who were reported to be completely under the influence of their priests and to be growing increasingly disaffected. In some regiments the presence of active Orange sympathizers threatened to stir up religious strife within the army.

Before Parliament separated for the summer recess Peel asked Anglesey whether he thought he ought to be armed with any more legal powers to cope with the unrest. Anglesey had already put this question to his law officers more than once and their reply had always been that it was not necessary or advisable. Yet they invariably discouraged any prosecution of inflammatory words or deeds on the grounds that it would be impracticable or inexpedient. Peel, for

instance, suggested that some of the Catholic leaders, in particular
Sheil, should be prosecuted for inflammatory speeches at a meeting of
the Association on 12 July. The law officers in London as well as
in Dublin agreed that a prosecution was unlikely to succeed and
therefore had better not be attempted. Anglesey pointed out to Peel
that Sheil would not easily be caught in this way. He wrote down
what he intended to say and stuck to it, unlike O'Connell, Lawless
and others who weighed their words less carefully and were apt to get
carried away by their emotional eloquence.[10] Peel accepted the law
officers' opinion, but at Wellington's suggestion he urged Anglesey to
make sure that government shorthand writers were always present at
the Association's meetings, as they used to be in Wellesley's day; their
reports would carry much more weight in prosecutions than would
newspaper reports.[11]

It does not seem to have occurred to Peel or Wellington that if
Ireland was really in such a combustible state as they feared, the
prosecution of highly popular Catholic leaders for saying out loud
what many were feeling would very likely set the country ablaze. That
was the last thing they wanted to do. Their aim was to prevent a
conflict and the best way of doing so, they felt, was to demonstrate the
government's readiness to use the law and, if necessary, the military,
against the Association and any signs of violent unrest. 'Whatever our
hopes', wrote Peel to Anglesey, 'that there will be no actual collision,
it is true policy and true mercy to be well prepared. All parties
will agree that any attempt at insurrection must be promptly and
effectually put down – the more promptly and the more decisively, the
less would be the ultimate evil.'[12]

With this sentiment Anglesey wholeheartedly agreed. Although he
sympathized with the Catholic cause, he had no use for the Catholic
'agitators', whose proceedings he described as 'very daring and very
insulting', and he would not have hesitated to snuff out any signs of
armed revolt. But he had become convinced that if the government
was content with a negative holding operation, the situation could
only grow worse. The Catholics' grievances must be removed and he
thought he saw how this could now be done. Although he had at
first feared that O'Connell's election would prove a disaster for
the Catholics, he quickly realized that if the Catholic leader could
actually take his seat, 'it would be a perfect Godsend, and would
get rid of this odious question'.[13] Before the election result had
been officially announced, he wrote two long letters to Lord Francis
Leveson-Gower in London setting out, with unvarnished frankness,
his view of the situation and what should be done about it. He

insisted that the Catholic Association had achieved such extraordinary power that it could provoke open rebellion at a moment's notice, and it was only the Catholic leaders' belief that they could carry their cause by incessant agitation and intimidation that prevented an outbreak.

> I believe their success inevitable – that no power under heaven can arrest its progress. There may be rebellion, you may put to death thousands, you may suppress it, but it will only be to put off the day of compromise; and in the mean time the country is only more impoverished, and the minds of the people are, if possible, still more alienated, and ruinous expense is entailed upon the empire.

He argued that the Association could only be suppressed by suspending habeas corpus and introducing martial law, and the present House of Commons would never agree to such drastic measures unless there was open rebellion. On the other hand, if nothing was done, things could only go from bad to worse:

> and I see no possible means of improving them but by depriving the demagogues of the power of directing the people; and by taking Messrs O'Connell, Sheil, and the rest of them from the Association, and placing them in the House of Commons, this desirable object would be at once accomplished.

Finally, he declared:

> I abhor the idea of truckling to the overbearing Catholic demagogues. To make any movement towards conciliation under the present excitement and system of terror would revolt me; but I do most conscientiously, and after the most earnest consideration of the subject, give it as my conviction that the first moment of composure and tranquillity should be seized to signify the intention of adjusting the question, lest another period of calm should not present itself.[14]

With considerable misgivings Leveson-Gower obeyed Anglesey's instructions to show these uncompromising letters to the Prime Minster and Peel. On 12 July Peel read them out to the Cabinet, which decided to stave off the need for positive action by deputing Wellington to show them to the King. To Anglesey, Peel sent only a noncommittal assurance that the letters were being shown to those who ought to see them. Anglesey could hardly hope to get a considered reply at once. But he was an impatient man, all the more so since he realized that his advice would not be palatable and might be dismissed as too partisan. On 16 July he solemnly solemnly assured Peel that if he took an opposite view of the Catholic question, his advice would be exactly the same.[15] Ten days later he again warned Peel of the danger of delay and urged him, while the country was comparatively tranquil, to indicate publicly that the government intended to bring forward the state of Ireland when Parliament reassembled.[16] He was immensely self-confident – his critics would say arrogant – and he was convinced he could secure a sufficiently law-abiding atmosphere for the government to be able to grant emancipation without appearing to give way to fear or panic. 'How it is, I hardly know,' he wrote to his brother Arthur,

> but I have got hold of these people *surprisingly*, and unless the people on the other side of the water are *mad*, this great question may be satisfactorily adjusted early in the next session. I would pledge my life that I made an arrangement that would be satisfactory to *all* the Catholics and to *all but* the ultra Orangemen, and I have converted several even of these. In short, I really do see my way, if I am confided in and meet with fair play from the ministers . . . you may rely on it that I have the game in my hand, if I am allowed to play it. But I sadly fear the Duke of Wellington has not the nerve to let me play it. He is temporizing, vacillating, and every minute lost is an advantage thrown away.[17]

After Anglesey had so frankly stated where he stood, it was inconceivable that any Tory government would let him play 'the game' in Ireland in his own way. Wellington realized that emancipation could no longer be avoided if Ireland was not to slip out of control. Indeed, for months past he had been pondering how to remove the obstacles which, in his view, stood in the way of emancipation. He did not want Anglesey's gratuitous advice which was not the less uncongenial for being basically correct. (It would have been much more uncongenial if he had known Anglesey was suggesting he had lost his nerve.) Anglesey felt it was his duty (as well as his inclination) to offer advice to the government; Wellington, on the other hand, felt that the Lord Lieutenant's duty was simply to maintain order and leave policy-making to the government in London. The two men might not be far apart on the policy which it was necessary, for whatever reason, to adopt, but the basic difference in their attitudes towards the Catholic question combined with a clash of temperament to create a gulf into which all mutual trust disappeared.

In Wellington's eyes Anglesey could soon do nothing right. 'I beg you', he wrote to Peel, 'to look at Lord Anglesey's memorandum!! I cannot venture to express what I think of such a document from the Lord Lieutenant to the Commander-in-Chief in Ireland.'[18] In the offending document, which was bound to pass through many hands, Anglesey had expressed his opinion that Catholic soldiers in the army were no longer to be trusted. It was, as Ellenborough commented, 'very imprudent' of him.

But what angered the ministers most was Anglesey's insistence on cultivating friendly relations with Catholics as well as Protestants, like Lord Cloncurry, who supported emancipation. To Anglesey this was simply a necessary part of the process of tranquillizing the country through the creation of mutual trust. He did not, however, as he should have done, hide the fact that he personally was in favour of emancipation, and the distinction he carefully made between his own views and those of the government, on which he insisted he was not authorized to speak, was all too easily lost or ignored. His listeners tended to hear what they wanted to hear, and what they passed on grew in the telling, so that the *Dublin Evening Post* went so far as to report that 'the noble Marquis' would resign if the government refused to bring in emancipation early in the next session of Parliament.

Anglesey was well aware of the danger of being misrepresented, and when at the end of July O'Connell put him in 'rather an awkward predicament' by asking for an interview, he took the precaution of telling Peel beforehand. With the approval of all his advisers he had decided to grant the request, but he would insist on having a witness present. 'It will be my business', he assured Peel, 'to be very patient, very guarded, but not severely reserved, and whilst he is endeavouring to penetrate me, to try if I can make anything out of him.'[19]

So far as Anglesey was concerned, this mutual probing was highly satisfactory. 'I rejoice', he told Peel afterwards, 'that it [the meeting] took place for I had an opportunity of taking a very high tone.' He had found O'Connell 'most respectful and gentlemanlike' and was inclined to believe in the sincerity of his protestations that he wanted to gain emancipation only through constitutional and peaceful means.[20] Anglesey made it abundantly clear that he intended to maintain order and had ample resources to do so. He complained that many Roman Catholics, including priests, were behaving very irresponsibly, and he criticized O'Connell for his frequent public abuse of Wellington. He pointed out that the duke was the only man who could settle the Catholic question and he did not despair of his making the attempt. Anglesey made a memorandum of the interview, but neither he nor O'Connell commented publicly on it. The

Orangemen were left to make what they could of it and, as Anglesey had foreseen, they made it 'a subject of much vituperation'.

Anglesey sent Peel three letters about his interview with O'Connell, and his annoyance at the failure of Peel (who was having something of a busman's holiday at Brighton) to answer any of them was typical of their increasingly uneasy relationship. He had usually got on well enough with the Home Secretary, but he was not comfortable with him. He had no idea that Peel had come to accept the expediency of emancipation, and found it very difficult to work confidentially with someone whose aim he believed to be the opposite of his own, especially when he felt that he himself did not enjoy that person's confidence. 'I am not satisfied with these ministers', he told Lord Holland. 'They leave me in utter ignorance of their intentions. They have not the straight forwardness to approve of my proceedings if they like them, or to point out their objections if they have any.'[21] He was driven to unburden himself from time to time to Holland, although he knew he should not write in a confidential way, let alone send documents, to a leading member of the Whig Opposition, but he relied on his friend's discretion, he was desperate for a sympathetic listener and he was coming to feel increasingly beleaguered.

Early in August Anglesey began to fear that the King was being turned against him by '*secret* advisers [who] are busily engaged in poisoning his mind with regard to my measures and conduct'.[22] But the King did not need any secret advisers to turn him against his viceroy in Ireland. Anglesey's letters to Leveson-Gower and Peel were quite enough to do that. The King had read them all. He noted, not unfairly, that the writer seemed unable to make up his mind whether rebellion was a distant or an imminent possibility, and concluded that such undecided language was 'certainly not suited to the present perilous situation of Ireland'.[23] On 5 August he summoned Wellington to Windsor and proposed that Anglesey should be recalled from Dublin. The duke replied that it was certainly very inconvenient to have him there but to remove him would be still more inconvenient. Although Wellington did not put it so bluntly, in his opinion, Anglesey had made himself too popular with the Irish Catholics by his reluctance to prosecute their leaders for their inflammatory speeches and by seeming altogether too sympathetic to their cause. But these could hardly be given as reasons for sacking him, and to recall him without a plausible excuse would be to risk increased unrest in Ireland. The King reluctantly acquiesced.[24] So did Peel, although he felt that it 'would be very easy to get a much better man' than Anglesey, and if 'the Crown's advisers' should think a settlement of the Catholic question was practicable, they might well wish to replace him.[25] He appeared to feel that if Catholic emancipation had to be granted to the Irish, it had better not be under the auspices of someone who actually believed in it.

In any case, Wellington was by no means sure that emancipation was a practicable proposition. At a Cabinet dinner in June he confessed that no one wanted a settlement more than he did, but he did not see daylight on it.[26] Mrs Arbuthnot, to whom the duke unburdened himself while walking up and down Birdcage Walk, felt that emancipation 'occupied and puzzled him more than any question I have ever seen him think about'.[27] According to her account, he saw the issue as primarily one of law and order. 'Mr O'Connell and his gang' were pushing the Irish people towards rebellion and the authorities in Dublin seemed unable to stop them. Parliament, however, would not authorize any stronger coercive powers to forestall rebellion unless the government first produced a scheme that would remove the Catholics' disabilities without endangering the constitution or the Protestant establishment.[28] But if Wellington managed to devise a scheme that satisfied the Irish Catholics and the pro-Catholic majority in the House of Commons, how was he to overcome the opposition of those – the King, the Protestant majority in the House of Lords and the country as a whole – who were opposed to any settlement at all? Above all, how was he to get round the King, whose influence, quite apart from any constitutional rights he might claim, might make or mar a settlement?

According to Lady Holland, if George IV had not been a prince he would have been a most amiable man. Even as a prince he had many amiable qualities – kindness, generosity, humanity, tact and charm among them. But in affairs of state he could be, and in his declining years increasingly became, vacillating, frivolous and appallingly indolent. He tended to take refuge in ill-health, which was often genuine enough. He suffered from gout and rheumatism and a wide variety of other unpleasant complaints. He dosed himself alternately with alcohol and laudanum which eased his pain and discomfort but befuddled his brain and made him even more reluctant to exert himself over affairs of state.

He tried to fend off business discussions with his ministers by embarking on irrelevant and interminable monologues. Wellington dealt firmly with this diversionary tactic. 'I make it a rule', he told Charles Greville, 'never to interrupt him [the King], and when in this way he tries to get rid of a subject in the way of business which he does not like, I let him talk himself out, and then quietly put before him the matter in question so that he cannot escape from it.'[29] The duke might preen himself on his skill in pinning the King down, but his victim naturally felt differently. The King had been greatly angered by Wellington's refusal to serve under Canning but had been forced to turn to him to replace Goderich because there seemed no alternative. As Prime Minister, the duke had not made any particular effort to regain the royal favour. He did not flatter his royal master and made little allowance for his weaknesses. (Two years earlier he had told Mrs Arbuthnot that there was nothing the matter with the King 'excepting what is caused by the effects of strong liquors taken too frequently and in too large quantities'.[30]) He would not fall in with the King's wishes unless he himself thought it right to do so. During July and August there was a continuing crisis over the Duke of Clarence's rather cavalier conduct as Lord High Admiral. The King dutifully obeyed Wellington's injunction to reprimand his brother, but after Clarence had resigned, he had a change of heart and wanted the issue reopened. Wellington's refusal to do so did not improve his popularity at Windsor. Nor did his rather autocratic manner conciliate the King, or make him more willing to accept his Prime Minister's advice on the Catholic question or anything else. According to Princess Lieven, the wife of the Russian ambassador, the King had been heard to declare: 'King Arthur must go to the devil, or King George must go to Hanover.'[31]

When George IV came to the throne and was told that the coronation oath could not be modified, he said to Castlereagh: 'Remember, once I take that oath, I am for ever a Protestant King, a Protestant upholder, a Protestant adherent.'[32] After having sworn to uphold the Protestant religion as by law established, he could not, he believed, sign any bill conceding political equality to the Roman Catholics. His attitude was based four-square on that of his father; it was emphatically confirmed by his first Lord Chancellor, Lord Eldon; and it was bolsterd up by two of his brothers, the Duke of York (until his death in 1827) and the Duke of Cumberland.

Ernest Augustus, Duke of Cumberland, was one of those people of whom the worst is invariably assumed. His reputation was not improved by his somewhat sinister appearance, although this was in fact the result of sabre wounds received when fighting bravely against the French. In the popular imagination, fed entirely by rumour and the gutter press, he was a wicked ogre, guilty of an astonishing variety of crimes and vices. Better-informed political and court circles simply found him thoroughly disagreeable. He always spoke his mind forcefully, without tact or inhibition. He could be offensively sarcastic and was altogether much better at making enemies than winning friends. He held strong ultra-Tory opinions, and although he spent most of his time in Berlin (he had married a German princess), he kept himself well informed about English politics and was widely regarded as a meddlesome behind-the-scenes intriguer. His relationship with his brother George was close, although it had been periodically punctuated by sharp quarrels. His influence with him had always been considerable; it was all the greater now that the King was increasingly indolent and ill.

In April 1828 rumours that Wellington's government might not be entirely sound on the Catholic issue brought Cumberland on a visit to England. He arrived in time to cast his vote in the House of Lords against the repeal of the Test and Corporation Acts, which the government had reluctantly decided to support. It was an indication of his hostility to any measure of toleration that he decided to vote against Wellington's wishes. Afterwards he wondered 'who would have said or believed that I, the friend, the great worshipper of Wellington, should have found myself obliged to give my *vote* against him, I, who was come to give it for him?'[33]

Wellington, far from reciprocating Cumberland's warm feelings, had once called him 'the most mischievous fellow he had ever met'. He had no intention of letting the King's brother upset his plans even if it meant lying to his face. During a three-hour interview with him on 9 August Wellington flatly denied (according to Cumberland's account) that he would ever consent to Catholic emancipation.[34] Cumberland was determined to keep him to his word. He could not desert his family in Berlin any longer, but he let it be known that he would return at once if the Catholic issue was raised in Parliament. Before setting out on his return journey he assured Princess Lieven that he would fight to the last against any Catholic relief bill, and his visit to England had so greatly strengthened and increased his party that he felt sure he would win the battle.[35]

It was not an altogether idle boast. During his stay in England Cumberland had worked hard to build up a movement to oppose Catholic emancipation, and there were enough fanatical Protestants of weight and influence to give the impression that a formidable opposition might be mounted if the government showed signs of wanting to conciliate the Catholics. Even before the Clare election had brought matters to a head, some members of both Houses of Parliament had met to discuss what the Protestant response should be to the Catholic Association's renewed agitation. At a further meeting early in July, attended by the Duke of Cumberland and with the Marquess of Chandos in the chair, it was decided to establish a Protestant – later Brunswick – Club which would meet on the first Monday in the month while Parliament was sitting.

Some ultra-Protestant peers felt that a less discreet method of stirring up anti-Catholic feeling was needed. On 8 August the *Shrewsbury Chronicle* reported that after dusk the previous Friday a man huddled up in a greatcoat had been observed distributing songs and pamphlets, throwing them into shops and pushing them under the doors of houses. He had refused to give his name or that of his employer, but later it was discovered that Lord Farnham, who was staying in the town that night, was responsible. Lord Farnham, a nephew of John Foster, the last Speaker of the Irish Parliament, had been present at the inaugural meeting of the Brunswick Club in London. The message which he caused to be distributed was on the following lines:

> Wake, Protestants of England, awake the time is come,
> The Papist foe is prowling near; why are your voices dumb?
> Let not your Church be thus overthrown, your pleasant vine be felled;
> Rise up and SPEAK, or ye must soon FIGHT.[36]

Other Protestant peers attempted more conventional anti-Catholic publicity. Chandos suggested to Lord Kenyon that a declaration of support for the Protestant constitution should be drawn up 'in firm and temperate language' and distributed to every parish for signature by all who were 'anxious for the good of their country'. Kenyon advocated this plan in four 'Letters to the Protestants of Great Britain' which were published widely in the anti-Catholic press. The first, published on 30 August, argued that as the House of Commons did not represent the anti-Catholic feelings of the people, the Protestants must rely on their own efforts. If it was made clear to the King that his subjects wanted him to honour his coronation oath, he would do so.[37]

On 18 September the Duke of Newcastle published in the *Morning Post* a letter to Kenyon supporting his appeal for Protestant action. Newcastle, described by Greville as 'one of the silliest of the High Tories', never held any political office, seldom attended the House of Lords and thoroughly disliked London and London society. But any threat, as he conceived it, to the British constitution, which he believed he had a sacred duty to defend, stung him into action. In

March 1821 he had published a pamphlet opposing a Catholic relief bill then being debated in the House of Commons. In 1824 he had tried to stir up opposition to the government because of its failure, as he saw it, to deal firmly with the Catholic Association. In 1827, during the crisis caused by Lord Liverpool's stroke, he had tried hard to drum up support for an anti-Catholic ministry and to persuade the King that it was his duty to form one. Little more than a year later a Tory government, headed by the Duke of Wellington, was being inexplicably tardy in stamping on a new threat to the constitution, emanating this time from Ireland where 'the Popish Association, day after day, audaciously asserts its omnipotence'. Newcastle was not at all comfortable to find himself wearing a demagogic mantle and appealing to the people against the executive government, but he saw no alternative, and, as Eldon commented after reading his letter to Kenyon, he was 'no flincher'.

> Deserted or unsupported by those in power, we see ourselves on the brink of ruin . . . An appeal to the nation is our only resource – it must be made – and the voice of the nation must decide whether Protestantism or Popery shall prevail . . . whether these kingdoms shall be at once the cradle and the citadel of Protestantism and real liberty, or the hot-bed of Popery, with its scarlet train of mental and political despotism . . .

There was much more in the same vein, and by the end of his long letter Newcastle had worked himself up to declare that the nation must 'demand' the annihilation of the Popish Association, the abolition of all Popish establishments, the withdrawal of the franchise from all Catholics and, in short, 'full and undisputed Protestant ascendancy'. He called on Protestant associations from one end of the country to the other to petition the King, since Parliament was not in session.[38]

Newcastle's letter was reprinted a few days later in *The Times*, which seemed to have decided that mockery was now the best weapon against the anti-Catholics. On 26 September it published a ballad entitled 'Write on, Write on', in which it rejoiced at the help the foolish letters of Kenyon and Newcastle were bound to give to the Catholic cause.

> Sure never, since the precious use
> Of pen and ink began,
> Did letters, writ by fools, produce
> Such signal good to man.
> While intellect, 'mong high and low,

Is marching on, they say,
Give *me* the Dukes and Lords that go,
Like crabs, the *other* way.

Up and down the country, however, a good many people preferred to
go 'the other way'. Those already active in Pitt or Orange Clubs
began to organize Brunswick Clubs with the aim of opposing any
further concessions to the Catholics. (Some people complained that
the name was a calumny on the present reigning house which had
come to the throne as upholders of religious liberty.) The first to be
set up outside London was the Kentish Brunswick Constitutional
Club. The inaugural meeting on 16 September was to have been held
in a large room at the Bull Inn at Maidstone, but so many turned up
that it had to be transferred to the town hall. The proceedings were
opened by the fanatically ultra-Tory Earl of Winchilsea who, in the
opinion of Sir Arthur Paget, must be, with the exception of the Duke
of Newcastle, 'the very greatest ass that ever breathed'. His resolution
to form a club was seconded by Sir John Brydges, MP, who told his
audience they were there to decide whether the established Protestant
Ascendancy in church and state was to continue to exist.

> The Papists have joined issue with us; they have thrown down the
> gauntlet, and unless we mean to yield to them (cries of 'Never', 'No fear
> of that') we must take it up. ('Yes, we're ready') – we have no choice. I
> thank God they have done so – that they have exposed the cloven hoof;
> and the sooner we measure our strength with them the better (Cheers)
> – of the result there can be no doubt . . .

Sir John went on to denounce the 'timid minds' who argued that it
would be expedient to grant the Catholics what they asked.

> They [the Catholics] will never be satisfied until they destroy the
> Protestant ascendancy in church and state and substitute Popery in its
> place (hear); to extirpate heretics is part of their creed. Shall we then be
> such fools as to place power in their hands to enable them to cut our
> throats? ('No, never') Shall we be guilty of an act of suicide? Forbid it
> heaven! There must be no surrender; it would be nobler to die in the
> trenches.

In spite of such stirring stuff – another MP declared he would fight up
to his knees in blood to defend 'our glorious constitution' – some
cautious and disapproving voices were raised. To mingled cheers
and hisses, several speakers warned of the danger of civil war and
condemned the Orange Clubs. Another called the meeting ill-timed

and injudicious and declared that there would be no tranquillity in Ireland until the claims of the Irish Catholics were met. Sir Edward Knatchbull, a prominent local MP and a back-bencher of independent views, tried to bring the two sides together. He would, he said, support the formation of the club, but he would also support a measure to give the Catholics what they wanted provided it included securities to keep the Protestant constitution inviolate.[39]

The doubters and dissenters at the Maidstone meeting did not prevent the Kent Brunswick Club from being enthusiastically set up, but their fears were quite widely shared. There was a widespread distrust of self-constituted permanent political clubs which seemed bent on usurping the constitutional functions of Parliament. 'If these [Brunswick] clubs are general,' wrote *The Times*, 'it is evident that the Duke of Wellington can only govern the country in the sense of the clubs or retire from his station.' Those who did not anticipate such extreme consequences were alienated by the verbal violence of some members of the Brunswick Clubs and feared that they would only stimulate a pro-Catholic reaction. (There were similar feelings on the other side. Lord John Russell dropped his proposal to form a society to publicize the Catholic cause after the Whig leader Earl Grey had flatly refused to join, and another prominent Whig, Lord Althorp, in an extremely discouraging letter, had expressed the fear that it would only stir up the anti-Catholics.[40]) The ultra-Protestant Lord Eldon had very mixed feelings about the Brunswick Clubs, his approval of their aims contending with his fear that they might do something 'not perfectly constitutional'. By the end of November he had come to feel that 'the strong language used in many of the clubs is most mischievous, and deters many from meeting to express in sober and temperate petitions their feelings'.[41]

Wellington and Peel did not welcome either temperate or intemperate support for a cause they had privately decided to abandon. The duke was heard to say that a Protestant explosion would particularly hamper and embarrass the government. The Duke of Rutland, a convinced but reasonable Protestant, was not puzzled or alarmed when he heard this indiscreet remark because he was aware of the rumours current in London society that the Prime Minister meant to 'conciliate' the Catholics.[42] What was not then suspected, not even probably by Wellington himself, was the eventual extent of the conciliation.

As soon as Parliament rose for the long summer recess at the end of July Wellington began to consider seriously exactly what measure of

Catholic relief should be adopted and then how to persuade the King to accept it. The King's position was not as strong as Wellington believed it to be, because he had misinterpreted a memorandum in which Canning had defined where he stood on the Catholic issue. This document had been accepted by Goderich and Wellington when they in turn took over the government. It made the Catholic issue an 'open' one, as it had been for the past fifteen years, on which each member of the Cabinet could be guided by his own conscience, but it did not specifically deny the Cabinet the right to raise the issue collectively should they choose to do so. In other words, it was not, as Wellington seemed to believe, a self-denying ordinance which in effect conceded to the King a right of veto on any government initiative on the Catholic issue. The King should have understood this since Canning had told him plainly that he could give no pledges on this issue, and Goderich's Cabinet had told him in writing that they did not consider Canning's formula prevented them from making Catholic emancipation a Cabinet issue if they chose to do so. The King had neither denied nor accepted this interpretation, and he did not feel obliged, when Wellington succeeded Goderich, to draw it to the attention of his new Prime Minister.[43] Peel, who also had not been a member of Canning's or Goderich's Cabinets, also believed that the King could prevent the Cabinet from discussing Catholic emancipation as a government measure.[44]

In any case, even if Wellington had felt – as Canning had assured the King *he* did – as 'free as air' on the Catholic issue, he would still have had to face a stiff battle with his royal master.[45] However much he may have prevaricated over what his Cabinet could and could not do, the King had always stood firm on his personal opposition to Catholic relief, and no piece of paper would have shifted him on that.

Wellington opened his campaign to break down the King's resistance by composing a lengthy memorandum in which he spelled out in the starkest and most uncompromising terms how the influence and powers of government had been 'usurped' by the demagogues of the Catholic Association 'who hold in their hands at the present moment the political power and the fate of Ireland'. He explained why the government had virtually no chance of suppressing the Association and then bleakly summarized his analysis.

> This, then, may be considered as the real state of the case. We have a rebellion impending over us in Ireland, excited, organized; and this organization directed by the leaders of the Roman Catholic Association; and their directions carried into execution by the Roman Catholic

priests; and we have in England a Parliament which we cannot dissolve, the majority of which is of opinion, with many wise and able men, that the remedy is to be found in Roman Catholic emancipation, and they would unwillingly enter into the contest without making such an endeavour to pacify the country.

It was very doubtful, Wellington concluded, whether emancipation *would* avert a civil war, but it was the duty of King and ministers 'to look our difficulties in the face and to lay the ground for getting the better of them'. They must try to conciliate Parliament and people so that if civil war did come, they would have the support of the great majority of the country.[46]

Wellington sent this alarming document to the King on 1 August, together with a covering letter in which he explained that his memorandum's object was 'to obtain your Majesty's permission to take into consideration the whole case of Ireland, with a view to the adoption of some measure to be proposed to Parliament for the pacification of that country'. And he tried to sweeten the pill by assuring the King that his approval would be sought for every stage of the policy-making process in the Cabinet.[47] 'I fear', replied the King, 'your picture of that unhappy country [Ireland] is but too true.' He agreed that Wellington should consult Peel and Lyndhurst, the Lord Chancellor, but that was as far as he would go. It must be understood, he emphasized, 'that I pledge myself to *nothing*, with respect to the *Cabinet*, or any *future proceeding*, until I am in possession of your plan'.[48]

Lord Lyndhurst had presumably been chosen as a second confidant because of the high office he held and also perhaps because, as Solicitor-General, he had played a leading part in the trial of Queen Caroline in 1820 and consequently was *persona grata* with the King. John Singleton Copley, Lord Lyndhurst, was the son of the American painter of the same name who had moved to London in 1774 when his son was two years old. He was a handsome, vain man with expensive tastes which his wife shared. Although not an outstandingly able lawyer, he had climbed rapidly up the legal profession. In the House of Commons between 1818 and 1827 he had always spoken against Catholic emancipation. In March 1827 his opposition to Burdett's relief motion had earned him a withering reply from Canning, 'under whose sarcasms', according to an eye-witness, 'he seemed to writhe'.[49] But only a few weeks later he did not refuse when Canning, anxious to keep a balance between Protestants and pro-Catholics in his Cabinet, offered to make him Lord Chancellor. Indeed, he appeared to be far

more interested in his career and finances than in politics. When he
discussed with Charles Greville the 'speculation' he had made in
giving up the Mastership of the Rolls with £7,000 a year to become
Lord Chancellor with uncertain tenure, 'political opinions and
political consistency', noted Greville, 'seemed never to occur to him,
and he considered the whole matter in a light so businesslike and
professional as to be quite amusing'.[50] In July 1828, when the
Catholic question seemed likely to upset the stability of the government, he was anxious for a settlement to be found. But when
Wellington sought his advice he was not very helpful. Lyndhurst,
the duke complained, was very ready to do anything that 'will not
occasion confusion in which he may lose his place. But he does not
look to the real efficiency of the measure to be proposed.'[51]

That complaint could not be made about Peel. He had retreated to
Brighton soon after Parliament rose and from there, on 11 August,
sent Wellington some critical but constructive comments on the proposals for a Catholic settlement which the duke had sent him. Peel
was still reluctantly convinced that to settle the Catholic issue would
be a lesser evil than to leave it an open question on which the
government could take no decisive action while the unrest in Ireland
became steadily more menacing. And he still firmly believed that it
would not do for him to pilot a relief bill through the House of
Commons. But he was willing to give Wellington help in drawing up
a settlement and then to support it firmly from the back benches. He
spelled out his position in a long memorandum to Wellington which
was, one feels, an attempt to assure himself as much as the Prime
Minister that he was doing the right thing. He would, he concluded,
resign whenever seemed the most convenient time.[52] For Wellington,
no time could seem convenient for his right-hand man's resignation,
but he recognized that Peel might feel obliged to go.[53] The rumours
flying about London were much more positive about the Home
Secretary's imminent departure from office and the reasons why he
was going.

Ignoring the rumours, Wellington assured Charles Arbuthnot that
any chance of getting a Catholic settlement depended on the very
profoundest secrecy.[54] He was, presumably, thinking of the King
whose opposition, he feared, would be greatly strengthened if he felt
he was being by-passed. His fear was amply, if unwittingly, confirmed
by the repercussions of a speech made by George Dawson, MP
for Londonderry, at the annual Orange dinner on 12 August to
commemorate the lifting of the siege of Derry in 1689. Dawson,
hitherto known publicly as an unbending defender of the Protestant

Ascendancy, had become convinced that Catholic emancipation must be conceded, and he chose to devote his speech to persuading his fanatically Orange audience to share his conviction. He emphasized the power of the Catholic Association in stark terms: 'The peace of Ireland depends not upon the government of the King but upon the dictation of the Catholic Association.' And he declared that the only alternative to crushing the Association was 'to look at the question with an intention to settle it'.[55] His speech was received with noisy hostility by his audience, it was read with anger and dismay by Peel and Wellington, and with unbounded astonishment by everyone else.

Dawson was not merely the local Tory MP. He was financial secretary to the Treasury in London and he was married to Peel's sister Mary. As a member of the government and Peel's brother-in-law, it was universally assumed that he would and could speak publicly on such a delicate subject only with the knowledge and approval of the government. 'Good God,' wrote William Peel to his brother, 'what can Dawson be about? I know no plea but insanity which can justify his conduct.' Dawson justified himself on other grounds in letters to Peel and Wellington (which went unanswered) but he did not apologize for having set the cat among the pigeons. Months later he told Greville that so many of his friends knew about his changed opinions that he thought it more 'fair and manly' to declare them publicly to his constituents.[56] Peel could hardly blame him for having changed his mind. But his public announcement of his change and the reasons he had given for it – emphasizing the power of the Catholic Association – aroused Peel's bitter anger. 'I was astonished', he concluded a long diatribe to William Gregory, 'and hurt – at the unfairness – the folly – and the indecency of his late exhibition.'[57] (Dawson, however, was not given the sack.)

The full extent of the damage Dawson had caused was revealed to Peel only when he attended a council meeting at Windsor. The King, who had only just heard about the speech, said that Dawson must be mad. But this did not prevent him from suspecting that Dawson had had his wits sufficiently about him to act as the mouthpiece of ministers who wanted to have the ground prepared in Ulster for Catholic relief. It was almost impossible to eradicate this mistaken idea from the King's mind, and the feeling that his ministers were slyly pursuing a policy directly contrary to his wishes reinforced his determination to resist it. 'The King', reported Peel delicately to Wellington, 'has a deeper *tinge* of Protestantism than when you last saw him.'[58]

Wellington's last visit to Windsor had been a fortnight earlier when he stayed there for a couple of nights on his way to Cheltenham. According to Princess Lieven, he arrived looking 'out of humour' – not surprisingly in view of his manifold worries and his rather strained relations with his host. He had, it seems, been burning too much midnight oil over the Irish problem and had been advised to take a fortnight's holiday and some medicinal waters. At Cheltenham he proved to be, in the words of the *Spectator*, 'a magnet of extraordinary attraction'. The number of visitors soared and the public walks where he was likely to stroll were unusually thronged. When he attended a ball in the Assembly Rooms, the ballroom was appropriately decorated in his honour and he entered it through a triumphal arch of laurels. When he attended the theatre, he was received 'with honours little short of those paid exclusively to royalty'.

In spite of the attentions of his admirers Wellington managed to get away for some healthy country walks and he returned to his country home, Stratfieldsaye, early in September much improved in health. Mrs Arbuthnot reported that he had got 'a brown healthy colour, and seems to have got his head and stomach quite right'. But his worries loomed as large as ever. He was faced with the loss of the invaluable Peel and all the tiresome personal complications that a Cabinet reshuffle always seemed to cause. He still had to work out how to satisfy the Irish Catholics in a way that was acceptable – or at least tolerable – to King, Parliament, Orangemen and the British public. With barely concealed irritation he pointed out to a Tory supporter that although the Catholic question had been debated for twenty-five years and had been the subject of more speeches and pamphlets than any other issue, the government was expected 'at once to find the way out of chaos'.[59]

And time was not on his side. Presumably, O'Connell would try to take his seat when Parliament reassembled in the new year. Even more urgent, the popular unrest in Ireland, among both Catholics and Orangemen, was growing more menacing every day. It was beginning to look as if the Catholic leaders could no longer control their supporters even if they wanted to. And to make matters worse, Wellington was rapidly losing confidence in the Lord Lieutenant's ability to do so either. In the early autumn of 1828 Ireland seemed to be slipping towards civil war.

4

Ireland on the Brink

(August–December 1828)

'It is clear the people neither mind the magistrates nor their priests when they are in opposition to their wishes – and I suspect their leaders are beginning to find out that they have but little power to control them. The mine is prepared, and it is very evident there is but little wanting to make it explode.'

Lord Clare to Lord Francis Leveson-Gower, from Nenagh,
Co. Tipperary, 22 September 1828

'You and I', wrote Peel to Gregory towards the end of August, 'have seen bad times in Ireland – but I agree with you – we never saw anything like the present.'[1] In a sense, the country seemed strangely – ominously – quiescent. Incidents of violent crime had noticeably decreased. When the Tipperary summer assizes opened at Clonmel, the judge congratulated the grand jury on the absence of violent and turbulent crime. At the Galway assizes there was only one criminal case, which was dismissed for lack of evidence. One reason for the unwonted calm was the peasants' preoccupation with getting in the harvest which that year promised to be good. A further reason was that the agrarian secret societies, which traditionally provided an outlet for the peasants' violent frustrations through house-burning, cattle-maiming and murder, had decided not to compete with O'Connell and the Catholic Association. With its stirring propaganda and its countrywide organization, the Association offered a new ex-hilarating focus for discontent. But it eschewed violence, and the peasants, who assumed they would still have to fight for their rights, waited impatiently for O'Connell's call to arms. When he was in Clonmel the question 'When will he call us out?' was heard in the streets. According to the contemporary historian of the Association, it was frequently answered 'with a finger on the mouth, and a significant smile and wink from the bystanders'.[2]

But O'Connell gave no sign and the peasants were reduced to fighting each other, a traditional occupation which some years later de Tocqueville noted when he was travelling through Ireland. Almost every village, he wrote, forms a faction with a code name: 'Factions which start nobody knows when, and which continue nobody knows why, and which take on no particular political colour.'[3] The Catholic Association tried to stop this pointless feuding. In the middle of August O'Gorman Mahon and Tom Steele went to Newport, near Limerick, summoned two factions to meet in the large Catholic chapel, and with the help of the priest persuaded them to be reconciled. They were sworn into O'Connell's Order of Liberators* in couples, each couple afterwards shaking hands.[4] On another occasion a local schoolmaster, who was an agent of the Association, assembled between 5,000 and 6,000 men, assured them that Catholic emancipation was nearly achieved and told them to stop fighting at fairs and go home peacefully.[5]

Soon, however, large crowds of men were assembling apparently of their own accord, particularly in Tipperary, Limerick and Clare. They marched through the towns and villages in orderly processions. They caused no rioting and dispersed peacefully, but there was something ominous about the way they marched and manoeuvred at the command of unknown leaders. Many were dressed in green quasi-military uniforms; all wore a green sash or shawl or green ribbons in their hat. Some carried green flags or banners decorated with a harp or with two men shaking hands. Some carried large portraits of O'Connell or a crucifix covered with green ribbons. Mr Edward Wilson, the chief magistrate in County Tipperary, found some 4,000 to 5,000 men assembled in the village of Holycross, near Thurles, one Sunday morning early in September. He rode through them asking who was in command but no one would tell him. They said they had assembled to make peace and settle their disputes for ever, and they seemed delighted that he had had the confidence to come among them. One of the speakers told the crowd that if they lived in peace and harmony with each other 'they would soon gain what they had

---

* The Order of Liberators was founded by O'Connell in July 1826 in imitation of a society founded by Bolivar in South America. Members were supposed to have performed some act of service for Ireland and could wear a very flamboyant uniform designed by O'Connell. It was not a success.

long looked for – Emancipation'. A priest asked them to stop assembling in this way. They promised to do so, and about six o'clock
went home peacefully.[6] From Limerick the chief magistrate reported
on 2 September that large bodies of men, each man wearing a green
sash, had been assembling to make huge bonfires. The previous
Saturday evening at least thirty bonfires in Clare and Limerick could
be seen from rising ground. The local people were being compelled
to make large contributions towards the cost of green ribbons and
materials for bonfires, and they were 'beyond conception alarmed'.[7]

Inevitably, the Protestants felt gravely threatened, not only by the
Catholics' restlessness, but also by the Lord Lieutenant's failure, as it
seemed to them, to give them wholehearted support. William Gregory
complained to Peel that 'the belief that they [the Protestants] are
deserted by the Government is driving them into clubs and associations amongst themselves'.[8] In the middle of August the Brunswick
Constitutional Club of Ireland was formed in Dublin 'on the principle
of preserving the Protestant constitution'. The president was
Wellington's brother-in-law, Lord Longford, at whose London house
the first English Brunswick Club had been founded early the previous
month. Of the thirty vice-presidents only one was not a peer; the
rank and file were mostly former Orangemen. By the beginning of
September contributions, one at least of as much as £1,000, were
pouring in. The movement spread rapidly, especially in Ulster, and
by the end of September the *Spectator* claimed that there was scarcely a
town in Ireland without its Brunswick Club. With a membership
largely of artisans and farmers, these local clubs were led by lawyers
and clergy and other members of the professional classes. They held
meetings, prepared petitions designed to deter the government from
granting emancipation and began to organize the collection of a
'Protestant rent'.

To the more extreme Orangemen such low-key activities did not
seem enough to keep the Catholics in their place. They made provocative speeches at public meetings. They celebrated the King's
birthday on 12 August with processions and demonstrations. The
inhabitants of Enniskillen and Tempo in County Fermanagh were
kept awake one night by Orangemen, mostly yeomanry, who charged
up and down the streets for hours on end firing as they went. The
priest's house was a favourite target; by morning all its windows were
shattered.[9]

> The Orangemen [wrote Lord Anglesey], by which I mean the most
> violent of the Protestants, are almost in a state of frenzy. It seems to me

that they feel their cause is going down ... and that they are therefore anxious for any mischief rather than allow matters to be quietly settled. I am persuaded there are many who are living upon the hope of driving the Catholics to violence as the last hope of averting the measure they dread by deeply committing them with the Government.[10]

Anglesey did not believe that the Catholic leaders wanted to oblige the Orangemen by allowing themselves to be provoked into full-scale violence. Yet O'Connell could not afford to let the Orangemen make all the running if he was to keep control of his own wild men, and his speeches sometimes veered perilously close to incitement to violence. After some particularly provocative Orange speechifying, he exclaimed to a big provincial meeting at Clonmel: 'Oh! Would to God that our excellent viceroy, Lord Anglesey, would but only give me a commission, and *if* those men of blood should attempt to attack the property and persons of His Majesty's loyal subjects, with a hundred thousand of my brave Tipperary boys, I would soon drive them into the sea before me.'[11] O'Connell assured the same meeting that he expected to take his seat in the House of Commons when Parliament reassembled in February. Three days later he was at a large meeting in Cork where he moved a resolution of thanks to Peel's brother-in-law, George Dawson, whose speech at Derry in favour of emancipation had so greatly upset the authorities. The motion was carried amidst deafening applause.

Meanwhile the alarm which Dawson had stirred up among the Ulster Protestants was being greatly heightened by the activities of one of the Catholic Association's most reckless demagogues. John ('Radical – or Honest – Jack') Lawless was a Catholic lawyer from Belfast who had been excluded from the Bar because of his extreme political views. As a radical politician his career was not helped by his turbulent and erratic temperament. On public platforms his performances were invariably rousing but not always comprehensible. A foreign visitor who heard him speak in Dublin called him the Don Quixote of the Association. 'His fine head and white hair, his wild but noble dignity, and his magnificent voice, excite an expectation of something extraordinary when he rises; but the speech ... soon falls into the most incredible extravagancies and sometimes into total absurdity.'[12] He had no use for O'Connell's attempts to steer a moderate statesmanlike course towards emancipation and heckled him mercilessly at public meetings. O'Connell, who once referred to Lawless in a letter to his wife as 'that miserable maniac', found him a difficult ally.[13] Perhaps that was partly why he agreed to Lawless's offer to go up to the northern counties to drum up support and organize a more efficient collection of the Catholic 'rent'. It would be a useful outlet for Lawless's energies. But to conduct such a mission in districts where Orangemen were violently denouncing the Catholic Association was a delicate undertaking, and moderate Catholics felt that Lawless was hardly the most suitable man to lead it. He proceeded as far as Counties Louth and Meath, where Catholics predominated, and hung about there for several weeks, holding meetings and organizing the collection of the 'rent'. His threatening presence and his enthusiastic reception by the Catholic peasants raised the temperature in the north still further.

The authorities in Dublin, however, were chiefly alarmed by the disturbed state of the southern counties – Tipperary, Limerick, Clare – and during August Lord Anglesey tried, so far as his gout would let him, to find out for himself what was going on there. He went to the notoriously troubled county of Tipperary and visited the most disturbed villages. 'Nothing', he told his brother, 'can exceed the enthusiasm with which I have been received everywhere. I have had some of the most *affect.* addresses from the poorest and most disturbed *villages.*'[14] He found the road-building scheme, by which he set great store, proceeding satisfactorily and the local gentry willing to help.[15] A visit to Carlingford was cut short by illness, but at the end of the month he visited the famous Donnybrook fair, accompanied only by his son William Paget and two friends. The absence of any soldiers or policemen made his reception all the more friendly. But these attempts to create trust between government and people laid him open in Ireland – as the *Spectator* indignantly pointed out – to 'the animadversions of the Church and State party'. When people received him with affection and he repaid them with 'an urbanity never exercised by former viceregents', it was inferred that he 'had "given himself up to the Catholics"'. When he told the people he hoped all religious distinctions would soon be forgotten, 'these courteous and not very uncommon words' were construed into a promise that the demands of popery would soon be met.[16]

Anglesey's reluctance to cultivate relations with 'the Church and State party' naturally increased their dislike and distrust of him. He did not share their extreme views and did not wish to discuss them. Instead he surrounded himself with a small inner council of men who sympathized with the Catholic cause and whose names, consequently, 'stank in the nostrils of good Protestants'.[17] According to one of these unofficial advisers, Lord Cloncurry, they were frequently summoned by the Lord Lieutenant to give him information and advice.[18]

The distrust created by Anglesey's choice of advisers was compounded by O'Connell's unfortunate habit of referring to him in public in the friendliest terms and in general doing his best to foster the impression that the Lord Lieutenant and his Chief Secretary were on the Catholics' side. O'Connell even went so far as to issue a placard which purported to place the Lord Lieutenant under the Association's protection. He also tried private blandishments, sending Leveson-Gower a letter full of compliments and offers of information and assistance. Lord Francis sent him a civil reply and then did his embarrassed best to explain to Peel that although it would be improper to correspond officially with a member of the Catholic Association, to treat O'Connell with discourtesy would not help either. 'The line of conduct in such cases is a matter of some difficulty, and if you see any reason to doubt the judgment of mine, I should be grateful . . . for your unbiassed opinion.'[19]

Inevitably in the circumstances, there were failures of communication between London and Dublin which generated mutual exasperation. Peel felt he was being kept short of reliable information by which he could judge the wild exaggerations and misinformation in the Irish press.* When he found two letters on his desk, one from George Dawson and the other from the Commander-in-Chief, Sir George Hill, reporting that the disbanding of the (largely Protestant) yeomanry was causing the greatest alarm in the Protestant north, he immediately asked Leveson-Gower whether the yeomanry were in fact being disbanded. By return Lord Francis assured him they were not. The arms and ammunition of some yeomanry regiments had been removed to a safer place and that was all.[20] Anglesey added his rather barbed assurances. The report, he told Peel, was 'so absurd that I really did not think it necessary to contradict it'. And he added: 'It is not easy to foresee what importance may on your side of the water be attached to the idle and frequently malicious reports that are put forth here.' Peel agreed that the reports which Hill and Dawson had mistakenly believed 'had very likely originated in the spirit of mischief'; but he added that it would be a great advantage to him if he could say not merely that he *believed*, but that he *knew* a report to be false.[21]

Wellington's mounting irritation with the Lord Lieutenant made

---

* Leveson-Gower asked Peel if he had, when he was Chief Secretary, any means of 'stating an occurrence, occasionally, as it really was? The newspapers here are mere channels of fiction . . .' Peel replied that a government newspaper would not work. If it was moderate no one would read it, and if 'highly seasoned enough for the Irish palate', it would be mischievous. 'I am very much afraid there is no appetite for the truth in Ireland.' (BL Add. MSS 40335, 26 August and 2 September 1828.).

him less scrupulous. He was ready to believe whatever he was told about Anglesey and condemn him without further ado. Anglesey, he complained to Peel, was behaving 'in a very extraordinary manner'. He was apparently making no attempt to hide his criticism of the government: 'He has been repeatedly heard to say that his hands were tied up by the ministers, otherwise he would do everything that was wished.'[22] Anglesey's impatience and self-confidence led him to talk in private with a freedom and lack of discretion that was only too easily transmitted by the gossips of Dublin and London in a mischievously garbled form. He might well have restrained himself if he had known that Wellington had accepted the expediency of granting emancipation and was planning how to carry it out. All he had been told about the government's intentions was contained in a letter from Peel in the middle of August which stated, in the most formal terms, that the Cabinet intended to consider the state of Ireland and what should be done about it before the next session of Parliament.[23] Peel did not ask for the views of the man on the spot, who continued to offer them all the same.

But the more ministers suspected Anglesey's pro-Catholic leanings and doubted his determination to maintain order, the less willing they became to confide their plans to him. 'What more can I say to him?' asked Peel of Wellington. He himself thought that 'the most prudent course' with regard to the Lord Lieutenant was to 'maintain as much reserve as possible'.[24] Shortly afterwards, on 24 September, Anglesey made a determined effort to break down that reserve in a long letter to Wellington. His frustration emerged plainly in his opening remarks. He had, he wrote, been doubting for a long time whether to write to him about Catholic emancipation, 'for, as you have never named the subject to me, I have had a delicacy in introducing it'. His advice to Wellington was that if he went for a settlement now he could get one on better terms and with less opposition from the Catholic bishops and the Association than ever before. Even the Protestants, he believed, felt that something must be done, and would acquiesce in moderate concessions to the Catholics.[25]

Wellington's reply was not encouraging. He had not, he said, written to Anglesey about emancipation because he had nothing to tell him. The first step was to reconcile the King's mind to it, and until that was achieved, he thought he should not talk about it at all. He doubted whether a settlement of the Catholic question would solve Ireland's difficulties. But 'it is quite clear that nothing can be done now; that our affair now, and indeed in Ireland always, will be to preserve the peace . . .'[26]

Anglesey might have penetrated this verbal camouflage and deduced that Wellington would move when he had won over the King. But he did not take the hint (if such it was intended to be), perhaps because he did not attach so much importance to royal opposition. In his reply the duke had referred to Canning's memorandum on the Catholic question. Anglesey, who, unlike Wellington, had been a member of both Canning's and Goderich's Cabinets, must have had a better understanding of how that document should be interpreted. He may, consequently, have felt that if Canning had still been in charge, he would have felt free to accept the logical consequences of the Clare election and insist that his royal master should do so too – as indeed Wellington was eventually to do. So he may not have realized the strength of the duke's inhibitions about confronting the King's prejudices on this issue.

By the middle of September the meetings and marches in the south of Ireland showed no sign of abating, and the Protestant minority living there in a sea of Catholics was becoming increasingly frightened. An English clergyman, Mr Derby, who was staying in Killenaule, County Tipperary, reported that those Protestants who could not afford to go to America were arming themselves in their own defence. But he himself, unnerved perhaps by a recent alarming experience, believed these preparations were too late and 'the Protestants of the south will fall a sacrifice'. On Sunday, 14 September, he and his family were returning from church when they ran into a crowd at least 10,000 strong, who were marching into the town, carrying green flags and accompanied by bands and officers wearing red sashes. A cross ten feet high was carried in front of one contingent. Mr Derby got his family out of their carriage and they escaped out of the town on foot with the help of a priest who clearly disliked what was going on, although the purpose of the march was said to be simply to reconcile different factions. No Protestant was molested or insulted and the chief constable had assured Mr Derby that there would be no outrage until Mr O'Connell had been rejected by the House of Commons – that would be the signal.[27]

Lord Francis Leveson-Gower forwarded Mr Derby's letter to Peel with the comment that it was merely a repetition of the reports he was sending to London daily. He took the view that the meetings were clearly illegal and that it might be necessary to suppress them, 'possibly with much loss of life', long before O'Connell was refused his seat in the House of Commons. Later that same day Lord Francis had a long talk with the Lord Lieutenant about the unrest in Tipperary.

Remembering, perhaps, his friendly reception there a few weeks earlier, Anglesey was still reluctant to suppress the meetings by force so long as they remained peaceful.[28]

Two days later, on 20 September, Anglesey reluctantly made up his mind to prepare for the possibility that they might not stay peaceful. 'It is', he wrote to Peel, 'most distressing to me to feel that I may now be compelled to bring on a crisis which it has been my most anxious wish to avoid.' But the meetings in Tipperary had become more frequent, much larger and altogether more formidable. Moreover, the priests, who had tried without success to stop them, seemed to have lost all control over the people. So Anglesey suggested it would be prudent to issue a proclamation declaring that the meetings were illegal and would, if necessary, be dispersed by force. He hoped the warning would be sufficient, but in case it was not, he asked that troop reinforcements should be stationed on the English and Welsh sides of the Irish Sea. Finally, he asked for authority to bring them over himself, without an order from the Horse Guards, in case of emergency.[29]

Next day, Sunday, the 21st, there were more marchings and meetings. Among the more or less agitated reports sent to Dublin Castle was one from the mayor of Clonmel. He described how about 5,000 people came from about ten miles round and assembled in the town. About half of them, dressed in various costumes, were divided into regiments, each headed by fifes and drums and banners with harps and other devices. Accompanied by 500 to 600 horsemen, they marched to the barracks, wheeled by command, marched back and dispersed. In the evening three or four patrols went round the public houses, removed the drunks and tried to get them to go home; a few refractory ones were put under the pump. There were no outrages and the marchers carried only sticks. To the mayor, watching in the background, 'there seemed to be a system throughout'. His restrained and respectful language did not hide his alarm.

> . . . from the language used by many of the bye standers, it was very apparent, the strong excitement created by this most novel display of so great a body, marching in military array through the chief town of the county. And allow me to say, that fears are entertained, if some check be not put to those meetings, they will end, and that ere long, in a subversion of good order and a spirit of resistance to the laws which may not easily be controlled.[30]

The day after this appeal was despatched from Tipperary, the development that the authorities feared most – an armed clash between

Catholics and Protestants – was narrowly averted by a British officer, General Thornton. After Lawless had hovered for weeks south of the Ulster border, uttering threats to exterminate the 'Orange reptiles' and whip them into the walls of Derry, he began to lead his motley force of Catholic peasants north through County Monaghan, where the two creeds were more or less evenly divided. General Thornton, with about a hundred soldiers, rode into Ballybay, the first place of any size in Lawless's path, very early on the morning of 23 September. He found a large well-armed body of Orangemen about to set out to prevent Lawless from entering the town. He persuaded them to stay where they were while he intercepted Lawless and persuaded him to turn back. His mediation was successful. Lawless stopped short at a Catholic chapel not far from the town, and then beat an ignominious retreat eastwards to Castleblaney, leaving the Orangemen to claim a splendid victory.[31] In the opinion of Leveson-Gower, only General Thornton's 'prompt and judicious exertion' had prevented an explosion in the north, and he warned Peel that Ireland must be considered 'as on the eve of rebellion, or civil war, or both'.[32] Less than a week later Lawless – that 'pestilentious agitator' – had turned up in Carrickmacross where he was daily, almost hourly, making 'mischievous and abusive harangues'.[33]

On the same day as the Ballybay incident, Anglesey's letter of the 20th reached Peel at his home in Staffordshire. It crossed an immensely long letter from Peel in which he forcefully argued that the meetings in Ireland must be banned at once by proclamation if, as he assumed, the law officers pronounced them to be illegal.* He was extremely anxious that whatever the risk of bloodshed the government should not give the impression that it was afraid to act.[34] A few days later the Cabinet, meeting in London, agreed to authorize the Lord Lieutenant to ban the Irish meetings. All the troops that could be spared – six regiments of infantry and two of cavalry – were ordered to the west coast and Anglesey was authorized to summon them across the Irish Sea himself.[35] ('I must say,' he told Wellington, 'you do not do things by halves.') The Cabinet, according to Ellenborough,

---

* As usual in its dealings with the Irish Catholics, the English government was punctilious about remaining within the law. The English law officers ruled that the recent meetings in Ireland were illegal under common law, although no act of violence was committed, because they had no definite legal object and were 'formed with such apparent concert and organisation ... as to strike a well-founded fear into the peaceable and well-disposed inhabitants of the neighbourhood where they meet ...' (Peel, *Memoirs*, vol. 1, p. 226).

felt it would be easier to put down the meetings now rather than later. 'Still, it is a fearful step and may precipitate the crisis.'[36]

Anglesey still hoped that he would not have to risk precipitating a crisis. He assured Peel that he only wished 'to be prepared at all points'.[37] But the news of Ballybay greatly increased the alarm of the ministers in London. Peel at once urged Anglesey, in peremptory and unusually agitated terms, to consult his legal advisers about prosecuting Lawless and thus bringing his northern progress to an end.[38] Wellington – and he was not the only one – saw a connection between Lawless and the unrest in Tipperary. He interpreted the latter as 'a notification to the Protestants of the north that their scattered brethren in the south will be massacred some Sunday, if Mr Lawless's progress should be impeded'.[39]

Anglesey, however, knew that the Catholic leaders, both lay and clerical, were seriously alarmed by the spontaneous unrest, and he had indirectly let it be known that he hoped they would not make it necessary for him to intervene. Sheil took the hint and on 18 September gave a public warning of the danger of conflict between Catholics and Orangemen. A week later, at a meeting of the Catholic Association in Dublin, he attacked the government for its 'strange procrastination and almost imbecile indecision' in not granting emancipation, denied that the Association had any responsibility for the unrest and warned his audience that the Association was in danger of losing the 'useful despotism over the passions of the people' which it had been able to exercise in the past. The meeting resolved that the demonstrations in the south should be stopped, and sent an urgent appeal to O'Connell in his remote County Kerry home to exert his powerful influence to calm things down.

Several thousand copies of an address prohibiting, in the name of the Catholic Association, any further meetings and marches, were immediately despatched to Tipperary. A few days later, O'Connell issued an 'Address to the Honest and Worthy People of the County Tipperary' in which he appealed to the people to give up their huge meetings, which had now served their purpose, and leave it to the Association to carry the Catholic cause to final victory.

> We will plant in our native land the constitutional Tree of Liberty ... Beneath its sweet and sacred shade, the universal people of Ireland, Catholics and Protestants, and Presbyterians and Dissenters of every class, will sit in peace and unison and tranquillity. Commerce and trade will flourish; industry will be rewarded; and the people, contented and happy, will see Old Ireland what she ought to be,

Great, Glorious and FREE,
First flower of the Earth, first gem of the Sea.[40]

In Dublin Castle, and among the Protestant establishment generally, the news that the Catholic Association had intervened – and, as it soon appeared, to good effect – to curb the unrest, was not well received. The Solicitor-General, John Doherty, told Anglesey bluntly that the Irish government had been made to seem weak and indecisive. Even his loyal lieutenant, Leveson-Gower, thought the same. Anglesey disagreed, and he defended himself stoutly in a letter to Peel. He hoped, he wrote, that tranquillity would now be preserved, but if he did have to act, he was confident that 'my arm will have been amazingly strengthened by the moderation and forbearance I have shown'. As for the Catholic Association, there was 'some vanity and some insolence' in its conduct, 'but if the course it has chosen to pursue tends to preserve tranquillity, much good will have been obtained'. And he continued, with what could be called, according to taste, either robust common sense or deplorable naivety:

> It seems to me to be absurd to condemn people for their (their very first) act of retribution – the first symptom they have shown of repentance of former follies and of returning moderation, when for years past the Government has . . . allowed the agitation . . . of these dangerous principles which have brought the country into its present state.[41]

For two more days Anglesey went on hoping that the situation was under control. But on Tuesday, 30 September ('a very harassing day') General Byng placed before him a letter from General Thornton written from Armagh the previous day and enclosing a printed proclamation full of the most inflammatory Orange propaganda. It called on the Protestants of the north to assemble in Armagh next day (the 30th) to oppose an expected attempt by Lawless to enter the town. Thornton thought that as many as 40,000 Protestants might respond to the appeal if Lawless really approached the town. But the previous Saturday the local Catholics had held a meeting, with their priest in the chair, and had passed a resolution begging him to stay away. Thornton believed Lawless would obey, but as a precaution had ordered two companies of infantry, who were on their way to Newry, to halt in the town.[42]

The news from Armagh made civil war seem imminent. With the urgent backing of all his advisers, Anglesey immediately decided to issue a proclamation banning all meetings, whether of Catholics or Protestants. He also ordered a modest reinforcement of the troops at his immediate command: one battalion was summoned from Liverpool to Belfast, and another from Bristol to Waterford. On 9 October Leveson-Gower reported that they had arrived safely 'in the teeth of a tremendous gale'.

These precautions proved unnecessary. The unrest in the south died down, although the Orange yeomanry in the north remained unsettled. Yet the ministers in London still felt that Anglesey had bungled the crisis disgracefully. They believed that a proclamation declaring certain acts illegal should be given weight and authority by the signatures of privy councillors, especially those of the law officers. But Anglesey had let his Lord Chancellor, Sir Anthony Hart, as well as the Attorney-General and the Solicitor-General, leave the country on their private affairs. Peel complained to Wellington that if the state of Ireland was really as bad as Anglesey said, it was 'an odd time for the chief law officers of the Crown . . . to be at Spa or on the Rhine'.[43] He asked Lyndhurst to write privately to Hart, suggesting he should return at once to Dublin. But Hart was not back at his post by the 30th, and when the proclamation was published next day, it bore only the Lord Lieutenant's signature. Anglesey's excuse was that the very few privy councillors who were immediately available would have given the proclamation very little weight.[44] (Privately, he thought they would have attached ridicule rather than importance to the document.[45]) But the English ministers were furious. Peel sent Leveson-Gower a measured reproof, and assured Wellington that it would have been very much stronger if the damage had not already been done. 'Nothing can be more foolish than these uncalled-for supersessions of ancient usages in matters of this nature.'[46]*

Whether angry Orangemen or Catholic peasants would pay much attention to 'ancient usages' seems doubtful. Perhaps Peel and Wellington would not have done so either if they had had more confidence in the Lord Lieutenant. But by this time they had precious little. He had been so obviously reluctant to put down the unrest by force. Even on the 30th he had yielded only reluctantly to the urgent

---

*In his reply to Peel on 4 October, Leveson-Gower remarked that if the proclamation continued to escape public criticism for lacking legal authority, as it had done so far, 'the result will probably be little affected by the form in which it has been issued . . .' Later, after doing some research in the Castle archives, he sent Peel various precedents which could justify Anglesey's proclamation, adding, rather disingenuously, that he did not mean to combat Peel's 'mature opinion' (BL Add. MSS 40336, 13 Oct. 1828).

advice of those around him, and he was unwise enough to reveal this afterwards to both Wellington and Peel. He might have been more inclined to assert his authority if he, for his part, had had more confidence in the government's intentions – or even if he had had some idea what they were.

When Palmerston saw the Lord Lieutenant during a visit to Ireland in October, Anglesey was undisguisedly anxious to know what the government intended to do about Ireland. To his surprise, Palmerston found himself being begged to pick up what information he could in London and pass it back to Dublin.

> The Lord Lieutenant of Ireland [he commented in his journal] begging a private gentleman to let him know, if he could find out, what the prime minister meant upon a question deeply affecting the peace and welfare of the country which that Lord Lieutenant was appointed to govern, and upon which question he was every week stating to the Government the opinions he himself entertained – a strange instance of the withholding of that confidence which, for both their sakes, ought to have existed.[47]

He would have thought it even stranger if he could have known that the measure that the Prime Minister refused to reveal to the Lord Lieutenant was precisely the one that the Lord Lieutenant was most anxious to see adopted.

After the Ballybay incident Lawless continued to make a nuisance of himself. The Association recalled him to Dublin and soon after his return early in October, he went too far in his inflammatory speechifying and was duly arrested. According to Leveson-Gower, he 'took his arrest with good humour, admitted that his bail was not excessive and predicted a certain and joyous triumph for himself'. Lawless was not far wrong, for instead of being prosecuted – as Wellington and Peel strongly believed he ought to be – the case against him was quietly dropped several weeks later.

Tom Steele and O'Gorman Mahon also attracted the unfavourable attention of the English government. Leveson-Gower found it hard to take Steele seriously. He assured Peel that Steele was 'a decided lunatic', who would probably some day get into a 'scrape', in which case a jury would very probably bring in a verdict of insanity.[48] Steele rode around the countryside wearing a broad green sash and attending meetings in Catholic chapels at which he urged the people to keep off alcohol and live in peace with one another. These worthy sentiments did not reconcile the authorities in London to his activities. It was also alleged that he had indulged in insurrectionary talk – how, if there was a rising, information could be conveyed by signals – and Peel told Leveson-Gower that if these allegations were well-founded, there was 'no punishment consistent with [the] law which Mr Steele does not most richly deserve'.[49]

Worst of all was the behaviour of O'Gorman Mahon when the high sheriff of County Clare called a meeting in Ennis to set up a Brunswick Club and brought some soldiers into the town in case of trouble. Mahon, accompanied by Steele, went to Ennis to oppose the meeting but was refused admittance. During an ostentatious parade through the town he and Steele came across the soldiers who were returning to the gaol yard after finding no disturbances to put down. Mahon addressed himself to the officer in charge, Major Grierson, and used such strong language to criticize the sheriff for his 'shameful' conduct in needlessly calling in the troops that Grierson felt obliged to report him to the sheriff, who immediately got him to repeat Mahon's words to as many magistrates as he could find.

Wellington and Peel agreed that both Steele and Mahon should be dismissed instantly from the bench of magistrates. 'Is it possible', asked the duke, 'to expect that the gentlemen of Ireland will continue to act as magistrates if this conduct is persevered in? If they have the spirit of men, they must resent it.'[50] At the same time both he and Peel privately deplored the conduct of the sheriff at Ennis who had summoned a political meeting although he had felt that the presence of troops might be required to prevent a breach of the peace.[51] Anglesey felt that neither Mahon nor Steele were really fit to sit on the bench, but his law officers advised him that he lacked sufficient grounds to dismiss them.[52] These were not found until the following January, and in the meantime Steele continued to ride round the countryside in Clare and Limerick, undermining the authority of the local magistrates by his opprobrious comments. To Wellington such leniency was completely unjustified and served only to inflame the Protestants. He tried himself to redress the balance and his friends were reported to be speaking out strongly against concessions to the Catholics. 'Can he possibly', asked Henry Brougham, 'have made up his mind to a civil war?'[53]

In the middle of October that ultimate disaster did not seem entirely out of the question. The Catholic peasants' meetings and marches had died away, thanks to Anglesey's proclamation and – probably even more – to the exhortations of O'Connell and the Association and the efforts of the 'pacificators' sent by the Association into the most disturbed districts. But the feelings which had produced them were as strong as ever. When a foreign traveller met a lad of about eighteen on a country road in Cork and asked him about the state of the country, he was told it was quiet enough there, but in Tipperary

> they know how to stand against the Orangemen. O'Connell and the Association have organized us there, like regular troops: I belong to them, and I have a uniform at home; if you saw me in it, you'd hardly know me; three weeks ago we all met there, above 40,000 men, to be reviewed. We had all green jackets . . . with an inscription on the arm – King George and O'Connell. We have chosen our own officers; they drill us, and we can march and wheel already like the redcoats. We had no arms to be sure, but they could be had too if O'Connell chose. We had flags, and whoever deserted them or got drunk we threw into the water till he was sober again; but that very seldom happened.[54]

A Cambridge student, travelling back to the university after his long vacation in County Clare, found as he went along that nobody was interested in anything but politics.

> The very cabin children, that run out in their rags to stare at the passing traveller, cry 'High for O'Connell!' while perhaps a rustic politician within reads aloud with note and comment from some Catholic journal the speeches of the orators of the Corn Exchange [Catholic Association] to an agitated circle of hereditary bondsmen.[55]

Catholic orators were not the only stimulant. Reports of Orange aggressiveness in the north and the spread of Brunswick Clubs to most parts of the south stirred up the Catholic peasants' hostility to their Protestant neighbours. More than 180 clubs, with funds amounting to £60,000, were said to have been set up throughout Ireland by the middle of November. There were reports of Catholic servants leaving their Protestant masters, of labourers refusing to work for Protestant employers, and of men who were digging potatoes for Protestants being chased off the fields. One striking example of the sectarian hostility that could sweep through a small community occurred in a small parish in Galway. On Sunday, 12 October, two petitions to Parliament in favour of emancipation were delivered to the two Catholic churchwardens in the village. They had been drawn up by the Catholic Association and the churchwardens were instructed to obtain Protestant signatures to them. When the local Protestant clergyman, Mr Huleath, heard about this, he got on his horse and rode through the village cautioning his parishioners to sign no document unless he had seen it first. The following Friday, at a meeting in the school hall with Mr Huleath in the chair and several local gentry present, 135 Protestants were enrolled as members of a Brunswick Club. The Catholic priest, Mr Sheehy (who had played an active part at Ennis during O'Connell's election), tried unsuccessfully to stop the meeting. Mr Huleath accused him of being the leading agent of sedition for the last four years, and – in the words of the chief constable's report – 'very warm words passed between the two reverend gentlemen'. The following Sunday a large meeting, held in the Catholic chapel after Mass, decided on various measures to ostracize Protestant tradesmen, landlords and other members of the minority.[56]

This was an extreme case, in a district particularly prone to unrest and exacerbated by the intolerant and fanatical character of the clergymen involved. But the practice of 'exclusive dealing', whereby all intercourse with Protestants was banned (usually by the Catholic priest) wherever a Brunswick Club was established, was reported by Leveson-Gower to be 'very generally adopted'. In Wexford a run on the local provincial bank was organized because some of its members had joined a Brunswick Club. This example was followed in Clonmel and Kilkenny, but the government rushed over supplies of gold and this particular anti-Protestant threat failed to develop. But there were also the beginnings of a movement to refuse payment of rent and tithes and, as Wellington pointed out to the King, if this spread it would be virtually impossible to force millions of peasants to obey the law.

Wellington's task of persuading the King to accept emancipation was not made any easier by the King's gout, which attacked him mercilessly that autumn in his right hand and arm and then spread to his knees and feet; his arm was reported to be so swollen that he could not get a shirt on. The constant pain and the frequent bleedings which the royal doctor thought necessary to reduce the inflammation, combined to make the King extremely irritable and even more reluctant than usual to discuss business with his Prime Minister, or even to see him at all. When Wellington was granted an audience on 10 October he was treated to a monologue three hours long during which the King suggested, among other things, that Anglesey should be recalled, Eldon brought into the Cabinet and Parliament dissolved. Wellington did not find any of these suggestions helpful and, since the King refused to listen to him, politely told him so in writing. There was no remedy for the Irish troubles, he concluded, 'excepting by means of a consideration of the whole state of Ireland' – and the King presumably knew what he meant by that.[57]

When the King's attention was not absorbed by the excruciating pains of gout, he could not be accused of ignoring the Irish crisis. He bombarded Wellington with complaints about Anglesey's short-comings, in this way fending off any discussion of a long-term solution of Ireland's problems. The duke complained that Anglesey and Leveson-Gower could have no idea how much they were increasing his difficulties with the King by their failure to deal firmly with trouble-makers and their partiality – as it seemed to him – for opponents of the government.[58]

Wellington himself was in favour of prosecuting everybody who could be prosecuted, and that included errant magistrates and the Catholic Association itself. He gave no credit to the Association for its efforts to stop the meetings and marches in the south. To him it was quite unacceptable that the King's peace should be maintained, not by the King's representatives, but by a body of dubious legality whose members were given to near-treasonable utterances. Peel agreed and asked the law officers in London and Dublin to scrutinize the acts and pronouncements of the Association for anything that could be inter-preted as a breach of the law. When, for instance, the Association 'recalled' Lawless from his Ulster mission, was it not accepting legal responsibility for his probably illegal acts?[59] Messrs Doherty and Joy dutifully perused all the shorthand reports of the Association's pro-ceedings for the past six months. They concluded (and their English colleagues agreed) that a successful prosecution of the Association was highly unlikely, although individual members might be indicted for conspiracy to, among other things, excite discontent and disaffection in the minds of the people.[60]

At the Association's meetings in the Dublin Corn Exchange the wilder spirits, like Lawless, did not care how far they went. Some members, especially if they were lawyers or were in commerce or had American contacts – funds were received from well-wishers in New York – looked beyond emancipation and talked of parliamentary reform, repeal of the Union and even republicanism. Something of the frenetic atmosphere of these meetings was recorded by a German traveller who attended some of them during November.

> The room is not very large, and as dirty as the English House of Commons. Here too every man keeps his hat on, except while he is speaking . . . The heat was suffocating, and I had to sit out five hours; but the debate was so interesting I scarcely remarked the annoyances.

O'Connell was undoubtedly the best speaker. Although idolized by the greater number, he was severely attacked by several, and defended himself with equal address and moderation; on the other hand, he assailed the Government without reserve; and in my opinion in too strong expressions . . .[61]

During these oratorical free-for-alls O'Connell could not afford to be eclipsed if he was to keep control of the movement. But he kept his eyes firmly fixed on the goal of emancipation which he hoped and believed could be achieved without violence. He realized that the English government would not give in until it had to, but – he wrote in September – 'I do think *the necessity* for Emancipation is nearly created already by the state of Ireland . . .'[62] He intended to present himself at the door of the House of Commons when it reassembled in the new year and he trusted to the sheer inflexible pressure of the popular Catholic demand to get him inside. His problem was to keep up the pressure without letting it boil over. Liberal clubs, Catholic churchwardens, parish reading-rooms supplied with free newspapers, all helped to keep it up. So did the collection of the Catholic 'rent' which after the Clare election brought in enormously increased amounts. But the mainspring of all these activities, the Catholic Association in Dublin, was easily carried away by the rhetoric of its more extreme members. Its enthusiasm for 'exclusive dealing' grew all the greater because Orangemen were beginning to resort to the same tactic against Catholics. O'Connell, who realized that it would cause great disruption and suffering, had to exert all his authority to persuade the Association, at a particularly crowded and excited meeting early in December, not to endorse the practice.

In England, meanwhile, the Protestant agitation rumbled on. Early in October Peel spent several days in the north being fêted by fellow Lancastrians. He returned 'satiated with good dining and deaf with four times four and nine times nine'. But he can hardly have had a comfortable time distancing himself from his hosts' enthusiastic cheers for the Protestant Ascendancy. At a public breakfast in the town hall at Salford, his speech was described as 'the affectionate effusion of an overflowing bosom at the manner in which he had been received by ancient friends in a place . . . associated with many pleasant reminiscences'. But when a toast to 'the pride of Britain and the admiration of the world – our glorious constitution' was drunk twice to rapturous cheers, Peel had nothing to say. When at another public breakfast at Bolton a local magistrate expressed his belief that Peel and his colleagues would make no more concessions to the Catholics, Peel failed

to respond and soon after left the table. At a big public dinner in
Manchester his speech concentrated on compliments to his hosts
and their town. But there was gloom and disappointment when he
remained seated and silent, contemplating his glass, while the rest of
the company drank a toast to the Protestant Ascendancy with nine
times nine cheers.[63] Afterwards the *Leeds Intelligencer* reported that
Peel had persuaded his Protestant friends in Lancashire to refrain
from publicly expressing their sentiments on the Catholic question.
This naturally led to speculation that he himself had changed sides.[64]

By the end of November it was reckoned that some thirty-six
Brunswick Clubs had been formed in England since the first one was
set up in Kent in September. Presumably there would have been more
if ministers had not been so discouraging. (But it was whispered,
correctly, that the King was privately in favour of them.) Lord
Talbot, a strongly anti-Catholic former viceroy, wrote anxiously
to Peel for advice when he realized that, as Lord Lieutenant of
Staffordshire, he was going to be asked to call a county meeting for
the purpose of forming a Brunswick Club. How was he to preserve
harmony and good feeling when 'the weight of interest and number of
principal personages is against us . . . [while] . . . the yeomanry and
middling classes are generally (I think) with us?'[65] (Similarly in
Lancashire, where a sizeable minority of Catholics mingled with their
Protestant neighbours, another Protestant peer, Lord Skelmersdale,
was worried by the 'break-up' of county society that a Brunswick
Club would cause.[66]) Peel firmly advised Talbot against holding a
meeting. Like many of his contemporaries, he thought clubs were
'dangerous instruments'. If he were a private person in England, he
told Talbot, he would not join a Brunswick Club, but he admitted
he did not know what he would do if he were living in Ireland
'menaced by such scoundrels as those who direct the Roman Catholic
Association'.[67] Lord Westmorland turned to Wellington for advice when he was approached about forming a Brunswick Club in
Northampton. He received a very dismissive answer. 'The difficulties
of the times', wrote the duke testily, 'have been accumulating for
nearly forty years; and I must find a way out of them!!! It is not by
means of Brunswick clubs.'[68]

Nor was it, as it turned out, by means of huge public meetings,
although the men of Kent, again in the van in the Protestant cause,
put on a very impressive show. Their meeting, billed as a debate
between Protestants and pro-Catholics, was held on 24 October
on Penenden heath, outside Maidstone. The scene was set by the
Spectator's correspondent:

About eleven o'clock the host assembled appeared to be countless. All
parts of Kent seemed to have been drained of their population. The
branches of the trees were studded with human forms; and beyond the
range of carriages . . . were thousands of people. The ceaseless din of
music, and the astounding cheers and hisses of the different parties as
their friends arrived on the ground added to the grandeur of the scene.

The two sides were assembled on either side of hustings set up for the
sheriff, either crowded into wagons or drawn up on foot. Many
landowners had brought their tenants, and the Brunswick side was
distinguished by an impressive array of Anglican and Methodist
clergy, the latter, according to an unfriendly witness, being easily
recognizable by their 'lugubrious and dismal expressions'. The motion
to be debated – that the Protestant constitution might be preserved
'entire and inviolable' – was not in itself controversial. But everyone
knew that political equality for the Catholics was the real issue. The
speakers on both sides had to contend with almost continuous noise
and heckling. Lord Darnley, who led off for the Catholic side, was
received with prolonged hooting which his uninspired style was ill-
suited to quell. But the tricks of demagogic oratory came naturally to
his principal opponent, the eccentric Lord Winchilsea, who waved his
arms, beat his breast and bellowed for half an hour. Even Richard
Sheil conceded that Winchilsea's 'rude sincerity' had made a much
greater impression than the cold didactic Darnley. Sheil himself made
several unsuccessful attempts to speak, and when at last he caught the
sheriff's eye he had to make himself heard – 'with piercing sounds and
violent gesticulations' – through such an uproar that he was virtually
inaudible. But the most hostile reception of all seems to have been
reserved for Henry Hunt and William Cobbett, whose stormy relationship was going through a brief co-operative phase. They had come
to the meeting in the hope of taking it over, but had merely added to
the general confusion. Their attempt to present a petition against
tithes was drowned in the tumult and sank without trace.[69]

At the end of the meeting, after the motion had been carried
by a large majority, Lord Winchilsea proposed three cheers for the
Protestant Ascendancy, and then asked for one more cheer which
he hoped would echo in the meanest cottage in the county. The
Brunswickers could claim a triumph, thanks to their greater numbers,
much superior organization and the partiality of the sheriff (which the
pro-Catholic *Morning Herald* called 'glaring' but attributed to 'sheer
stupidity rather than a corrupt motive'). On the other hand the
Catholics could, and did, take comfort from the fact that their cause

had not been allowed to go by default on Penenden heath. Sheil claimed that the Brunswickers did not represent 'the people', who really were indifferent to the whole affair.[70] Although equally partisan, his view was probably nearer the mark than Winchilsea's extravagant outpourings. The meeting was too much of a circus to influence or frighten anyone, with the important exception perhaps of the King. Lord Goderich called it 'one of the most ridiculous proceedings ever known . . . highly disapproved of by many very strong anti-Catholics'.[71]

There was indeed no rush to emulate the men of Kent, but the issue was widely discussed and as on Penenden heath the Catholic cause was not without its champions. (In Liverpool an attempt was even made to organize the collection of a Catholic 'rent'.) At Exeter a crowd estimated at 12,000 rejected two pro-Catholic motions before passing a Protestant one. At Leeds the two sides, each supported by one of the local newspapers, issued rival addresses and a huge crowd attended a public debate in the Cloth Hall Yard. After the speakers on both sides had contended with much confusion and uproar, an indecisive show of hands was taken. The chairman, a local manufacturer and an MP for Yorkshire, was pro-Catholic, but he was surrounded by Protestant supporters who urged him to pronounce in their favour. In the end he adjourned the meeting without deciding either way.[72] In other large manufacturing towns, such as Sheffield and Birmingham, anti-Catholic petitions were supported by thousands of signatures. In the smaller towns up and down the country the issue was debated at meetings and dinners. At a civic dinner at Bury St Edmunds in Suffolk the head of the local leading family, the Marquess of Bristol, spoke firmly in favour of emancipation, and after he had departed, an attempt to toast the ultra-Protestant Duke of Newcastle was greeted with groans, hisses and laughter. By contrast, a meeting at Bewdley in Worcestershire adopted an anti-Catholic petition, proposed by the Reverend John Cawood, without any discussion at all.

Many Anglican clergymen were, like Mr Cawood, actively involved in organizing anti-Catholic petitions. Few of them sympathized with the Catholics, let alone followed the example of Sydney Smith who robustly condemned the anti-Catholic laws and extolled the virtues of tolerance in a sermon preached in Bristol cathedral before the astonished mayor and corporation. 'They stared with all their eyes', he wrote afterwards with obvious satisfaction. The Evangelicals were divided between those who feared that emancipation would ruin Protestantism in Ireland altogether, and those who felt that discriminatory laws would not help to make the country more Protestant. Most Methodists were as bigoted as most Anglicans, but many of the older Dissenting congregations spoke up for the spirit of toleration from which they themselves had recently benefited. In January 1829 the standing committee representing the Presbyterians, Baptists and Congregationalists approved a motion in favour of emancipation and urged their congregations throughout the country to get up pro-Catholic petitions. After emancipation was won, O'Connell publicly thanked them for their contribution to the victory.

For his fellow Catholics in England, however, O'Connell felt no gratitude at all. A British Catholic Association (BCA) had been set up in 1823 in imitation of O'Connell's Association, but it never became an effective pressure group in spite of much worthy effort to arouse sympathy through the distribution of pamphlets. The English Catholics were divided by class distinctions; they were always anxious to show that their loyalty to the Crown was beyond question; and they were always afraid of being compromised by the unwelcome support of radical political agitators. In Preston, for instance, almost all the 'respectable' members of the local BCA withdrew after the Irish Catholic Association was banned in 1825. According to its secretary, it was 'deemed most prudent' to dissolve it altogether the following year because its proceedings had become 'most irregular in entertaining political and other objectionable questions'.[73]

But what fatally damned the English Catholics in O'Connell's eyes was their apparent willingness to settle for less than unconditional and unrestricted emancipation. At a meeting of the BCA in November 1828, the secretary, Edward Blount, hinted that they should be willing to accept emancipation on certain conditions. O'Connell described this as 'scandalous and discreditable'. Several weeks later, after the BCA had failed to pronounce decisively in favour of unconditional emancipation, he broke off all links with the English Catholics. On 21 January 1829, after a heated debate lasting more than ten hours, the thirty-five members of the BCA who had stuck it out decided by one vote against insisting on unconditional emancipation. The association did not meet again; it was finally wound up the following June.[74]

On 11 November Wellington's patience with Anglesey ran out and he sent him a sharply disapproving letter.[75] He criticized Anglesey's failure to dismiss O'Gorman Mahon and Steele from the magistrates' bench and deplored his decision to take his family to stay with Lord Cloncurry at his home in County Kildare for the Curragh races. To Wellington this was accepting the hospitality of a man who was no better than a traitor. In his youth Cloncurry had been a member of the United Irishmen, the nationalist organization responsible for the unsuccessful revolt of 1798. He had twice been imprisoned on suspicion of treason but never brought to trial. He was now a member of the Catholic Association and had outraged Wellington by attending a meeting of the Association immediately after he had 'had the honour of receiving the King's representative in his house'. In the reply he despatched three days later Anglesey stoutly defended his handling of O'Gorman Mahon and Steele, emphasized the Ennis sheriff's dubious conduct and firmly declared his belief that Cloncurry was 'a sedate loyal subject, and one of the best and most impartial magistrates of Ireland'.[76]

There was a further exchange of letters in which neither of these two proud, angry and opinionated gentlemen gave an inch of ground. Behind all the sparring over individual cases each had a profound grievance for which he blamed the other. Anglesey felt he was left in complete ignorance of the government's intentions towards Ireland, by which he meant how it intended to deal with the Catholic question. Wellington felt that the Lord Lieutenant's behaviour was making his own attempt to pacify Ireland much more difficult. He made a distinction between the Catholic question and the practical administration of Ireland. 'Whatever may be the determination of the King and his servants upon that [Roman Catholic] subject, it is the duty of the government of Ireland to enforce the existing law.'[77] In other words, policy was none of the Lord Lieutenant's business. (That had not been the view of William Pitt who had fully consulted the then Lord Lieutenant, Cornwallis, when planning the legislative union of England and Ireland in 1798/9.)

Anglesey, on the other hand, argued that a knowledge of the government's future policy towards Ireland would greatly help him to govern the country; 'for although it is quite clear that a country must be governed by existing laws, yet it may well be thought to be a matter of expediency to what extent they are to be exercised.'[78] (Later, however, Anglesey acknowledged privately that in his letter of 28 September Wellington had told him '*something*' of his general views on the Catholic question, 'but he certainly does not give me that sort of information of which I could make use in regulating my style of intercourse with the influential men'.[79])

Wellington, for his part, was preoccupied by the problem of overcoming the King's resistance to emancipation. The King, he told Anglesey, had convinced himself that there was a formidable conspiracy in Ireland and he felt that his representative there (Anglesey) seemed to make no distinction between the chief conspirators and his most loyal subjects.[80] Anglesey replied that he was not aware of any conspiracy and 'peremptorily' denied that he made no distinction between his treatment of 'agitators' and loyal subjects. Who could the duke be thinking of? He had had one interview with O'Connell on which he had reported fully to Peel. Sheil, Steele and O'Gorman Mahon he had never even seen. He had met Lawless once when he was a member of a delegation of manufacturers; once he had bowed to him at a ball at the Rotunda; and once come across him in a very crowded room at Kingstown; his last involvement with him was to order his arrest.[81]

It was a dialogue of the deaf in which each merely succeeded in making the other extremely angry. In his second letter Anglesey felt obliged to reserve the right to make any of this correspondence public in his own defence if necessary. For Wellington this was the last straw and the end of the correspondence. 'Lord Anglesey', he declared, 'is gone mad. He is bit by a mad Papist; or instigated by the love of popularity.'[82] Peel thought Anglesey's second letter was 'a very shabby production', and the King called it 'nothing but a proud and pompous farrago of the most *outré* bombast'. Only Lord Francis Leveson-Gower, who by chance had read the first two letters, stuck up for his chief. He assured Wellington that only the 'clear and decided opinion' of the law officers had stopped the Lord Lieutenant from prosecuting several inflammatory orators; there was 'no systematic reluctance on his part to act with decision against the agitators'.[83]

To make matters worse, O'Connell chose this moment to ask for another audience with Anglesey in order to present evidence about the partisan behaviour of some Orange magistrates in the north. Leveson-Gower, who was already feeling 'harassed to death', thought it was a mischievous request, but he told Peel he could see no reason against granting it. Peel, who had been greatly incensed by one of O'Connell's recent speeches, replied by return: 'I would not, if I were the Lord Lieutenant, receive a man who has been holding the language which that man [O'Connell] has been holding within the last two months.'[84] By the time this letter reached Dublin Castle O'Connell had already had his audience with the Lord Lieutenant.

Wellington probably hoped that his sharp epistolary reproof to Anglesey would pacify the King and make him more willing to consider concessions to the Catholics. The King was certainly pleased. He read the duke's first letter twice and commanded Sir William Knighton, his doctor and confidant, to tell Wellington that he '*most highly approves*' it. 'His Majesty', continued Knighton, 'says (I use his own words) that it is quite a cordial to his feelings.'[85] A few days later Wellington sent the King a long memorandum (it took Mrs Arbuthnot six hours to copy out the final draft) on the Catholic problem and how it might be solved. In his accompanying letter he pointed out that the situation in Ireland was steadily deteriorating, and Protestants in England and Ireland were ready for 'some arrangement' of the Catholic question. There was little encouragement for the duke in the King's brief acknowledgement. He was willing for the memorandum to be shown to Peel and the bishops, but he himself did not wish to be involved. 'I consider your paper to be very able; but on the point in question I need not tell you what my feelings are.'[86]

For several weeks Wellington could not see his way forward, either with the King, who would not listen to him, or the Lord Lieutenant, whose dismissal (since he would not resign) might dangerously increase the tension in Ireland. He consulted the law officers about the oratorical excesses of the Catholic Association, brooded on the 'terrible' state of Ireland and tried to prepare influential Protestant peers, like the Duke of Rutland, for a settlement of the Catholic issue – although 'God alone knows how such a settlement can be effected'.[87] He hoped that Anglesey might restore a working relationship between them by reporting the dismissal of O'Gorman Mahon. But Anglesey, whose last letter to the duke had not even been acknowledged, remained silent. He did in fact dismiss Mahon early in December after the latter had made a particularly inflammatory speech, but apparently the dismissal was not officially reported to London. Anglesey was perhaps too proud to make use of this olive branch.

Eventually Wellington made up his mind to get rid of him. On Christmas Eve he summoned the Cabinet and read out his latest exchanges with Anglesey. The Cabinet agreed without difficulty that cordial co-operation with him was no longer possible and that he should be recalled. On the 28th, after obtaining the King's delighted agreement, Wellington told Anglesey that he was to be recalled. The only reason he gave was that their relations had become 'such as ought not to exist between the Lord Lieutenant and the King's Minister . . .'[88] Anglesey had become too involved with the Irish to let himself be forced into resigning. But in an increasingly impossible situation to be forced to go was not altogether unwelcome.[89] He would, he told Wellington, be ready to obey the King's commands as soon as he received them.

He received them sooner than anyone had anticipated through the innocent agency of Dr Patrick Curtis, the Roman Catholic Archbishop of Armagh and Primate of Ireland. Curtis had become friendly with Wellington during the Peninsular war when he had been rector of the Irish College at Salamanca and had been able to provide useful information about the movements of the French forces. He had returned to Ireland to become Primate and after the formation of the Catholic Association gave it a cautious blessing while deploring the wilder speeches of its members. On 4 December Curtis wrote to Wellington begging him to settle the Catholic question without delay.[90] Wellington evidently felt able to reveal more of his feelings and intentions to the Archbishop – a harmless old man in his late eighties – than to the man who was responsible for governing Ireland. Without even marking his letter 'confidential', he replied that he was 'sincerely anxious to witness a settlement of the Roman Catholic question; which by benefiting the State would confer a benefit upon every individual belonging to it'. But he saw no prospect of getting a settlement. 'If we could bury it [the Catholic question] in oblivion for a short time, and employ that time diligently in the consideration of its difficulties on all sides (for they are great), I should not despair of seeing a satisfactory remedy.'[91]

Since the Dublin Post Office was the leakiest of leaky sieves, and since the duke had advertised the origin of his letter by franking it himself, it is hardly surprising that its contents were known in the streets of Dublin before it had reached the Archbishop in his palace at Drogheda. Several days later, after various versions of Wellington's letter had been bruited abroad, Curtis decided he had better send the original to the Lord Lieutenant. Although it did not really go much further than Wellington's statement to the House of Lords on 10 June, it made Anglesey realize for the first time that the duke really did want a settlement, but did not yet see how to bring it about. His immediate reaction was to write to Curtis urging that the Catholics should do nothing to hamper Wellington's efforts. He admitted he disagreed with the duke about burying the question in oblivion for a time because that would be impossible; but he pointed out that Wellington was more likely than anyone else to be able to overcome the difficulties and very strong prejudices that impeded a settlement; and he urged that the duke should not be personally abused or obstructed in any way.

Let the Catholic trust to the justice of his cause, to the growing liberality of mankind. Unfortunately, he has lost some friends, and fortified his enemies within the last six months, by unmeasured and unnecessary violence ... Brute force, he should be assured, can effect nothing. It is the legislature that must decide this great question; and my greatest anxiety is, that it should be met by the Parliament, under the most favourable circumstances, and that the opposers of Catholic Emancipation shall be disarmed by the patient forbearance, as well as by the unwearied perseverance of its advocates.[92]

Anglesey took precautions to keep this letter from prying eyes and told Curtis that it was to be regarded as secret. He changed his mind a week later when the news of his dismissal began to spread through Dublin. People came to him with alarming stories of the violence of the Catholics' reaction to the news, which they interpreted as a sign that the government had decided against any concessions. (O'Connell was reported to be 'dreadfully dejected'.) Anglesey was begged to do something to calm things down. He knew it would be quite improper for him to issue a public statement on his own recall, but he felt 'the immense importance of giving some safe and prudent direction to the popular feeling'.[93] He remembered his letter to Curtis and arranged to have it published on New Year's Day. Its effect was all that he could have wished. The Catholic Association met next day and passed some unusually moderate resolutions, including a recommendation to all Catholics to follow the Lord Lieutenant's guidance.

In London, however, the publication of Anglesey's letter to Curtis raised rather than lowered the temperature. In Anglesey's mind there was a clear distinction between issuing a formal statement in the Lord Lieutenant's name and publishing his private letter to Curtis. But to the ministers in London it was a distinction without a difference. The Lord Lieutenant had once again exceeded his proper functions. The motives for his action, as well as its beneficial effects, were ignored. Peel at once sent him a formal command to place the government of Ireland in the hands of lords justices and return to England immediately. Anglesey was reported to be very angry but declared that he would do exactly the same again if he had the choice.[94]

On 19 January 1829, Lord Anglesey sailed away from Dublin Bay amidst the undisguised grief of an immense crowd who lined the route from the Castle to Kingstown harbour and watched the procession, one and a half miles long, slowly pass by. Many people wore crêpe in their hats, many houses were draped in black. Lady Anglesey's maid, who mingled with the crowd, reported that there 'was no joking amongst the lower orders ... there was not one smile nor scarcely a word uttered amongst them'.[95] On every gate there were placards proclaiming 'Lord Anglesey for Ever', or 'Civil and Religious Liberty', or 'Down with Wellington'. Outside one large private house four poles were erected, each carrying some black crêpe and a placard which read:

> May Heaven's power
> Protect each hour
> Of Anglesey – and may
> The Duke and Peel
> For ever feel
> The grief of Erin's sons this day.

It was not only the Catholics who deplored Anglesey's departure. On the quay at Kingstown, Sir Harcourt Lees, a militant Orangeman, made a speech regretting the Lord Lieutenant's recall. He feared a clash between Protestants and Catholics, and had already appealed to the King, through Lord Conyngham, not to remove Anglesey. The short speech which Anglesey himself made on the quayside reduced him and everyone who heard him to tears. And after he had been rowed away in his barge 'there was not a dry eye from the highest to the lowest. The Duchess of Leinster and all the great ladies as well as the lower orders cried most dreadfully.' Even the Lord Chancellor could only restrain his tears until he reached the privacy of the viceregal lodge.[96] It was all a world away from the stern, upright, unimaginative men who controlled the fate of Ireland from Whitehall.*

---

* During his second term as Lord Lieutenant (1830–3) under the Whig government, Anglesey lost his popularity with the Irish Catholics because of his opposition to the agitation for the repeal of the Union then being organized by O'Connell.

5

Protestant Protests

(January–February 1829)

'Do not believe that emancipation will give the Catholics power. It will
only make them *eligible* to accept of office; the power of *appointing* them
will still be vested in a Protestant King, controlled by a Protestant
Parliament...'

Bristol Mercury, 9 February 1829

On 11 January 1829, Croker noted in his diary that the Duke of
Wellington seemed thoroughly upset about the Catholic question. He
had never seen the duke speak with so much emotion or with so little
confidence in his own ability to deal with a problem successfully.[1]
And it was clear that this particular problem would not go away. In a
few weeks' time O'Connell would come knocking on the door of the
House of Commons and if it remained shut all Ireland would be
ablaze.

O'Connell's reaction to Anglesey's dismissal was to set about
strengthening the organization – and hence the influence – of the
Catholic Association in preparation for a renewed campaign of agitation. He called for the appointment of five local inspectors in each
county to supervise and galvanize the 'rent' collecting and other
activities of the churchwardens. He also wrote to all the Catholic
bishops asking them to support a new drive to collect the Catholic
'rent'. According to one of Wellington's correspondents, writing from
Nenagh in County Tipperary, the peasants were being promised that
tithes, taxes and high rents would all go if they paid the 'rent', and
that after O'Connell had entered Parliament in February they would
only pay fourpence an acre for their land. 'The minds of the deluded
people are worked up to the highest state of agitation.'[2]

The Orangemen, for their part, were organizing meetings all over Ireland to petition against any concessions to the Catholics. In some parts of the north, Orange agitation spilled over into violence. They 'are acting most outrageously', wrote William Gregory, 'and exactly as their opponents must wish'.[3] Gregory would have been equally disgusted with the liberal Protestants whose open support O'Connell had been trying for months to enlist. On 20 January they came off the fence at last. In the Rotunda at Dublin an impressive gathering of Protestant noblemen and landed gentry agreed that a delegation led by the Duke of Leinster should go to London to present a pro-Catholic petition to the King. In short, everyone was taking sides either for or against whatever the government decided to announce when Parliament reassembled on 5 February.

What intentions the government would announce was quite unclear – perhaps sometimes even to Wellington himself. He had not thrown in his hand but he was greatly discouraged by the lack of influential support for Catholic relief. In November he had sounded out some of the leading bishops, with very discouraging results. Early in the new year he met the Archbishop of Canterbury and the bishops of London and Durham and tried to persuade them that Catholic emancipation was essential to the peace of Ireland. He failed completely. Archbishop Howley, deceptively timid in appearance and manner but indomitably firm in his opinions, was well known to be an unbending opponent of Catholic relief. Blomfield of London and Van Mildert of Durham were also hostile. This setback, however predictable, was all the more disheartening because episcopal support might have helped to reconcile the King to the government's wishes. As it was, a member of the royal Household was reported to have said 'he verily believed the King would go mad on the Catholic question, his violence was so great about it'.[4]

Worst of all, the threat of Peel's resignation, which had been hanging over Wellington since the previous summer, was, it seemed, about to be carried out. In the first week of January the duke and Peel had several long but indecisive discussions about where Peel's duty lay, and their unsatisfactory outcome must have helped to provoke Wellington's outburst to Croker that 'he found people so unreasonable and obstinate as to be quite unmanageable'.[5] On the morning of the following day, the 12th, the duke had yet another discussion with Peel which left him under the impression that he himself had been 'nicely worsted'.[6] But it was Peel whose resolution, undermined by the bishops' unyielding opposition, had at last started to crumble. Later that day he sent Wellington a letter in which, after insisting that he still thought it would be best if he supported Catholic relief from outside the government, he undertook not to insist on resigning if the duke felt this would be 'an *insuperable obstacle*' to a settlement. With the letter he sent a long memorandum setting out the case for a Catholic settlement (without suggesting what exactly it should consist of) which he hoped would help Wellington to convince the King.[7]

On the 14th Wellington handed in Peel's memorandum and next day the six ministers who had hitherto opposed emancipation – Wellington, Peel, Lyndhurst, Bathurst, Herries and Goulburn – told the King in separate audiences that it could no longer be avoided. Faced with this united front, the King agreed that the Cabinet should consider what to do about Ireland, but he emphasized that he would not pledge himself to accept whatever was proposed.

Two days later Peel's capitulation was signed and sealed. On the morning of 17 January Wellington marched round to Peel's house in Whitehall Gardens with a letter. It was an eloquent plea to the Home Secretary to stay at his post because if he did not, the duke did not see 'the smallest chance' of overcoming the difficulties that were impeding the settlement of 'this most difficult and important crisis'.[8] Peel read the letter in Wellington's presence and at once agreed not to resign. It was a painful and brave decision, although surely more straightforward, and therefore easier to justify, than resigning over a measure which he would then have energetically supported from the back benches. What finally tipped the balance in Peel's mind may have been the King's shrewd comment at their interview on the 15th that Peel was asking him, the King, to make a sacrifice of consistency which he was not prepared to make himself.[9] In a letter to the ultra-Protestant William Gregory in Dublin Castle, Peel argued that it was impossible to do nothing about Ireland, and Catholic emancipation was the only practicable course.

> Will I advise *the King* to take the only remaining course – I myself shrinking from the sacrifices and responsibility that it entails – or will I remain at my post – setting the example of sacrifice to others and abiding for myself the issue be it what it may? I have chosen the last alternative, painful as it is to me. I may be wrong – but at any rate I am prepared to make sacrifices which will prove that I think I am right.[10]

There was no comfort in Gregory's reply which began with the bleak statement that he had been overwhelmed with surprise and dismay by Peel's letter. In Gregory's opinion Peel was simply capitulating to

Wellington and Peel pay homage to the Pope. Peel is holding a crown encircled by the words 'Protestant religion', which Wellington is about to extinguish with a papal tiara (February 1829). Reproduced by kind permission of the Trustees of the British Museum, London.

'menacing rebels' who should be subdued before they were offered any concessions.

The day after Peel decided definitely not to desert his post Wellington learned that he had a replacement for Anglesey in Dublin. It was not an easy or attractive post at that particular time. When Lord Bathurst was approached he told the duke that nothing could induce him to go to Ireland as Lord Lieutenant. Eventually, with the aid of a little flattery, the Duke of Northumberland was persuaded to go. Charles Greville was surprised, but decided that Northumberland 'probably likes to do something and display his magnificence'.[11] Hugh Percy, Duke of Northumberland, was certainly very rich and liked to show off his wealth. When he led a special mission to Paris in 1825 for the coronation of Charles X, he did it in great style and paid all his own expenses; they came to four times as much as the magnificent diamond sword, worth £10,000, with which a grateful government rewarded his services. As a young MP he had held liberal views – in 1807 he had tried unsuccessfully to interest the Commons in a bill to abolish slavery in all the colonies – and in middle age he was one of the more moderate Tory grandees. His early opposition to Catholic emancipation had gradually been replaced by a feeling that an effort to settle the Catholic question ought to be made, and if it was made by the Duke of Wellington so much the better.

Northumberland's appointment was widely approved. Although extremely vain, he was a pleasant man, with a very good-humoured and sensible wife who was believed to rule him in all things. He was a prodigious talker and consequently was considered a tremendous bore. Like many bores, he was not considered very intelligent, but that judgement is not borne out by the letter he wrote to Wellington on accepting his appointment, in which he set forth liberal and sensible views on Ireland even though he had no first-hand knowledge of the country.[12] Wellington was delighted to get him, not so much because of his sensible views, as because he had the handsome presence and ample fortune that would allow him to represent the King in Dublin with suitable magnificence and even more suitable (in Wellington's view) regal aloofness. He assured Northumberland that his opinions would be consulted, but next day airily told Leveson-Gower that 'it does not much signify what are the particular opinions of the Duke of Northumberland'.[13] He was probably right because Northumberland admired Wellington too much to disagree seriously with him.

'It is really like a dream. How beyond hope it is that this question should be taken up in this King's life!'[14] Thus wrote Ellenborough in his journal after a Cabinet meeting to plan the campaign that was to win Catholic emancipation. The first step was to ban the Catholic Association and any similar body that might try to replace it. The Cabinet discussed how to make the law more effective than the 1825 one had been and then entrusted the details to the technical ingenuity of the law officers. Very much more difficult was the task of contriving a bill that would give the Catholics civil equality without creating an unmanageable amount of ultra-Protestant hostility. The Cabinet was to wrestle with it for more than five weeks. The third item in the legislative package – a bill to disfranchise the 40s. freeholders who had played such a crucial role in O'Connell's election – took almost as long to settle.

Parliament was due to reassemble on 5 February and the Cabinet's first hurdle was a form of words for the King's Speech that would make its intentions towards Ireland and the Catholics sufficiently clear without immediately arousing the King's opposition. It was a combined effort of drafting and redrafting and tinkering with the result. The final version heavily emphasized the importance of improving the maintenance of law and order in Ireland, particularly by getting rid of the Catholic Association, and underlined the government's commitment to preserving the 'full and permanent security' of the Protestant establishment in church and state. In between was sandwiched a recommendation that Parliament 'should take into your deliberate consideration the whole condition of Ireland; and that you should review the laws which impose civil disabilities on His Majesty's Roman Catholic subjects'. The King eventually accepted this wording, but when Wellington tried to enlarge on what lay behind the cautious formula, the King expressed surprise – 'Damn it, etc., you mean to let them into Parliament' – which was presumably feigned, and reluctance which was certainly genuine.[15] A few days later he tried to get the reference to Roman Catholics removed on the grounds that they were included in the 'whole condition of Ireland'. Wellington effectively countered this ploy by pointing out that the King's Roman Catholic subjects were to be found not only in Ireland. But he did what he could to sugar the pill, for example, by suggesting to Peel that in the King's Speech they ought to refer more frequently to his Majesty's commands.

On Wednesday, 4 February, the postbag received by Lord Grey at Howick was so full of positive reports that the government intended to bring in some Catholic relief measure that he decided to set out for London earlier than he had planned. In Leicestershire reports that extensive concessions were going to be made to the Catholics made the Duke of Rutland fear that the anti-Catholic petition with 15,000 signatures which he was to present to the House of Lords would be treated as so much waste paper. On the other hand, many government supporters tended to dismiss the rumours flying around London as simply incredible. Anglesey's recall had seemed a certain sign that the government did not intend to concede anything to the Catholics. Some of those who attended Peel's eve-of-session dinner could not believe that he would change his mind until they heard him actually read the King's Speech. Sir Thomas Lethbridge, an ultra-Protestant, had so little suspected the government's intentions that he had volunteered to second the Address of Thanks. He withdrew his offer when he learned what the Speech contained. Lord Clive, also hitherto firmly anti-Catholic, agreed, after consulting his father and brother, to move the Address in the Commons because he felt something had to be done about the Catholics and Wellington was the best person to do it. Lord Corry reluctantly agreed to second the Address for the same reason.

On 5 February rumour and speculation were at last put to rest. In the House of Lords, the Lord Chancellor, Lord Lyndhurst, who read the King's Speech, was obviously struggling with nerves when he came to the passage about Ireland. Lord Salisbury moved the Address with a marked lack of enthusiasm for Catholic relief. He admitted to feeling embarrassed and repeatedly emphasized that their lordships were only being asked to take the subject of Ireland into consideration; he himself would never vote for any measure without adequate securities for the Protestant establishment. But the Whig leader, Lord Lansdowne, unreservedly welcomed the announcement. So did Lord Anglesey. Since his return from Dublin he had given much time and thought to the account of his administration in Ireland that he was determined to give to the Lords at the first opportunity. But now he declared that he would not intrude his private concerns until the great measure just announced had been accomplished.[16]*

On the other hand, the ultra-Protestant peers – Eldon, Winchilsea,

---

* On 4 May 1829, Anglesey delivered his defence of his Irish administration to the House of Lords. He quoted extensively from his correspondence with Wellington and Peel, to the great annoyance and disapproval of the duke. Later, in their declining years, friendly relations were restored between the two old soldiers.

Newcastle, Redesdale – expressed their outrage and condemnation with no attempt to spare the feelings of the Prime Minister who sat listening to them. The Duke of Newcastle assured him that if he persisted in his dangerous course 'he would soon fall from his present high station, and what was more material, he would deserve his fall'.[17] Wellington did not deign to justify himself at length. He simply insisted that after the last two years something had to be done, one way or the other, to settle the Catholic question. He was, according to Mrs Arbuthnot, 'very much annoyed and mortified at the tone of the House', and when he came round to her house that evening he was 'quite out of spirits'.[18]

In the Commons on the same day Peel faced his critics bravely, carefully spelling out why he now felt they could no longer let the Catholic issue remain unresolved because of divided counsels in the government and in Parliament. He made it clear that having changed his mind he would have preferred to retire to the back benches; he only remained at his post at the Prime Minister's urgent request. He emphatically denied more than once that he had altered his opinion about Catholic emancipation. But the risks involved in doing nothing about the present turbulent situation in Ireland were greater than the risks involved in removing the Catholics' disabilities. That would at least quiet the public mind in Ireland; he could not, however, see that it would produce any other advantages.[19]

Peel earned full marks for honesty, but his explanation still seemed lame and unconvincing and earned him some stinging brickbats from his supporters. The bouquets came from the Whigs who cheered him warmly at every opportunity. They were amused to hear him urging arguments that he had so often opposed in the past, but they were so delighted that the Catholics were at last to be emancipated that they were inclined to let him off lightly. Sir Francis Burdett and Henry Grattan warmly praised him for candidly confessing his difficulties and agreeing to support something he had previously strongly opposed. But the former Canningites – Huskisson, Palmerston and Grant – who should have been as delighted as anyone at the government's volte-face, found it hard to hide their chagrin.[20] They had assumed that if emancipation was forced on the government, Peel would have to resign and Wellington would have to call on them to help him out. Peel's decision to stay on had dashed their hopes of an early return to office. (In any case their hopes were illusory. Wellington made it clear that he would resign if his own party deserted him. 'I cannot submit', he told the Duke of Rutland, 'to be the puppet of the rump of the Whigs and of Mr Canning.'[21])

'Nothing', wrote Charles Greville a few days later, 'is thought of or talked of but the Catholic question.'[22] Peel's change of heart, which nobody had foreseen, was as much, if not more, of a sensation as the decision to concede emancipation, which many had seen coming sooner or later. The anti-Catholic Tories had been given a double shock and, moreover, the government had not bothered to warn them of its intentions. That was what really riled them. During the recess they had gone on arguing against emancipation to their friends and constituents and now they were suddenly being asked to eat their words and make themselves look ridiculous. Sir Thomas Gooch, for instance, had been so sure that the government did not intend to concede anything to the Catholics that he had advised his county not to organize an anti-Catholic petition. Now he did not know what to do. He was not the only one. Wellington, feeling overworked and harassed, did not think he deserved all the complaints of secrecy and duplicity that were reaching him. 'They forget that if I had breathed a whisper to anybody, the factions of all colours would have set to work, and the plan would have been defeated.'[23]

Now that the cat was out of the bag, the Prime Minister did his best to explain and justify his change of policy. He composed a long letter to the Duke of Rutland carefully explaining all the consequences that had flowed from the Clare election and made concessions to the Catholics essential.[24] He sent a copy of this letter – not having time to compose a separate one – to Lord Lonsdale. Neither peer was convinced by his arguments; neither would definitely promise to support him on the Catholic issue. Rutland, who greatly admired Wellington, uncomfortably explained: 'I am the centre of a circle, which has for its watchword the maintenance not only of the Protestant ascendancy but of our Protestant constitution as it has been handed down to us'; and he had been entrusted with an anti-Catholic petition from the county of Leicester with his own name at the head of it.[25]* Lonsdale accepted Wellington's analysis of the dangerous situation, but wondered whether it was not better to meet difficulties rather than yield to them. This must have infuriated Wellington, and the rest of the letter was scarcely less scathing. Lonsdale could not at present say 'how far I may judge it just, for I think justice should precede expediency, to make any inroad upon the constitution, whatever the object that may

---

* In April 1827 Rutland had written to a friend: 'I believe him [Wellington] to be so firm in principles that those on which he acts this year he will be found to act steadily upon ten years hence.' Lady Frances Shelley, *Diary*, vol. 2 (1913), p. 154.

seem to require it...'[26] Expediency was Wellington's principal – indeed, only – excuse for conceding Catholic relief.

Lonsdale's doubts were all the more unfortunate because they were likely to influence his anti-Catholic son, Lord Lowther, who held a junior post in the government and immediately began to wonder whether he ought not to resign it. Another Protestant office-holder, George Bankes, who was secretary to the Board of Control, was nearly reduced to tears when told of the government's intentions. A few days later he gave Wellington his letter of resignation. The duke was extremely annoyed and said he did not know what to do with it.[27] He feared that Bankes's resignation would have a domino effect on other office-holders, and the last thing he wanted was vacancies that he might be reduced to filling with Whigs or Huskissonites. So he ignored the letter of resignation and Bankes continued to turn up at the India office. On the other hand, some members of the royal Household, who were trying to wriggle out of their obligation to support the government, were firmly told that they must toe the line or be dismissed, although that might risk unsettling the King's reluctant acquiescence. Ellenborough, however, felt that all the government's supporters had been given a great shock and they ought to be given time to come round. Rumours, after all, could always be discounted, but not the contents of the King's Speech.

The announcement was also a shock to the general public. On 13 February the (anti-Catholic) *Courier* wrote: 'Men's minds are so engrossed by this one [Catholic] subject that foreign relations, financial measures, the state of trade and manufactures are scarcely mentioned either in Parliament or out.' In Ireland the news was received with unrestrained anger and alarm by the Protestant minority. The *Dublin Evening Mail* declared that Wellington might drive them to rebel or banish them from their native land, but he could never 'coerce them into passive submission to a measure, which places their lives and their liberties, their institutions and their religion at the mercy of a faction who thirst for their blood'.[28] In Dublin so many applied to attend a meeting in the Rotunda, to be presided over by the lord mayor and sheriffs, that it had to be transferred to the spacious lawns of Tyrone House. Soon after the meeting began, the platform collapsed with a tremendous crash. Among the casualties was the speaker, a Protestant clergyman who was hit on the head by a statue of King William, installed at the back of the platform, just as he was singing the praises of that ungrateful monarch. (The wound was slight but bled copiously.) Although a noisy, confused and turbu-

lent meeting, it managed to approve an address to the King begging
him to dismiss all pro-Catholic ministers from his councils.

A few days later the Brunswick Constitutional Club condemned
the granting of any concessions to the Catholics. It met in the Rotunda
which was decorated with flags inscribed 'Remember 1688 and 1798'
and 'Protestants, Up Now or Sink for Ever'. When one of the speakers
mentioned Peel by name, there was such an angry uproar that it was
some minutes before he could be heard. Afterwards there was rioting
around College Green, windows in O'Connell's house were smashed
and the magistrates had to summon the military to reinforce the
police. The Catholic Dubliners, however, regarded with complacent
contempt the 'puddle in a storm' violence of the Protestant minority.

In England the ultra-Protestant press was, as the *Spectator* scornfully put it, 'perfectly rabid'. In addition to its own fulminations,
the weekly *John Bull* gave space to those of ultra-Protestant peers.
Lord Kenyon appealed at length to the Protestants of Britain to
'rescue your Sovereign and this free country from the foulest disgrace
that can befall this Protestant island. If you don't wake from your
slumbers, Protestantism will soon be extirpated from Ireland.' Lord
Winchilsea's appeal was short and to the point:

> Let the voice of Protestantism be heard from one end of the Empire to
> the other. Let the sound of it echo from hill to hill, from vale to vale.
> Let the tables of the Houses of Parliament groan under the weight of
> your petitions; and let your prayers reach the foot of the Throne.[29]

The right to petition Parliament was undisputed and carefully preserved; it was the traditional way of conveying public feeling to
Parliament. Throughout Britain and Ireland, in remote rural parishes,
in lethargic country towns, in busy industrial cities, the opponents
and supporters of Catholic emancipation embarked on what might
almost be called an orgy of petitioning. In London the lord mayor and
corporation patitioned in favour of emancipation. So did the Dissenting ministers. A meeting of London Anglican clergy took the opposite
view, with only one dissenting vote, that of the brother of Lord Grey.
But the clergy did not have it all their own way. The parishioners of
St Leonard's, Shoreditch, argued for nearly five hours over an anti-
Catholic petition 'with all the warmth of feeling and confusion com-
monly attendant upon the introduction of this exciting subject'.[30] In
the rural districts the Anglican clergy, taking their cue from their
(mostly) anti-Catholic bishops, played a leading part in organizing
petitions against Catholic relief. Some went round themselves from

house to house, from farm to cottage, urging their parishioners to sign petitions.

At Oxford, Convocation voted by more than three to one to petition against emancipation. But at Cambridge the Senate narrowly rejected a similar petition. One Cambridge MA, the young barrister Thomas Babington Macaulay, heard at the last moment that the vote was likely to be extremely close. He rounded up some Whig Cambridge MAs from the Inns of Court and packed them into a chartered stagecoach which arrived outside the Senate House just as the Senate was due to vote on an anti-Catholic petition. It was rejected by nine votes, and the party from the Inns of Court dined in triumph at Trinity before returning to London. The ultra-Protestant press was very indignant that the university's opinion should have been decided by a coachful of 'godless and briefless barristers'.[31] But in fact as only seven of the coach party were eligible to vote in the Senate, the petition would have been defeated without their help.*

In many places petitions for or against emancipation were approved and displayed for signature in an atmosphere of intense public excitement and interest. At Sheffield a meeting promoted principally by the clergy, at which pro-Catholics were not allowed to speak, voted for a petition against emancipation. The pro-Catholics immediately asked the Master Cutler to hold a public meeting in the town hall; so many people came that the meeting had to be adjourned to a square capable of holding several thousand. At the end of the meeting a pro-Catholic petition was overwhelmingly approved with only thirty to forty hands raised in opposition.[32] Bristol also held a huge open-air meeting to which many of the parish clergy marched their flock in procession. It voted in favour of an anti-Catholic petition which was placed in the Guildhall to be signed. No amendment in favour of a counter-petition was allowed, but afterwards the mayor agreed that one could be placed in the Exchange. This petition was attacked by the mob after a man who had changed his mind was not allowed to cross out his signature. The petition was saved, but the table on which it rested was wrecked. Next day the mob attacked again and succeeded in tearing the petition. The mayor then managed to get it

---

* When a pro-Catholic petition signed by 600 Cambridge undergraduates was sent to the House of Lords, Lansdowne said he disapproved of undergraduates presenting petitions – 'it would be better for them to pursue their studies than to be thus anticipating the passions of future life' – but since petitions from apprentices, schoolboys and charity children had been accepted, he would not reject this one. Bishop Lloyd said that in Oxford undergraduate petitions had been suppressed by the authorities (Hansard, XX, 1416–17, 24 March 1829).

withdrawn in the interest of municipal peace, and it was sent up to
London with fewer than 2,000 signatures and an explanation of its
mutilated state. The anti-Catholic petition continued to lie in the
Guildhall and eventually attracted 38,000 signatures.[33]

The anti-Catholic petitions clearly had the advantage in terms of
numbers of signatures. But their validity as genuine expressions of
'respectable' public opinion was hotly debated in both Houses of
Parliament and disputed in the pro-Catholic press. A correspondent
in *The Times*, writing from Cheltenham, claimed to have gone into a
shop in the High Street and found an anti-Catholic petition being
signed by an urchin, hardly tall enough to rest his elbow on the table,
who could not have been more than nine, although two men present
insisted that he was sixteen. Another correspondent, writing from
Sussex, alleged that anti-Catholic petitions were being taken round to
the local schools, and every boy who signed one was given a half-
holiday. Small boys, women, prisoners, vagrants, illiterates and
individuals who signed twice were all alleged to have swelled the
numbers of anti-Catholic signatures. Several MPs felt uncomfortable
about excluding the 'fair sex' (or 'the most interesting part of the
creation') since the issue was as important to them as to the men. One
MP even defended double signatures on the grounds that they showed
'a zealous feeling on the subject'.[34]

There were also many complaints about the way in which the anti-
Catholic petitions were organized and signatures obtained. Meetings
held to authorize them sometimes excluded pro-Catholics, or would
not let them speak (as at Sheffield), or were not advertised beforehand
so that opponents did not hear about them. At a Manchester meeting
it was claimed that police were posted at the door to keep them out.[35]
A petition from Ripon was dismissed as a 'hole and corner affair', got
up at a meeting in a public house and not signed by the mayor and
corporation.[36] In Norwich, where the common council thanked the
King for recommending emancipation to Parliament, an anti-Catholic
petition was carried from door to door and signatures were demanded
on the grounds that the Protestant establishment was in the most
imminent danger.[37]

There were frequent allegations of over-zealous activity by the
clergy and of appeals to religious fanaticism reinforced with blood-
curdling handbills and pamphlets provided by the Religious Tract
Society. In Surrey handbills portraying Protestants being burned and
tortured during Mary's reign were distributed before a meeting. At
Truro a table on which an anti-Catholic petition was placed was
covered with inflammatory pamphlets. One of them was called 'Look

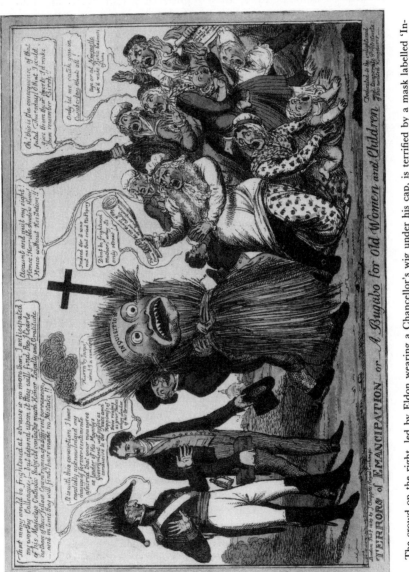

The crowd on the right, led by Eldon wearing a Chancellor's wig under his cap, is terrified by a mask labelled 'Inquisition' attached to a huge sheaf of straw. On the left, Wellington assures Peel that in time people will find he has made no mistake. This cartoon is unusually favourable to emancipation (c. April 1829). Reproduced by kind permission of the Trustees of the British Museum, London.

about You' and had a picture of Irish Catholics burning Protestants.[38] When Lord Torrington asked some petitioners why they had signed an anti-Catholic petition, they replied they had been told that if the Romanists got the upper hand they would fry the Protestants over faggots, and in confirmation of this they produced pictures of Protestants being fried over faggots.[39] In parishes near Glasgow the clergy were accused of urging the people to sign anti-Catholic petitions or else have their throats cut by Papists, who were described as worse in the sight of God than the inhabitants of Sodom and Gomorrah.[40] In Cornwall the vicar of Mylor called at a charity school just as the children were going home and ordered them to tell their parents to come at once to the school to sign a petition in support of the Protestant Ascendancy. (But a pro-Catholic patron of the school, who happened to be there, objected to the school being put to this use, and after some argument the vicar was forced to withdraw with his petition to a private house.[41])

No doubt the allegations about the anti-Catholic petitions were often exaggerated and sometimes fabricated. No doubt, as Sir Robert Inglis complained, some MPs were impossible to satisfy. 'If petitions were adopted by vast multitudes of the people, they were represented as the offspring of a riotous and ignorant rabble; and if they proceeded from more select meetings, they were designated "hole and corner productions".'[42] Yet there was enough substance in the allegations for the pro-Catholics to be able to claim, over and over again, that whereas their petitions were signed by the educated, professional, 'respectable' classes, many of the signatures on their opponents' petitions were worthless. As Lord Darnley told the House of Lords, it was not difficult to procure anti-Catholic petitions; the question was whether the signatories understood what they were signing. 'A country squire had only to take a piece of parchment in his hand, and ask every poor labourer or old woman he met to sign it. His request would be sure to be complied with, especially if he told them, as some had done, that the Catholics would burn them all.'[43]

Neither side in the parliamentary debates was prepared to give any ground to the other. Again and again, when an MP or a peer solemnly declared his complete conviction that a certain county or town was for or against emancipation, someone else would immediately get up and flatly contradict him. Since most minds were already so firmly made up, the petitions to Parliament and the discussions about them, which dragged on for weeks, could have had little influence on the outcome of the crisis. But they were a useful safety valve which demonstrated the strength of feeling on the Catholic issue but did no harm – apart from taking up an inordinate amount of parliamentary time.

For the Catholic leaders in Ireland the news that emancipation really was imminent posed two important tactical questions. Should O'Connell insist on taking his seat in Parliament immediately? And should the Catholic Association be wound up at once or should it continue to agitate until the relief legislation was actually on the statute book? The Irish peasants had been led to believe that O'Connell's entrance into the House of Commons would herald the dawn of a new age for all of them. A correspondent of William Gregory's in Limerick reported that if O'Connell was not allowed to take his seat, it would be a *'miracle'* if some violence were not attempted; 'you can have little idea of the present state of things, their telegraphic arrangements *by lights* are so complete that the entire province could be in motion in half an hour.'[44]

O'Connell's wishes coincided with the popular demand. He published an address to Parliament justifying his right to take his seat in Parliament, and he sent a second address to the freeholders of County Clare, committing himself to go to London to claim his seat as soon as Parliament reassembled. Before setting out on 6 February he told the Association that it ought not to dissolve itself until the royal assent had been given to a bill for immediate and complete emancipation. Victory might be in sight but it was not yet clear how complete it would be.

His reception on the journey from Holyhead to London was generally friendly, except at Coventry, where there were some cries of 'No Popery' and 'Down with O'Connell', and at one point the crowd seemed so hostile that O'Connell's friends felt it was prudent to show that they were armed.[45] At some of his stopping places leading Dissenters waited on him to thank him for his exertions in the cause of civil and political liberty. He and his entourage arrived in London on 10 February and established themselves in Batt's Hotel in Dover Street. But O'Connell did not go on to Westminster to claim his seat in the House of Commons. In the cooler, less heady atmosphere of London he let himself be overruled by those who thought that in the circumstances this would be an unnecessarily provocative step.

The same anxiety not to rock the boat hastened the demise of the Catholic Association. When the news of the King's Speech arrived in Dublin, the Catholic bishops happened to be holding their annual synod in the city. They recommended unequivocally that the Association should be immediately dissolved. Influential friends in England –

Anglesey, Holland, Brougham – sent the same advice. But from Shrewsbury, on his way to London, O'Connell sent a letter strongly advising the Association not to dissolve itself until it was certain of unconditional emancipation. His letter was read out at a meeting on 10 February, but Sheil still insisted that the Association should be dissolved immediately. His proposal was greeted with loud cheers and cries of 'No, No'. Eventually the meeting accepted Maurice O'Connell's plea that a decision should be put off for a couple of days until they had heard again from his father. O'Connell's second letter was not much help. He conceded that all the friends of emancipation in Parliament wanted the Association to dissolve itself at once, but he could not bring himself to recommend it. In effect, he left the Association to make up its own mind. After nearly six hours of debate, it voted by acclamation to dissolve itself. Lady Morgan wrote in her diary after attending the meeting: 'The *great question* – the dissolution of the Catholic Association, was the subject of debate; and every ardent mind came worked up to the contest. All the best feelings, cool judgment, and tact, was evidently for the prompt and voluntary extinction of this great engine of popular opinion.' Two days later she attended a party 'of the débris of the ascendancy faction; but the Orange ladies all looked *blue,* and their husbands tried to look green'.[46]

So far as Peel was concerned, the voluntary liquidation of the Catholic Association did not merit a mention – let alone a word of commendation – during the debates on the bill to suppress it. The bill banned any association considered to be a danger to the public peace, but was to remain in force for only a year because of its arbitrary nature. It received its third reading in the Commons on 17 February. The friends of the Catholics poured scorn on it.

> Put down the Association [exclaimed Palmerston]! They might as well talk of putting down the winds of Heaven, or of chaining the ceaseless tides of the ocean...The Catholic Association was the people of Ireland. Its spirit was caused by the grievance of the nation and its seat was the bosom of seven millions of its population. It was therefore idle to talk of putting down the Association, except by removing the cause to which the Association owed its existence.[47]

The Whigs voted for the bill on the clear understanding that that cause was going to be removed. The Protestants could hardly oppose a measure they had long been demanding, but several of the ultras took the opportunity to launch bitter personal attacks on Peel for his inconsistency. He was shaken out of his customary glacial composure and rebuffed the charges with spirit. On one of his persecutors, Henry Bankes, he neatly turned the tables by quoting a speech made by Bankes in 1812 in which he had defended the right of politicians to change their minds.

Peel gave short shrift to his critics in the House of Commons, but towards his Oxford constituents his conscience was extremely tender. Twelve years earlier he had defeated the pro-Catholic Canning and won the university seat largely because he had shown himself to be an outstanding champion of the Protestant cause in the House of Commons. He was in no way obliged to resign his seat because he had changed his views; indeed, Croker told him that to do so was 'democratical and unconstitutional' and a dangerous precedent for the independence of the House of Commons.[48] But Peel felt that to represent his university was an exceptional honour which imposed exceptional obligations on him. (He did not share Ellenborough's contemptuous view of university dons. 'God forgive me if I am wrong, but from what I saw of them at Cambridge, the persons I least respect are Fellows of Colleges, and I believe the Oxonians are even less liberal than the people of Cambridge.'[49])

Peel's letter of resignation reached the Vice-Chancellor of Oxford, Dr J. C. Jones, on the morning of 5 February. Rumours that the government intended to emancipate the Catholics had already reached the university and Convocation was due to meet that afternoon to vote on an anti-Catholic petition. After the petition had been approved by an overwhelming majority – 164 votes to 48 – Peel's letter was read out. Although it could hardly have been made public in less propitious circumstances, a good many people thought that Peel would be re-elected if he chose to stand again. It was assumed that his friends would propose him, and four days later the Christ Church common room, encouraged by the degree of feeling in Peel's favour, did unanimously decide to support his candidature.

Peel himself was not at all sure that he wanted to stand again for Oxford. He was a proud and sensitive man and he did not relish the prospect of the rough handling that his reputation and motives were likely to get in the hurly-burly of an Oxford election. 'For God's sake', he wrote to his former tutor, Charles Lloyd, 'take no step, directly or indirectly, that could appear to intimate a wish on my part to be returned. I have no such wish, and I think a protracted contest, even if it ended successfully, would be very embarrassing and painful to me.' But if he was elected again, he would not resign again, or do

'anything which would appear peevish and ill-humoured, or dis-
respectful'.[50] Indeed, in his heart of hearts he probably could not help
wanting to be re-elected for his old university. But he knew it would
be much less painful to be brought in quietly for a pocket borough,
and he had no objection to using this time-honoured but increasingly
discredited expedient. So he told the Vice-Chancellor he would apply
for the Chiltern Hundreds on 20 February and took the necessary
steps to secure his election elsewhere. Whether his candidature should
go forward in Oxford he left to his supporters to decide.

It was very soon apparent that if he did stand in Oxford he would
not have a clear run. Even among those who were sympathetic to
Catholic relief there was a feeling that Peel was no longer worthy to
represent the university. They also felt – as John Henry Newman, a
young Fellow of Oriel put it – that it would be 'an infamous thing if
Oxford was to be blown round by the breath of a Minister, signing a
petition one day and approving the contrary the next'.[51] The dignity
of the university was at issue as well as the emancipation of the
Catholics. On 11 February an influential group of dons decided that
Peel must be opposed, although at first they were not sure by whom.
Three days later they met again and unanimously chose Sir Robert
Inglis, MP for Ripon, as their candidate. They could hardly have
made a better choice. Not only was Inglis also a Christ Church man,
so that his candidature was bound to deprive Peel of the unanimous
support of his own college; he was also an old-fashioned Tory, who
wholeheartedly embraced the outlook and prejudices of the typical
country gentleman. Brougham might dub him 'the bigoted baronet',
but his upright character and friendly manner made him widely
respected and liked in the House of Commons. He was a devout
Evangelical, a friend of Wilberforce and other members of the Clapham
sect. In the House of Commons he was always a stout defender of the
Anglican Church whenever he thought its interests under threat. On 5
February he had greeted the references to the Catholics in the King's
Speech with anger and dismay – to a Whig listener he made a 'crazy
and laughable harangue'[52] – and in the following weeks he was
indefatigable in presenting and defending anti-Catholic petitions in
the Commons.

Peel's chief confidant in Oxford was his devoted friend and admirer,
Charles Lloyd, Bishop of Oxford. Lloyd had been opposed to Catholic
emancipation, but such was his respect for Peel that he accepted his
change of mind, albeit with many misgivings. It was perhaps his
unhappy mixed feelings that caused him to over-react badly when he
heard about the anti-Peel meeting on the 11th. He took it upon

himself to tell the Christ Church dons that Peel did not want them to take any further steps on his behalf. To Peel he explained that he had done so because the 'malevolence' of his opponents was so great.[53]

Peel's cause, however, was not allowed to go by default. It was taken up by Richard Whately, whose combination of intellectual distinction and spectacularly unconventional manners and appearance had made him one of the best known figures in Oxford. (Two years later he was made Archbishop of Dublin.) On 12 February a committee including seven heads of houses and other 'highly respectable individuals' was set up under the chairmanship of Dr Marsham, the Warden of Merton, to work for Peel's re-election. It hired an election room in the High Steet and issued a manifesto. Shortly afterwards a similar committee was set up in London and began to canvass on Peel's behalf, especially in the Inns of Court.

When Peel heard of these developments he sent Marsham a distinctly discouraging letter. He was in the unhappy situation of sympathizing with the feelings of his opponents, and he suggested it would be much better if he removed himself from the Oxford scene by quietly obtaining a seat elsewhere. His committee, however, refused even to listen to his letter to Marsham. They were, they said, acting on their own responsibility without any communication with Mr Peel, who could not be allowed to interfere in a university election.[54] Peel accepted this novel and high-handed interpretation of the rules and agreed – perhaps not altogether reluctantly – to take no steps to secure another seat before Monday, 2 March.[55] Later that week it was essential for him to be in his place in the House of Commons to introduce the Catholic relief bill.

When the polling opened on 26 February Oxford was crowded with MAs who had come from all over the country to register their votes, as well as with strangers impelled by interest or simple curiosity. Not a horse or a carriage was for hire, not an inn room was vacant. As soon as the doors of the Convocation hall were opened at twelve o'clock a large crowd pushed and shoved their way in and the hall was instantly crowded to suffocation. There were cries of 'let me out' and 'break the windows'. The first was impossible, the second was achieved with the help of umbrellas which, as *The Times* commented, were thus put to a use – letting in the weather – 'the very reverse of that for which they were invented'. The noise, confusion and cries of 'poll, poll' showed no sign of dying down when Dr Jones, the Vice-Chancellor, tried to open the proceedings. A pathetic cry from the hall to have mercy on the clergy 'for we have come a great distance' only provoked shouts of laughter and still greater confusion.

Dr Marsham, who eventually got up to propose Peel, spoke against a heavy barrage of noise and had to sit down with his speech unfinished. Dr Ingram of Trinity, who got up to propose Inglis, only managed a few inaudible words. *The Times*'s correspondent thought that the noise and confusion equalled anything ever produced at the traditionally rowdy Westminster elections 'and demonstrated what apt imitators the higher classes sometimes are of the manners of the lower, in moments of political excitement'.[56] George Dawson, who had got into such hot water with his brother-in-law the previous summer, was unable to take such a detached view.

> During these speeches [he told Peel] the clamour, violence, and insulting language used by your opponents was almost beyond endurance. The common courtesy, every decency of life was forgotten . . . I never felt less proud of having been a member of the University and cannot but think the honour of representing it most overrated . . . their [the MAs'] coarse and base remarks upon your conduct were almost enough to make the blood of your friends boil in their veins.[57]

Somehow the voters struggled through the crush to the table where the Vice-Chancellor was installed to register their votes. By the time the poll closed that day Inglis had a majority of more than sixty. On the second day many more non-resident MAs (or out-voters) turned up to vote for Inglis than for Peel. 'The odium theologicum has done it', wrote an eye-witness; 'the outlying parsons are strong, Church against State. One of them told me just now, they could fight as well as vote, if necessary.'[58]

The gap between the two candidates was widening ominously and an express was sent to London in an attempt to round up a few more votes for Peel. By the third day, the 28th, it was clear that Inglis had won, and did not need the additional support that arrived during that morning. There were some country clergy from remote parts, two Orangemen from Armagh and someone who had come all the way from France after reading about the election in a newspaper. On the other hand, the coaches which Peel's committee had sent to the West Country, where the pro-Catholic Sir Thomas Acland had been actively canvassing, came back virtually empty.

When the poll was closed at two o'clock Sir Robert Inglis was declared the victor with a majority of 146 votes. Three cheers were given for the Vice-Chancellor (which he richly deserved) and then three more for that champion of Protestantism, Lord Eldon. When someone called for cheers for the King, the hisses equalled, if not outnumbered, the cheers, and when someone tried to raise a cheer for Peel, it was drowned in hisses and groans. He had been swept to defeat on a tide of Protestant prejudice which affected high and low alike, from erudite academics to country clergy and to the Thorntons' nanny, who during the election read Fox's Book of Martyrs all day and fervently believed that Inglis's return was her only hope of not being burned.[59]

Peel could console himself with the quality of the support he received. Thirteen out of 19 professors voted for him, 38 out of 40 MPs and 24 out of 28 prizemen. Whately assured him that with such support 'few will talk of the *sense* of the University being against you, if at least they have any sense of their own'.[60] But Newman, who certainly did not consider himself deficient in sense, was delighted with the outcome of his first active intervention in public affairs. 'We have achieved a glorious victory... We have proved the independence of the Church and of Oxford.' And he added, with that dismissive attitude towards Ireland and its troubles sadly typical of many of his educated contemporaries: 'No wonder that such as I, who have not, and others who have, definite opinions in favour of Catholic emancipation, should feel we have a much nearer and holier interest than the pacification of Ireland, and should, with all our might, resist the attempt to put us under the feet of the Duke and Mr Brougham.'[61]

Inevitably, some people suggested that after such a powerful display of Protestant feeling Wellington would not dare to press ahead with any Catholic relief. *The Times* was determined to nip such sentiments in the bud. On 3 March it published a resounding leading article in which it declared it had a duty

> to crush at once all pretence for those alleged hopes which some of the more foolish among the Brunswickers may have imbibed within these two or three days from the rogues who feigned them... The King's ministers are to a man unshaken; the promises held out in the King's Speech will be accomplished without favour or delay...

The Catholic relief measure – 'of British wisdom and of Irish peace' – insisted *The Times*, would be carried by ample majorities in both Houses and would satisfy 'all reasonable and upright minds... and leave incendiaries on both sides to burn amidst their own faggots'.

Members of the public who relied entirely on *The Times* for their knowledge of public events would have been very well informed about Peel's defeat in the Oxford election. But if they wondered how he still managed to appear in his place in the House of Commons on the following Tuesday, they would not have found any enlightenment in the columns of their daily paper. *The Times* apparently felt – perhaps wisely – that the events in the little Wiltshire town of Westbury did not merit a mention.[62] Westbury was a rotten borough which had been acquired by Sir Manasseh Masseh Lopes and for the past half-dozen years had provided him with a seat in Parliament. Lopes came of an old Jamaican family of Spanish Jews. His father, Mordecai, settled in England after making a large fortune from his sugar plantations. After Mordecai's death, his only son, Manasseh, inherited all his wealth. In 1798 he bought an extensive estate in Devonshire. Four years later he was converted to Christianity and entered Parliament as member for the pocket borough of New Romney. By 1805 he had ingratiated himself sufficiently with the government to be made a baronet. From 1812 to 1818 he sat as member for Barnstaple. But in the 1818 general election he overstepped the invisible line dividing the permissible from the impermissible in contested elections and his upwardly mobile career was ignominiously halted. After his re-election for Barnstaple he was unseated for having distributed £3,000 in bribes; he then laid out a further £2,000 on the notoriously corrupt (and soon to be disfranchised) borough of Grampound. For these two offences he was sent to prison for two years and fined £10,000. Nothing daunted, having served his sentence, he acquired Westbury and resumed his seat in the House of Commons. In 1829 he was persuaded to surrender it to Peel, presumably calculating that the sacrifice would be well worth his while.

The day after Peel was defeated at Oxford, Sunday, 1 March, William Holmes, a Tory whip, arrived in Westbury to make sure the surrender was carried through without a hitch. Next morning the formalities were duly observed in the presence of Lopes and the mayor, who happened to be his brother-in-law. The people of Westbury did not approve. Apart from the mayor, no member of the corporation would have anything to do with the proceedings, and outside the town hall a hostile crowd hurled stones and abuse. Lopes himself was hit by a missile and some windows of his house were smashed. (The ungrateful Holmes complained of the cold while waiting to eat his dinner with Lopes before returning to London.) Shortly after Peel's return had been announced from the town hall, a Protestant candidate drove up in a coach and four. In view of the feeling in the town, if he had arrived a few hours earlier Peel might well have had to look elsewhere for a safe seat.

As for Lopes, he had mixed feelings afterwards about the transaction in Westbury town hall. Although he claimed to feel great pleasure and satisfaction at Peel's election, the disapproval of his friends had, he felt, put him in 'an awkward situation'.[63] Apparently he had hoped he would be consoled with a peerage, but all he in fact got was the consulship of Pernambuco, in South America, worth £1,000 a year, for his nephew. And he only got that after repeated reminders to Peel. 'What a torment this Jew is!' exclaimed Peel before explaining to him that he had already made three or four applications to the Foreign Secretary. Lord Aberdeen was not sure whether Lopes's nephew would make a suitable consul, but eventually decided that he could not do much harm in Pernambuco. His uncle, Sir Manasseh, died two years later without again impinging on the political scene.

When Peel reappeared in the House of Commons on 3 March there seemed a real possibility that he need never have sacrificed his Oxford seat because the King seemed more inclined to dismiss his ministers than to let them carry Catholic emancipation. His consent had always been grudging and equivocal, and the arrival of the Duke of Cumberland in mid-February may have powerfully encouraged and stiffened his inclination to change his mind. Cumberland's suspicions had been aroused when he read in a newspaper 'that most curious letter' of Wellington's to Dr Curtis, the Archbishop of Armagh. On 10 January, he wrote to his brother, the King, urgently suggesting that he should be allowed to come to England so that he could be on hand to give him moral support, if needed, when Parliament reassembled.[64] The King passed this letter to the Prime Minister. A few days earlier, on the 14th, Wellington had himself written to Cumberland, explaining why he had felt obliged to dismiss Anglesey but making no reference to the Cabinet's efforts to persuade the King to accept Catholic emancipation.[65] He was determined that the apparent success of those efforts should not be undermined by Cumberland's counter-arguments. He managed to persuade the King to postpone his brother's visit, and on 2 February Sir William Knighton set out for Berlin, bearing his royal master's letter reinforced with a firm but tactful letter from Wellington and a copy of the King's Speech due to be delivered in a few days' time.[66] Knighton, making the best speed he could through atrocious winter weather, arrived in Berlin on the 15th, only to find – 'to my great mortification' – that his quarry had left a week earlier. They had missed each other on the way, somewhere between Frankfurt and Coblenz.

The same day that Knighton left London in order to head off

Cumberland, the duke, in Berlin, received letters from Lord Eldon and Lord Farnham which determined him to go to London without delay. Both were sure that emancipation was going to be introduced in the coming session. Eldon thought there might not be time enough to send a warning to Berlin, and Farnham believed that 'every engine is set on foot to gain the consent, in a certain quarter, which your royal highness alone can perhaps prevent'.[67] On the same day Cumberland received Wellington's letter of 14 January. Although it contained nothing that could warn or alarm him, it did not deter him from what he conceived to be his duty. Three days later he said good-bye to his wife and son and set off for England, travelling through snow and ice by way of Halle and Frankfurt, crossing the frozen Rhine on a sledge at Mainz and arriving in Brussels on 12 February in time to eat his dinner with Sir Charles Bagot, the British ambassador. Bagot, who had been a close friend of Canning's, was delighted to show the duke the King's Speech with its implied promise of Catholic relief. Cumberland was amazed. In spite of all the warnings he had already received, which had sent him hurrying to England, he could hardly believe that the Duke of Wellington, in whose staunch Protestantism he had always had the most complete confidence, really had gone over to the enemy. 'No words', he wrote to his wife, 'can express my astonishment, my sorrow and my internal rage.'[68]

Next morning Cumberland pressed on for Calais. He caught the packet-boat at five o'clock on the morning of the 14th and arrived at Dover some three hours later. News of his coming had gone before him, and when he landed he found himself in the unaccustomed role of popular hero. The cheering crowds that lined the quay were repeated all the way to London. Whenever he stopped to change horses he was enthusiastically welcomed. At Canterbury Protestant newspapers were thrown into his carriage. He arrived in London late that evening. 'I am *aghast* and surprised, as you may conceive', he told Eldon in a brief note announcing his arrival.

Early next morning Cumberland drove down to Windsor. The King, not realizing at first that Knighton had missed his brother, was extremely surprised to see him. He was also very surprised – or seemed to be – when he learnt why Cumberland had felt it necessary to come in such haste in the depths of a severe winter. He vehemently insisted that all the Prime Minister wanted, and all he himself had agreed to, was an inquiry into the state of Ireland. He had agreed to nothing else, he never would agree to anything else and he was sure the Duke of Wellington would protect him. Moreover, he was sure he could rely on the support of Lord Lyndhurst, a stout champion of

Protestantism. He could not, apparently, believe that the Lord Chancellor had really changed sides.

The two royal brothers talked for six hours. As he was leaving Cumberland ran into Lyndhurst, who also seemed surprised to see him. The duke said that he could never support Catholic emancipation, and after the speeches Lyndhurst had made he did not suppose he could either. Lyndhurst, more dedicated to his career than to Protestantism, replied: 'A political man must learn to forget today what he had said yesterday.' Cumberland was deeply shocked.

When Cumberland called on the Prime Minister in Downing Street that evening, Wellington made a rather implausible pretence of being surprised to see him. Had Cumberland, he asked, not received his letter, entrusted to Knighton, advising him not to come? Cumberland replied that he had not, but if he had, it would have made no difference. He was too exhausted by his travels for a serious talk that evening, but was persuaded to stay to dinner. Although domestic politics were not discussed by the other guests, Cumberland came away with the distinct impression that the government did intend to emancipate the Catholics. His impression was confirmed next morning when Wellington did his best to persuade him that it was the only safe and expedient thing to do. Cumberland was not convinced. Nor was his brother, the King, who 'flew out in the greatest *rage*' when Cumberland told him Wellington made no secret of his intention to try to carry a measure of Catholic relief. He vehemently insisted that he would not agree; and 'that if the Duke pretended to say that such was the meaning of the [King's] speech he had *deceived* him most grossly'.[69]

The King may well have genuinely felt he had been deceived. He may have really believed that the reference to Ireland meant only what it said and nothing more. He was in the habit of soothing his various aches and pains with doses of laudanum, and if he took too many too often he naturally became rather befuddled. That at any rate was the state Lady Conyngham, his constant companion, thought he was in when the Speech was read to him. If that was so, he would in any case have jibbed more than he did at the time when he had fully grasped the implications of what he had accepted. But the presence of his brother Ernest, so much more forceful, energetic and dominating in character, must have greatly stiffened his resistance. Wellington and his colleagues had no doubt about Cumberland's baleful influence.

Cumberland had come to England to fight for the cause in which he believed and he resolutely rejected all Wellington's suggestions that it would be much better if he went straight back to Berlin. 'No one', he told his wife, 'has ever been placed in such a terrible position as I am. But God will help me and I will do my duty as a man of honour. I have only one line to follow and that is the straight line.'[70] And having heard rumours that he would after all support the government, he determined to remove publicly at the first opportunity any doubts about where his straight line lay. He did not have to wait long. On 19 February he heard his brother Augustus, Duke of Sussex, make a robust declaration of support for Catholic emancipation in the House of Lords. Cumberland was stung into making a spontaneous off-the-cuff reply. He told the Lords that the only question that mattered was whether 'this country was to be a Protestant country with a Protestant Government or a Roman Catholic country with a Roman Catholic Government'.[71] Ellenborough commented scornfully that he 'might as well have said if a drop of wine was poured into a glass of water it became a glass of wine'.[72] But word of his declaration spread fast and by the time Cumberland left the House of Lords a crowd of several thousand had assembled to cheer him on his way.

The general stir caused by Cumberland's intervention made his brother William, Duke of Clarence, feel that he must clarify his own very different opinion. A few days later, in the House of Lords, he denounced the opposition to Catholic relief in stronger terms than their lordships were accustomed to hear. Cumberland angrily replied and Sussex also joined in the fraternal fray.[73] Charles Greville found it very amusing to hear the three royal dukes abusing each other in language that nobody else would venture to use in those surroundings.[74] But to Ellenborough, more sensitive to the dignity of the upper house, 'they all seemed insane'.

Two days after the 'Night of the Three Princes', as it was being called in London clubs and drawing-rooms, Wellington had a very disagreeable audience with the King. Since members of the royal Household were assumed to reflect the royal wishes, it was of the utmost importance to the government that they should support and vote for the relief bill. But the King was reluctant to ask them to do so, and even seemed to suggest that they might vote against it. Wellington came away furious – next day Mrs Arbuthnot thought she had never seen him 'so provoked and annoyed' – and decided that he must bring matters to a head. Before leaving the castle he wrote a letter to the King, announcing that he would bring him details of the relief bill on Friday, the 27th – instead of the following Monday – and begging him 'not to believe that it is possible for the government to go on unless this question [Catholic emancipation] is fairly brought

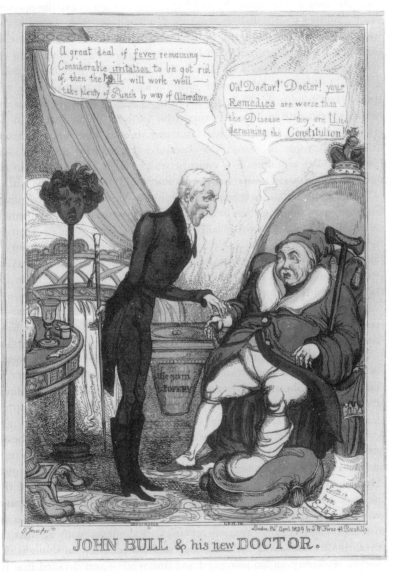

George IV, as a gouty invalid, tells his new doctor (Wellington) that his new remedy (the Catholic pill) is undermining his constitution (April 1829). Reproduced by kind permission of the Trustees of the British Museum, London.

forward and persevered in'.[75] In order words, the government would have to resign. The duke enclosed his letter in a note to Knighton, asking him to give it to the King as soon as he awoke, and adding some rather wild comments on the chaos he foresaw if the King did not form a government more to his own liking.[76] (How this was to be achieved he did not say.)

On 27 February Wellington went down to Windsor to have his confrontation with the King. It lasted five hours. The King began, as usual, by recounting at great length the story of his life, his political convictions, what his father had said and so on. After about an hour and a half of this the duke was allowed to explain his proposals for Catholic relief and why they were necessary. The King became very agitated, held forth about his conscience and his coronation oath, talked of abdicating, shed tears and at last gave way. He accepted the Catholic legislation, authorized Wellington to request his Household to attend the debates on it and promised to persuade his brother Ernest to go back to Berlin. Wellington found it all very distressing.[77] He hated having to browbeat someone who was obviously so much weaker than himself and who, moreover, continued to treat him with courtesy and affection.

In his account of these events Cumberland claimed that his brother sent for him as soon as the Prime Minister had gone and assured him that he had given up nothing.[78] If true, this would illustrate the King's painful predicament between two powerful, obstinate and autocratic men, one of whom he knew, in his calmer moments, he could not do without, and the other a brother to whom he was strongly attached and who knew exactly how to unsettle his conscience.

It was clear that as long as Cumberland stayed in England he would keep up a constant pressure on his brother, who was too weak and undecided to shut him up or close his ears to him. Cumberland was also a focus for the discontent of the ultra-Protestants and might instigate, and lend a spurious respectability to, an alternative anti-Catholic government which some ultra-Protestants might try to foist on the King. Before his audience on the 27th, Wellington had again tried, quite without success, to persuade Cumberland to go home. After leaving the King he arranged to have another talk with his brother next day in Downing Street. But when Cumberland turned up, Wellington had nothing to talk to him about except the weather and the state of the roads. Perhaps he suddenly realized that it would be useless to try to talk about anything more important.

The Cabinet met the following afternoon, Sunday, 1 March, without the Prime Minister who had gone to his Hampshire home,

Stratfieldsaye, to entertain the circuit judges. Soon after four o'clock Lyndhurst was brought a note from Windsor, asking him to go there immediately. The Cabinet assumed that the King had been unsettled by the news of Peel's defeat at Oxford and they feared the worst. Whatever the reason, the King was certainly unsettled and he may have felt that Lyndhurst, who had been so fervently Protestant, was the most sympathetic and malleable member of the Cabinet in whom to confide his doubts. At any rate, after dinner that evening he held forth to the Chancellor at great length and with increasing vehemence. Eventually he asked him to take a letter to the Duke of Cumberland. It was a typically equivocal letter, asking his brother to go back to Berlin but claiming that his mind was not yet made up and he might need his support later.[79] After reading it, Lyndhurst refused to make himself responsible for it without first consulting the Prime Minister. The King reluctantly agreed and Lyndhurst set off at once for Stratfieldsaye. He travelled through the night and roused Wellington from his bed at three o'clock in the morning. After briefing the duke on the King's unstable state of mind, Lyndhurst snatched a couple of hours' sleep and then set out for London where he arrived four hours later in time to carry out his judicial duties in the House of Lords.

Meanwhile Wellington called at Windsor on his way back to London and was received by the King in his bed. During an emotional three-hour audience the King confessed that he had tried without success to think of a suitable replacement for his present Prime Minister, and again talked of abdicating and retiring to Hanover. He also stubbornly insisted on withdrawing his agreement that the duke should require his Household to attend the Catholic debates. Not surprisingly, Wellington left the castle feeling thoroughly exhausted.[80]

He arrived back in Downing Street that evening to find his colleagues already assembled. They had heard Lyndhurst's report and were unanimously of the opinion that they had had enough and could not go on without the King's written commitment to the Catholic relief legislation. Peel produced the draft of a letter to the King which pointed out that the bill suppressing the Catholic Association had passed through Parliament without opposition on the understanding that it was the first of several measures. The Cabinet, therefore, could not advise the King to give his assent to it unless they had his written assurance that he approved the other bills and would support them will all the authority of the Crown. This ultimatum, signed by the Prime Minister, was sent to Windsor that evening.[81] Late the following evening, Wellington, Peel and Lyndhurst received a summons to appear at Windsor at twelve o'clock the next day, 4 March. 'I cannot tell you', wrote the King plaintively, 'how much your letter received this morning has embarrassed me.'[82] It was clear that he would not give in without a struggle.

Fortified with doses of brandy and water before and during his audience with the three ministers, the King was still holding out at the end of five hours. He asked Peel to explain the terms of the proposed Catholic relief bill in detail, and when he heard that the oath of supremacy would have to be changed for Roman Catholics, he expressed great surprise and declared that he had not understood this was intended, and that if he had, he would never have accepted it. The three ministers agreed that if the King had misunderstood the implications of the measure to which he had agreed, he ought to be allowed to withdraw his consent. Where, in that case, the King wondered, did that leave his ministers? Turning to Peel, he asked him what he proposed to do next day when he was due to introduce the Catholic relief bill in the House of Commons. Peel promptly replied that he would be obliged to resign. Wellington and Lyndhurst declared that there was no other alternative for them either. The King said he could not be surprised at their decision, kissed each of them on both cheeks and dismissed them in his usual courteous manner.[83]

That evening the Cabinet were being entertained to dinner by Lord Bathurst. Shortly before ten o'clock Wellington, Peel and Lyndhurst appeared and announced their dismissal. The news was not taken too tragically because nobody believed that the King could form a viable anti-Catholic alternative government.* The ministers suspected that the King merely wished to curry popularity by seeming to be forced to accept emancipation, and they had nothing but contempt for his conduct.[84] (Mrs Arbuthnot, at whose house the duke called on his way home, was outraged that the King's conscience should 'be made the bugbear! when everybody knows he has no more conscience than the chair he sits in.'[85])

The King, however, was saved from the humiliation he seemed bent on bringing on himself. Lady Conyngham, so greatly despised by polite society for her 'vulgarity' and plebeian birth (she was the daughter of a wealthy self-made merchant), was, when pushed, by no means deficient in determination and common sense. She also had pronounced pro-Catholic sympathies. As soon as she learnt that the

---

* According to Greville, after the three ministers had left the King, he sent for Eldon and asked him to form a government. Eldon deliberated, but eventually refused (Greville, *Journal*, vol. 1, p. 206).

King had dismissed his ministers, she set to work to persuade him to reinstate them. With the help of her husband and Knighton, she was successful. There and then the royal capitulation was written and despatched to Downing Street where it arrived that evening shortly after the duke's return. Since the country would be left without a government, wrote the King, he had decided to give way and agree to the Catholic legislation going ahead. 'God knows what pain it costs me to write these words.'[86] Wellington at once sent the letter round to Peel who feared that the King was trying to avoid a cast-iron commitment and urged the duke to try to get one.

At 7.15 the following morning the King was wakened by a messenger bringing Wellington's request for written confirmation that he approved and supported the Catholic legislation. With great reluctance the King gave it at once in a brief note that he wrote without getting out of bed.[87] He had lost the battle, but neither he nor his ultra-Protestant subjects were reconciled to defeat.

6

'Le Roi le Veut'

(March–April 1829)

'Really it seems like a dream! ... I must say with what delight I view the prospect of having Catholics in Parliament. I am sure it will do more for the happiness of Ireland, and for the strength of the Empire, than any measure that could have been adopted.'

Lord Ellenborough, *Diary*, 4 April 1829

Tremendous interest and excitement were created by the inevitable flood of rumours about the Cabinet's battle with the King and the likely break-up of the government. 'The degree of agitation,' wrote Charles Greville on 4 March, 'alternate hopes and fears, and excitement of every kind cannot be conceived unless seen and mixed in as I see and mix in it.' The previous day the Irish Whig MP, Thomas Spring-Rice, declared that the next four days would be the most important in the country's history for ages past.[1] Even the business community was said to have abandoned much of its buying and selling because no one could think of anything but the Catholic question.

People began collecting outside the House of Commons at ten o'clock on the morning of 5 March, and when the doors of the public gallery were at last opened shortly after six, there was such a frantic rush that in two minutes every seat was filled. In the scrimmage many got in without paying the usual fee, some who had been waiting for hours did not get in at all, others had their coats torn and everyone became most uncomfortably overheated. Peel took care to end the uncertainty about the government's future in the opening words of his speech: 'I rise as a minister of the King, and sustained by the just authority which belongs to that character, to vindicate the advice given to his Majesty by a united Cabinet.'

It was remarkable that the Cabinet should have remained united after the long hours of debate – sometimes rather heated – that had been spent on drafting and re-drafting the relief legislation. Gradually realism and common sense had replaced prejudice and fear so that – contrary to the usual tendency in such deliberations – the relief measures became bold and simple rather than timid and complicated. The bill giving civil and political equality to the Catholics gave rise to several difficult questions. In the first place, whom would it be prudent to exclude from its benefits? Peel was strongly of the opinion that the exclusions should be as few as possible in order to demonstrate the maximum trust in the loyalty of the Catholics; this, he felt, would in itself be a powerful 'moral security'. Eventually it was decided that the Catholics should not be allowed to hold the offices of Regent, Lord Lieutenant of Ireland, Lord Chancellor of England or Ireland, or any position connected with Church establishments, ecclesiastical courts, universities, schools of ecclesiastical foundation and public schools. At first the Cabinet had decided that Catholics must be excluded from the offices of Prime Minister and Home Secretary because of the amount of Church patronage they controlled. But on second thoughts this was felt to be too big a breach in the principle of equality (or equal opportunity) on which the bill was based, and it would be better simply to ban Catholics from any say in the disposal of Church property. Moreover, the title of Prime Minister could in theory be attached to any office; and the other two Secretaries of State – Foreign and War – would also have to be excluded since, it was argued, the office of Secretary of State was really one.

The second question was crucial to the acceptance of emancipation by the Catholics themselves. What form of oath should they be required to take if elected to Parliament or appointed to any office from which they had hitherto been excluded? In the past they had been kept out principally by religious tests, in particular a declaration against transubstantiation, which they could not conscientiously take. Most Catholics also would not take the oath of supremacy which included a denial of the Pope's religious authority.* The Cabinet

---

* Members of Parliament were required to subscribe to: (1) an oath of allegiance; (2) an oath abjuring any Stuart title to the throne; (3) an oath of supremacy ('I, A. B., do swear that I do . . . abjure as impious and heretical that damnable doctrine and position that princes excommunicated or deprived by the Pope . . . may be deposed or murdered by their subjects . . . And I do declare that no foreign Prince, Person, Prelate, State or Potentate hath, or ought to have, any jurisdiction . . . or authority, ecclesiastical or spiritual within this realm'); (4) a declaration against the doctrine of transubstantiation, the invocation of the saints and the sacrifice of the Mass. After April 1829, Protestant MPs still took the three oaths but the declaration was abolished.

decided to abolish all religious tests and to require Catholics to take a
new oath drafted by Peel on the basis of existing oaths which had
been introduced between 1771 and 1793 to allow Catholics to exempt
themselves from certain disabilities. The key points in this long oath
were a declaration of loyalty to George IV and the Hanoverian
succession; a repudiation of the right of the Pope or any other foreign
prince to exercise any civil jurisdiction in the United Kingdom; a
denial of any intention to subvert the existing Church establishment
(the Cabinet decided the Catholics could hardly be asked to *maintain*
it); and an undertaking never to use any privilege to disturb or
weaken the Protestant religion or government.[2]

Finally, the Cabinet had to decide what 'securities' should be
enforced to control the Catholic clergy and protect the Protestant
Church from Catholic 'aggression'. In all previous discussions of
Catholic emancipation, securities had loomed very large, both as
genuine safeguards and as sops to win the acceptance of the ultra-
Protestants. Even Lord Anglesey had taken for granted that 'the King
must have the same control as other sovereigns over the bishops
and the clergy must be paid'.[3] And when Bishop Lloyd reluctantly
accepted Peel's decision to support emancipation, he urged him
to prepare the strongest possible securities, warning him of the
'tremendous' danger of allowing the Roman Catholic Church to retain
the power it now had. 'I feel no doubt whatever that, if that power be
not *now* controlled, it never will be – there never will be such an
opportunity. And if it be not controlled, the Protestants of Ireland are
at an end.'[4]

Peel and his colleagues needed no reminder of the importance of
controlling the activities of the Catholic clergy. The methods they
discussed included the licensing of bishops and a provisional veto over
their appointment; state supervision of the education of priests; and
the payment, licensing and registration of priests. But could the
government strike a priest off the register for exercising his spiritual
functions, even if he was abusing them for a temporal purpose, such
as influencing elections? Opinions were divided and the Cabinet was
reduced to the expedient of surreptitiously seeking the advice of Leslie
Foster, a leading member of the Protestant Ascendancy in Ireland.
Hitherto a determined opponent of any further concessions to the
Catholics, Foster had become convinced of the necessity of a settlement. (He was smuggled into the Cabinet by Vesey Fitzgerald who
met him in the Park, and took him into the Foreign Office and along
the dark passages leading to the Cabinet room.[5])

In the end the ministers were forced to recognize, with varying degrees of reluctance, that the Roman Catholic Church could not be controlled without to some extent recognizing it and establishing with it a relationship that many Protestants would find highly objectionable and regard as possibly the thin end of a dangerous wedge. Moreover, every important security proposed was either impracticable, ineffective or unacceptable to the Catholics, a potential source of discord and mistrust undermining what was intended to be an act of reconciliation. (For the same reasons, any political securities, such as limiting the number of Catholic MPs, were also abandoned.) But religious securities had always been such an integral part of the emancipation debate that Peel, anxious though he was to keep the relief bill uncluttered by contentious provisos, still felt obliged to include a number of minor restrictions aimed principally at the male religious orders and public manifestations of Catholic worship. They annoyed the Catholics but in practice were largely ignored.

The Cabinet went on mulling over the details of the relief bill until a couple of days before Peel (unless dismissed by the King) was due to announce it in the House of Commons. The bill to disfranchise the 40s. freeholders – 'this most important, delicate and difficult measure', as Peel called it – caused almost as much anxiety. 'The object in view', wrote Peel, 'is to prevent a notorious abuse of an existing privilege, not to control the free expression of independent opinion in Ireland.'[6] The 40s. freeholders, it was felt, were not independent; they were either in the pockets of the landlords or under the influence of the priests. But although Tory politicians were opposed to extending the franchise, they had a strong instinctive reluctance to withdraw existing electoral rights. A vote was a form of property and should therefore be inviolate. At first the Cabinet agreed that open disfranchisement would be too 'violent' a measure; it could be attacked as unconstitutional and would create a fresh grievance. (The exception was Vesey Fitzgerald whom defeat in County Clare had made implacably hostile to the 40s. freeholders.) Might it not be better to devise strict regulations that would severely restrict the exercise of the 40s. franchise? A committee of four Irishmen (Vesey Fitzgerald, Leslie Foster, George Dawson and Lord Farnham) was set up to consider the technicalities as well as how to get round the tendency of Irish freeholders to inflate the value of their holdings. In the end, however, after long discussions inside and outside the Cabinet room, it was 'thought better to do the thing openly if it was to be done at all'.[7] The 40s. franchise in the counties would be abolished and replaced by a £10 qualification which would be established by an assistant barrister and a jury. The franchise in the towns was left untouched, and the bill applied to Protestants as well as Catholics, so that if, as Ellenborough feared, it created a 'ferment', at least it would not be an exclusively Catholic 'ferment'.

In his speech to the Commons on 5 March Peel did his best to reduce the chances of ferment, especially among the Protestants.[8] He gave a long and detailed account of the history of the Catholic controversy and the reasons why the government had decided it was imperatively necessary to get a settlement, and why there was no feasible alternative to emancipation.

> According to my heart and conscience I believe that the time is come when less danger is to be apprehended to the general interests of the empire and to the spiritual and temporal welfare of the Protestant establishment in attempting to adjust the Catholic question, than in allowing it to remain any longer in its present state.

He described the proposed legislation in detail, defending it robustly from the criticism that it conceded too much with too few safeguards, and he pleaded for an end to the mutual jealousies of Catholics and Protestants 'and that we may be taught, instead of looking at each other as adversaries and opponents, to respect and value each other, and to discover the existence of qualities, on both sides, that were not attributed to either.' He admitted that he was perhaps not so sanguine as others about the future. But

> if unhappily civil strife and contention shall survive the restoration of political privileges; if there be something inherent in the spirit of the Roman Catholic religion which disdains equality, and will be satisfied with nothing but ascendancy ... [t]he struggle will be – not for the abolition of civil distinctions – but for the predominance of an intolerant religion.

He felt perfectly confident about the outcome of that struggle, and for a reason that seemed for once to concede that emancipation was right and not merely expedient. 'We shall have dissolved the great moral alliance that has hitherto given strength to the cause of the Roman Catholics ... the rallying cry "Civil Liberty" will then be all our own.' In other words the Protestants would be able to seize the moral high ground now occupied by the Catholics and their supporters, and 'armed with the consciousness of having done justice and of being in the right', they could be fully assured of victory. Peel probably did not intend the peroration to his speech to sound so confrontational. It was perhaps a reflection of the immense effort it cost him personally to overcome his innate suspicion of Roman Catholicism in order to do what he believed was right for the country.

Peel was on his feet for more than four hours. He carried the House with him and was frequently interrupted by enthusiastic cheers. His speech was reckoned to be the best he had ever made. 'It is', wrote Greville, 'full of his never-failing fault, egotism, but certainly very able, plain, clear and statesmanlike, and the peroration very eloquent.'[9] Even the Protestants did not seem very ill-humoured afterwards. 'Such', commented Ellenborough, 'is the effect of a good speech.' As for the Whigs, Hobhouse, who thought that Peel spoke 'admirably', gave a lively account of their reactions as the speech unfolded.

> ... it was difficult to believe our senses, and that this was the Protestant champion, Robert Peel ... he rejected one security after another with the utmost courage and composure. Lord Sefton, sitting next to me, said to me, in his manner, every now and then: 'My G—! did you ever hear anything like that? There he goes, bowling them down, one after another – Wilmot Horton and all'. [Although] the disfranchisement of the 40s. freeholders was, of course, very unpalatable to us ... we cheered him long and loudly.[10]*

In the debate on that and the following evening the ultra-Protestants made no effort to restrain their anger and fear, which were all the greater after the government's virtual abandonments of the 'securities' which had always played such an important part in previous emancipation debates. Colonel Sibthorp condemned the ministers' conduct as 'a political apostasy that disgraced them'. George Moore, the member for Dublin, called the relief bill 'an utter subversion of the fundamental principles of Protestantism'. Henry Bankes claimed that the Catholics' ulterior motive was to get hold of all the property of the established Church in Ireland. Another member alleged that the Catholics would never be satisfied with what they were now being offered. In a violent attack on the government, Sir Robert Inglis, the new member for Oxford, claimed that the most dire consequences would immediately follow the moment one Roman Catholic entered the House of Commons. (Greville thought the university of Oxford should have been there in a body to hear the member they had rejected and the one they had chosen to replace him.) Lord Corry,

---

* Wilmot Horton proposed that Catholics should be excluded from voting on Church matters.

who had agreed to second the Address of Thanks on 5 February, turned round and opposed the relief bill on the grounds that it lacked sufficient safeguards. On the other hand, Sir Thomas Lethbridge, who had withdrawn his offer to second the Address when told of the government's plans, manfully declared that he had changed his mind. He now believed that the time had come to settle the Catholic question and he would support the government.

The debate was resumed next day and went on until the small hours of 7 March. When the House at last divided, the government's proposals were approved by 348 votes to 160. The majority was more than adequate, but the minority was larger than expected in view of the Opposition's decision to support the government.

The Whigs' decision had not been reached without much painful heart-searching. Their jubilation over the relief bill had been severely tempered by the plan to disfranchise the 40s. freeholders – which even Tory ministers had accepted with reluctance. On 6 March a meeting of about forty-five Whig MPs expressed strong hostility to the disfranchisement bill and deputed Lord Althorp and Thomas Spring-Rice to try to persude Peel at least to make it less objectionable by excluding existing 40s. freeholders from its provisions. But Peel would not budge. He insisted that the relief bill would be lost unless accompanied by the disfranchisement bill as it stood. When this was reported to the assembled Whigs they very reluctantly agreed to accept Peel's assessment.[11] As Brougham told the Commons later that evening, he would accept the disfranchisement bill as 'the all but extravagant price' of the 'inestimable good' of the relief bill. Lord Holland rejoiced that the Whigs were covering themselves with glory by their 'unaffected and disinterested support of the government', and he wrote to Lord William Russell in Florence to assure him there was no need for him to hurry home to support the Catholic relief bill.[12]

The disfranchisement bill created an even worse dilemma for O'Connell than for the Whigs, and it was all the more painful because the relief bill was so satisfactory. 'Great and glorious triumph', he told his wife, 'as far as the Emancipation bill goes – no veto – no payment of the clergy – no ecclesiastical arrangements.' He dismissed the minor securities devised by Peel and his colleagues as unenforceable or absurd. But the disfranchisement bill was another matter, and he ended his letter with mingled delight and despair. 'Darling, I am in perfect health and spirits. I tread on air. Oh! if I could support the 40s. freeholders! *That, that,* is the only blot.'[13]

O'Connell had never forgotten the opprobrium he had earned in Ireland in 1825 when he agreed to the disfranchisement of the 40s.

freeholders in return for Burdett's emancipation bill, and he was determined not to make the same mistake again. Moreover, after his election for County Clare he felt under a personal obligation to them, and while waiting in London for the government to announce its plans he had vehemently opposed their disfranchisement. He had even declared at a meeting of the East London Catholic Institute that if the 40s. freeholders were disfranchised, he would consume no excised articles – no tea, sugar, wine or spirits – until the law was repealed. Brougham, suspecting that the 40s. freeholders would have to be sacrificed, visited O'Connell two days before Peel made his speech and tried to persuade him to accept this sacrifice if it should prove to be the price for emancipation. He did not succeed. 'They [the Whigs] *trapped* me before', O'Connell told his wife afterwards. 'They cannot possibly succeed in that way a second time. Besides, darling, I really am too much indebted to the 40s. freeholders. You do not think I could ever turn my back on the poor fellows in Clare.'[14]

In this frame of mind O'Connell confronted his supporters at their usual meeting place, the Thatched House tavern, a few hours before the House of Commons was due to resume the debate on Peel's proposals. He urged that they should draw up a petition in favour of the 40s. freeholders and – according to the *Spectator* – even declared that he would rather risk losing the relief bill than see the disfranchisement of the 40s. freeholders become law. His more reckless supporters, such as Tom Steele, Jack Lawless and O'Gorman Mahon, supported him enthusiastically. But others took a more prudent view and it was only after a heated debate that the meeting accepted O'Connell's motion and sent a message, urging opposition to the disfranchisement bill, round to the Whigs who were debating the same issue in Burdett's house. Next day O'Connell issued an address to the people of Ireland in which he urged them not to let their jubilation at the relief bill prevent 'our decided, determined, energetic, but constitutional opposition' to the disfranchisement bill.

In London O'Connell also tried to enlist the help of Henry Hunt, with whom he had had something of a *rapprochement*, on behalf of the 40s. freeholders. He sent Lawless round to Hunt to persuade him to stir up the English radicals to agitate against the disfranchisement bill. But nothing came of this, and O'Connell's opinion of the radicals, especially of Henry Hunt, their leader, sank very low.[15] Hunt's opinion of O'Connell was no higher. The two men had different priorities and this put them hopelessly at odds. Parliamentary reform was much more important to Hunt than Catholic emancipation which, in any case, he felt was of little or no use to the starving Irish peasants. He wanted O'Connell to denounce the disfranchisement bill and seek immediate entry to the House of Commons. Fortunately, however, in spite of his rhetoric and genuine personal reluctance, O'Connell realized in time that he must abandon the 40s. freeholders. In the last resort, emancipation was his first priority and he was not prepared to risk losing it.

Nor were the Irish Catholics. Meetings were held in Dublin and elsewhere to organize support for petitions opposing the disfranchisement bill. But in the atmosphere of euphoric delight created by the prospect of emancipation, the 40s. freeholders lost much of their importance. They did not in any case arouse a great deal of sympathy – perhaps because they were perceived to be not truly independent, as too ready to obey either the landlord or the priest. During the assizes at Clonmel there was no public demand for a meeting to protest against the disfranchisement of the 40s. freeholders. 'Emancipation', wrote Sheil who was present, 'absorbs every mind and every heart, and the collateral terms, compared with the magnitude of the glorious boon, sink not merely into insignificance but into oblivion.'[16]

O'Connell also refused to risk delaying the relief bill by making an issue of his own seat in the House of Commons. The Whigs failed in their efforts to persuade Peel to alter the wording of the bill so that O'Connell could take his seat as soon as the bill became law. They raised the matter again during its committee stage, and when Peel insisted that it would not apply retrospectively, Spring-Rice made it clear, without naming names, that O'Connell did not want his own case to be an obstacle to the bill.[17] This gained him great credit and annoyed those who had always claimed that he only wanted to make trouble.

But nothing O'Connell and his supporters said or did could change the attitude of ultra-Protestants like Inglis or Sibthorp, Newcastle or Winchilsea. After Peel's speech on 5 March they could no longer delude themselves that the government would not really concede so much to the Catholics. 'The Protestants', wrote Mrs Arbuthnot a few days later, 'are very violent, and mean to oppose in every possible manner.'[18] One option open to borough patrons was to remove any pro-Catholic who sat for a seat they controlled. Before 1829 the Duke of Newcastle was reasonably tolerant about the voting habits of the MPs who sat for the half dozen seats he controlled. But when Sir William Clinton, the Lieutenant-General of Ordnance, who sat for Newcastle's borough of Newark, decided to support the Catholic relief bill, the duke forced him to resign and nominated a reliable ultra-Protestant, Michael Sadler, to take his place. But Newcastle did not have it all his own way. A pro-Catholic candidate came forward, and the seat was made safe for the Protestant cause only after a lively contest. Afterwards, when Newcastle was criticized for evicting some of his tenants who had failed to vote for Sadler, he replied: 'Is it presumed then that I am not to do what I will with my own?'[19] The Earl of Falmouth was another ultra who did what he would with his own, in this case the borough of Truro. The two sitting members, both pro-Catholics, were obliged to resign, and the mayor and corporation dutifully elected two suitably Protestant replacements. (One of them was a grandson of Lord Eldon.)[20] The practical consequences of these and similar gestures were negligible. But to frustrated ultras they were presumably both a duty and a source of satisfaction.

Feelings were indeed running so high that in the crucial division of 6/7 March there was an unexpectedly large number of defections by office-holders and others usually considered to be government supporters. One defection that was not unexpected was the Attorney-General's. Sir Charles Wetherell, vulgar in mind and manner and scruffy in appearance, was the most reactionary of Tories and the most bigoted of Protestants. Although he had refused to support the relief bill, let alone have any hand in drafting it, he had not thought it necessary to offer his resignation. But most office-holders who had voted in the minority, including Lord Lowther, Henry Bankes and Sir John Beckett, the Judge Advocate-General, sent Wellington their resignation. Some of the duke's supporters were shocked and angry at his failure to accept them immediately. But he believed he knew best and he was too self-confident to mind sending a signal of apparent weakness to his opponents. He suspected that the King would react badly to any changes in the government and he was determined not to upset him more than was absolutely necessary. Moreover, he hoped to reunite the Tory party once the divisive Catholic issue had been laid to rest. 'I am fighting this battle', he told Mrs Arbuthnot, 'for it is a battle like Waterloo. I must look only to the means of winning it and, to do that, I must keep the King quiet and the Tory party in as good humour as I can.'[21]

Neither task was easy, although Knighton's first report on the King's behaviour and state of mind was encouraging in spite of the Duke of Cumberland's descent on Windsor Castle immediately after the Commons debate on the relief bill. He was utterly outraged by the bill's lack of adequate safeguards and determined to do his best to stop it. The King, however, resisted his brother's pleas and admonitions on the grounds that he was already committed to his ministers. His resolution was presumably bolstered by Lady Conyngham, who was not only pro-Catholic but hated the Duke of Cumberland. An opportune letter from Dr Sumner, the Bishop of Winchester, also helped. The bishop argued, with considerable ingenuity and even greater faith in the superiority of his own creed, that the Catholic relief bill would be of great benefit to the Protestant Church in Ireland.[22] Wellington, who was shown Sumner's letter by Knighton, pronounced it to be the ablest letter he had ever read.[23]

Wellington was afflicted with a very bad cold – bad enough for him to be bled – and was unable to follow Cumberland down to Windsor to counteract his influence. But he was sufficiently recovered to take his place in the House of Lords on 10 March when he knew the eccentric Earl of Winchilsea intended to introduce a motion for a return of the number of Catholic priests and religious institutions. Predictably, Winchilsea used the occasion to launch a slashing attack on the Prime Minister whose conduct on the Catholic question he called 'more arbitrary and dictatorial than any act of any former prime minister'. Winchilsea's oratorical style when addressing his peers lent emphasis – if not substance – to his words. He always spoke very loudly and – according to Mrs Arbuthnot who heard him on this occasion – 'as if he was shouting to a mob on a windy day upon Pennenden [sic] heath'.[24] Wellington coolly replied that he did not object to a return of the number of Catholic priests and religious houses but he could not answer for its accuracy nor for the time it would take to compile it. As for the relief bill, he insisted, very deliberately, that he had 'his Majesty's firm and cordial support for it'. As he said this, he turned round and stared hard at the Duke of Cumberland. 'We all cheered', wrote Ellenborough, 'so did the Whigs, so did the doubtfuls, and I think since 1819 I have not heard so good a cheer in the Lords.'[25] The egregious Winchilsea had managed to lose votes for his side, and to make matters worse had infuriated them by announcing his conversion, for rather obscure reasons, to parliamentary reform. Lord Falmouth and the Duke of Richmond both assured the House that their agreement with Winchilsea's speech was limited to his views on the relief bill.

The King's attitude was an important factor in the minds of waverers in both Houses of Parliament, and Wellington's forthright declaration that he enjoyed royal support greatly encouraged the pro-Catholics. The ultras, for their part, were furious, all the more so since they knew that the King's support, if it really existed at all, was unlikely to be either firm or cordial for long. Wellington was as well aware of this as anyone. He even took the precaution of telling Goulburn, the Chancellor of the Exchequer, not to hurry with the money bills because until they became law the King would hesitate to dismiss his ministers or to dissolve Parliament, as some ultra peers were urging him to do.[26]

Some ultra-Protestant newspapers talked darkly of large-scale popular protests against the relief bill, and there were even rumours that Cumberland was planning to frighten his brother by sending a mob 20,000 strong down to Windsor. Wellington told Mrs Arbuthnot that if any such attempt was made, he would send the Duke of Cumberland to the Tower as soon as look at him.[27] But the only hired mob that actually materialized – it was presumed at Cumberland's instigation – was a group of about a hundred who assembled each day outside the entrance to the House of Lords to cheer or hiss according to instructions.

From the country as a whole the ultras at Westminster and Windsor looked in vain for a significant ebullition of popular Protestant feeling. The ultra-Protestant press fulminated against 'the Popish ascendancy bill', as the *Leeds Intelligencer* called it. Inflammatory anti-popish placards were posted up in some places. Members of the Protestant Society prepared themselves for martyrdom. 'Chains may be forged for us, we may be tortured and persecuted by triumphant popery, but we shall put our trust in the righteous cause . . .' In an extremely long and angry letter to the Bishop of London William Wordsworth gave vent to primitive anti-popish and anti-Irish sentiments.[28] And meetings to organize petitions, for as well as against Catholic relief, continued with varying degrees of excitement and disturbance.

In Edinburgh, for instance, a number of distinguished citizens, including Sir Walter Scott, called for a demonstration of support for emancipation after learning that an anti-Catholic petition was being got up. A meeting was held on 14 March in the Assembly Rooms in George Street. An admission charge of one shilling was paid by 1,700 people, but so great was the crowd and confusion that a good many more were thought to have squeezed in without paying, while hundreds were left stranded outside. Whigs and liberal Tories, for once forgetting their party labels, joined forces to support the Catholic cause, and many of Edinburgh's most eminent intellectual and professional men were on the platform or in the audience. The only disturbance was made by those at the back loudly demanding that the speakers should go up into the gallery where they could be better heard. (But the gallery was crammed with ladies.) The pro-emancipation petition approved at this meeting received about 8,000 signatures.[29] But Edinburgh had a long tradition of 'no-popery' agitation, and about 13,000 people signed an anti-Catholic petition.

Sir Walter Scott, however, was not disheartened. A week later he wrote: 'We shall all be good boys here. I think the great majority of everything like sense, or talent, or even property, is on the side of the Ministry, and though the roar may for a season be with the ultra Protestants, it will be *vox et praeterea*.'[30]

Elsewhere the moderate majority also seemed to be prevailing. When Macaulay arrived in Lancaster for the assizes a few days after the debate on Peel's speech, he found his fellow barristers all but unanimously in favour of the relief bill, and so far as he could see the townspeople were 'very well contented'. As soon as he arrived his landlady asked him how the debate had gone. She seemed surprised by the size of the majority. But when he asked her if she was against the measure she replied: ' "No; she only wished that all Christians would live in peace and charity together".'[31] She probably spoke for many.

Meanwhile, throughout the month of March the Catholic relief bill made its way through the House of Commons. Most of the arguments deployed for or against the bill had been heard many times before. But during the second reading debate on 17 March, Michael Sadler, who had just been imposed on Newark by the Duke of Newcastle, used his maiden speech to try, in an unusually forthright way, to stir the conscience of the Commons about the state of Ireland. Sadler was a Leeds merchant, trading in Irish linens, but his primary and passionate interest was social reform. (He was shortly to become a leading figure in the movement to limit factory hours.) He had recently published a book – *Ireland: Its Evils and Their Remedies* – in which he denied that the currently fashionable individualistic theory of political economy could or should be applied to the problems of Ireland. In his maiden speech he denied that emancipation would solve them either. His language was emotional and very blunt. The Protestant Ascendancy in Ireland was not, he assured the Commons, the cause of its troubles. 'Ireland, as it respects her connection with England, was a conquered country; that was her misfortune; but it has been our crime that she has continued to be treated as such.' Her lands were given to absentees who 'cruelly desert the people by whom they live, and persecute and oppress them by proxy'. The people are consigned to poverty and idleness and no provision whatever is made to relieve them. When the working classes in England recently lacked employment and bread, the demagogues told them to seek relief in parliamentary reform. In Ireland there was similar distress and the agitators told the people to ask for Catholic emancipation. What they really needed, declared Sadler, was investment, jobs, a poor law, education – 'dare to touch the culpable and heartless rich' by taxation for the benefit of the Irish people. These were the practicable means, 'though ridiculed by theoretic folly, and resisted by inveterate selfishness', which would regenerate Ireland.[32]

None of the subsequent speakers who referred to Sadler's speech suggested that he had exaggerated the economic and social problems of Ireland. But they denied that Catholic emancipation was an irrelevant issue. On the contrary, they argued, it was essential to remove the grievance of civil inequality before other remedies could be attempted.

After a two-day debate the relief bill was given a second reading by a majority of 180. The end of the debate was enlivened by an outbreak of hostilities between two members of the government – Peel and Wetherell. The Attorney-General stood in the middle of the Chamber, unbuttoned his braces and orated with such vehement gestures that his breeches slipped down and his waistcoat ran up, revealing a yawning gap which one spectator described as his only lucid interval. His harangue, variously labelled as violent, vulgar and brutal, was directed primarily at justifying his own conduct and condemning that of others. He complained several times that he had only been told (by Peel) of the government's intention to bring in a Catholic relief bill seven days before Parliament reassembled. He declared that he had refused to draft the relief bill – to be such a 'dirty tool' – because it would mean drafting the death warrant of the Protestant Church. And was he to be blamed for refusing to do what two years earlier the Lord Chancellor (then Master of the Rolls) had refused to do?

He dared them to attack him. He had no speech to eat up. He had no apostacy to explain. He had no paltry subterfuge to resort to. He had not to say that a thing was black one day and white another. He was not in one year a Protestant master of the rolls and in the next a Catholic lord chancellor.[33]

Wetherell's vicious attack on the absent Lyndhurst as well as, by implication, on Peel himself, put Peel in a towering passion. But he controlled himself and without losing either his temper or his dignity directed the full force of his cold contempt on the Attorney-General.

He did not need to make much of the delicate issue of Catholic relief. Wetherell had given him plenty of ammunition by his personal abuse of Lyndhurst and by committing – so Peel claimed – a breach of official confidence by revealing when he had been told of the Cabinet's decision to bring in Catholic emancipation.

Those who had long thought Wetherell was a disgrace to the government were delighted that he should at last have so obviously over-reached himself. Cumberland, on the other hand, told Lyndhurst that the Prime Minister would not dare to dismiss the Attorney-General because – he claimed – it would create such a feeling in the country. Wellington was not worried by the country's reaction, but all through these difficult days he was preoccupied with the importance of not upsetting the King, and he feared he would react badly if asked to dismiss his ultra-Protestant Attorney-General. He might even refuse, and his refusal would be a damaging demonstration of his lack of confidence in his ministers. But they decided it need not oblige them to resign. Nor would it reduce their authority any more than if they feebly ignored Wetherell's intolerable behaviour. So they made up their minds to try to get rid of him, and if they failed, to soldier on, putting emancipation above everything else.

In the event, the King reluctantly agreed that the Attorney-General must go. On 22 March Wellington informed Wetherell of his dismissal on the grounds that his recent conduct had been 'entirely inconsistent with your duty as a servant of the Crown holding a peculiarly confidential office'.[34] Wetherell was sacked but not silenced. He transferred himself to the Opposition benches and continued to protest vigorously against the Catholic relief bill.

Charles Wetherell was not the only thorn in the Prime Minister's flesh at this time. A more painful one was Lord Winchilsea, whose attack in the House of Lords on 10 March Wellington had adroitly turned to his own advantage. His second attack was launched more publicly in the press. On 16 March he published in the Standard a letter he had written two days earlier to the secretary of the commission responsible for establishing King's College, London; in the letter he withdrew his name from the list of subscribers. King's College had been set up the previous year as an Anglican foundation by those who disapproved of the secular character of the University of London (later University College) established in 1826. Winchilsea claimed in his letter that recent political events had convinced him that King's College 'was intended as a blind to the Protestant and High Church party' so that the Duke of Wellington (who was also supporting the new college) 'might the more effectually, under the cloak of some outward show of zeal for the Protestant religion, carry on his insidious designs, for the infringement of our liberties, and the introduction of Popery into every department of the State'.[35]

Winchilsea had already made such a fool of himself as a champion of ultra Protestantism that no one would have been surprised if Wellington had refused to take his latest effusion seriously. But to attack a man's private character and integrity was to go beyond the bounds of acceptable political hostility. Wellington felt he could not let it pass, and after several exchanges of letters failed to produced a satisfactory apology, he challenged Winchilsea to a duel.

They met in Battersea Fields at eight o'clock on the morning of 21 March. The duke's second was Sir Henry Hardinge; he brought along with him the surgeon, Mr Hume, who was astonished beyond measure when he saw who Hardinge's principal was. Winchilsea's second was Lord Falmouth who seemed to Hume to be an extremely unwilling participant in the affair. So also was Hardinge who, after measuring out twelve paces, read out a statement protesting that the affair should not have been allowed to reach such extreme lengths. According to his own account afterwards, Wellington reckoned that if he happened to kill his opponent, he would be put on trial and would lose his freedom before the trial took place. So in order not to risk this inconvenience he aimed at his opponent's legs. The bullet missed Winchilsea's legs but hit the edge of his coat. He, for his part, deliberately raised his arm and fired in the air. Falmouth then pulled out of his pocket a prepared statement which expressed regret but made no apology. The duke therefore rejected it. After some discussion between the seconds – all the more difficult for Falmouth because privately he believed his principal to be entirely in the wrong – the words 'in apology' were inserted in the statement. Wellington professed himself satisfied, touched his hat with two fingers, bade them 'good morning', and rode off with Hardinge.[36]

As sometimes happens, the resort to violence generated afterwards a little human warmth where usually none was to be found. Wellington told his Cabinet colleagues that on the battlefield Winchilsea had behaved like a gentleman and a man of courage and no one could have behaved better. And later that day, at Windsor, when the duke confessed what he had done, the King was warmly approving, declaring that if he had seen the 'atrocious' letter he would have sent it to Wellington himself.[37]

The news of the duel caused immense astonishment. Few had a good word to say for Winchilsea, but many thought Wellington should have treated his letter with silent contempt. Jeremy Bentham dashed off a very disapproving letter, beginning 'Ill-Advised Man' and asking the duke to think of the confusion into which the whole fabric of government would have been thrown if he had been killed.[38]

Wellington, however, had no misgivings about what he had done. He was in high spirits when he dined with the Arbuthnots on the day of the duel, and his hostess thought he 'seemed rather pleased at having had *a fight*'. He knew he was the object of misrepresentation, calumny and abuse from the ultra Protestants who believed he had betrayed their cause. 'If', he complained, 'my physician called upon me, it was for treasonable purposes.' By challenging Winchilsea he hoped he had cleared the air and placed his own position beyond the reach of calumny and misrepresentation. That was probably too much to hope for, but at least he had improved his own morale.

Two days before the duel, on 19 March, the bill to disfranchise the 40s. freeholders was also given a second reading. Only a tiny minority of oddly-assorted members – Tories and Whigs, Protestants and pro-Catholics – voted against it. In his winding-up speech Peel argued that 'it would be a serious objection to the proposed measure of emancipation, if it were to be conceded without an adequate security against the undue exercise of the Roman Catholic interest directed by the priests'. However much that argument may have commended itself to the anti-Catholics, it was Peel's statement that the bill was essential to the passage of the relief bill that made most of the Whigs reluctantly support it.[39]

By the end of the month both bills had completed all their stages in the House of Commons. During the committee stage of the relief bill all the amendments proposed by the ultras were rejected. During the third reading several of them – Wetherell, Inglis, Sadler – insisted on spelling out their opposition yet one more time. The Whigs, anxious not to spin out the proceedings, remained silent. When the House at last divided, the relief bill was passed by a majority of 178. Members cheered and threw their hats in the air. Before the House adjourned, at 3.45 on the morning of 31 March, the disfranchisement bill had also been given its third reading. On the same day Peel, accompanied by nearly a hundred MPs, carried the bills to the House of Lords and presented them to the Lord Chancellor. 'Little did I ever expect', wrote Lord Talbot mournfully to William Gregory, 'to have seen our friend [Peel] at the bar of our House upon such an occasion.'[40]

A few days earlier a meeting of ultra peers was held at Lord Kenyon's house with the Duke of Cumberland in the chair. Some strongly worded resolutions were passed and it was agreed to petition the King. If he would let his opposition to the relief bill be more widely known, this would stiffen the opposition to it in the House of Lords. But if, as now seemed likely, the Lords failed to reject the bill, only a royal veto could keep it off the statute book. Tories believed that the King was obliged by his coronation oath to refuse his assent to any bill that was likely to weaken the established Church, and the King himself had openly subscribed to this view. (The Whigs argued that the oath applied only to the King's executive authority as guardian of the laws already passed by Parliament.) Kenyon had already been to Lambeth to persuade the Archbishop of Canterbury to impress on the King his duty under his coronation oath. Howley himself was against emancipation, but he lacked the support of a united episcopal bench – the bishops had only been able to agree to disagree when they met to discuss the issue – and he refused to commit himself. Afterwards a disgusted Kenyon described him as 'personally very kind, but very sneaking, sophistical and cowardly'.[41]

If the archbishop was afraid to tackle the King, some of the ultra peers were not. Cumberland was often with his brother and always had a thoroughly unsettling effect on him. Newcastle, Eldon and Kenyon were among the peers who trooped down to Windsor to remonstrate or plead with the King. He professed merely to listen to his visitors, but he usually managed to convey a strong impression that he would like to get rid of the Catholic relief bill if he could.[42] The difficulty, as he was well aware, was that if he dismissed his ministers, or provoked them into resigning by vetoing the bill, he would be very hard put to find a viable anti-Catholic alternative. He might find some moderately competent volunteers among the peers, but not, by any stretch of the imagination, among the ultra Protestants in the House of Commons. When he asked Newcastle, who was urging him to dissolve Parliament, where he would find a government that would advise such a step, the duke had nothing to say. Similarly, if he vetoed the relief bill, he would lose one Tory government with no hope of finding another.

His helplessness in face of the Cabinet's determination did not reconcile the King to emancipation. He could not refrain from kicking against the pricks and pretending that he could still defeat the bill. One courtier, exasperated by his royal master's fractious ill-humour, once fled the castle without waiting, as he should have done, to dine with him; he called the King's opposition to the relief bill 'the opposition of a spoiled child'.[43] It was more than that. The King may well have deliberately emphasized his own helplessness in order to conciliate his ultra friends. Or he may have had genuine qualms about breaking his coronation oath as he had been led to interpret it. He was sick and old, and if he relieved his feelings by abusing members of his Household and accusing his ministers of tyrannically forcing the measure on him, it was , however unfair and undignified, very understandable.

Wellington, however, was furious when he heard reports of what the King had been saying about his ministers. Mrs Arbuthnot had never seen him so angry. He had always considered that his principal duty as a politician was to ensure that the King's government was carried on, preferably by ministers congenial to him. The Whigs did not fall into that category and Wellington, who also found them thoroughly uncongenial, was determined never to preside over a government dependent on their support. He was therefore doing his best to resolve the crisis without splitting the Tory party and letting in the Whigs. But the King's conduct and language seemed likely to do just that, although that was not his intention. In his anger, Wellington spoke of throwing in his hand and telling the King he must make a government as best he could without his help.[44]

The day after indulging in this private outburst, Wellington was back on course. Hearing that a procession was being organized, under the auspices of the Duke of Newcastle, to carry an anti-Catholic petition from the householders of London and Westminster to Windsor, he immediately set off to persuade the King to stop it. What was intended to be a dignified carriage procession might easily attract a dangerous mob of riotous 'no-popery' hangers-on, and even if it did not, it would have an unsettling effect on the King. At Windsor the duke had first to sit through a long saga about the amatory intrigues of the King's sisters, Amelia and Sophia, followed by an account of what Lord Eldon had said during an audience the previous day. When Wellington claimed that the real object of the proposed procession was not to present a petition but to frighten him, the King declared that he was not afraid, but with cavalry in one court and infantry in another he could defend himself successfully. Eventually, however, he approved a letter to Newcastle, drafted and signed by Wellington, which strongly hinted that the King did not approve of the proposed procession.[45] Newcastle took the hint and the procession was cancelled.

On 31 March the last-ditch struggle against Catholic emancipation was transferred to the House of Lords. Wellington, determined to keep up the momentum, successfully moved that the second reading of the relief bill should be held only two days later. Although reasonably sure of success, the government did not take it for granted. Weeks earlier a king's messenger had been sent off to secure the proxies of as many absent peers as he could find scattered about Italy. On 30 March Palmerston reported to his brother in the Berlin embassy that all members of the government had been ordered 'to redouble their attention[s] to the Tory opposers of the bill, and to be, if possible, more civil to them than to those Tories who have come round'.[46] Wellington gave a grand dinner for Tory supporters at which he dispensed gracious charm and complete confidence in the stability of his government. (But when assured that five minutes' civility could win him Lord Chatham's vote, he replied that it would take five hours and he could as little afford five hours as five days.)

A record turn-out of peers was expected and ministers were worried about how they were all to be squeezed into the modest chamber in which the Lords then held their debates. (Ellenborough also worried about the 'intolerable' heat.) Benches were placed before a blocked-up fireplace, providing twenty extra seats, and the possibility of erecting temporary galleries, as had been done for the trial of Queen Caroline, was discussed exhaustively but dismissed because it would require the King's permission – so anxious, apparently, were the Cabinet not to trigger off any further trouble with him. But the day before the debate began Wellington did, after all, write to Windsor for permission to put up the temporary galleries. The King had not the smallest objection, but the duke had left it too late; Black Rod, Sir Thomas Tyrwhitt, who was responsible for the arrangements in the Lords' chamber, said the work could not possibly be completed by four o'clock the next day.

Black Rod's authority does not seem to have extended to the ladies who had recently taken to invading the steps of the Throne in large numbers, to the great annoyance of members of the House of Commons and the eldest sons of peers who all had a right to be there. 'Every fool in London', wrote Greville indignantly, 'thinks it necessary to be there . . . they fill the whole space and put themselves in front with their large bonnets, without either fear or shame.'[47] It is not clear why society ladies should have been so anxious to endure long hours of heat and discomfort to listen to dull debates retracing ground that had been gone over so many times before. Perhaps they felt they were witnessing not only a great parliamentary occasion but a historic moment during which an issue which had periodically haunted governments and Parliaments for the past thirty years was at last, it seemed, to be laid to rest.

Wellington opened the second-reading debate on 2 April with a straightforward speech in which he rested the case for the relief bill largely on the state of Ireland. For the most part he spoke with his arms folded, without notes, 'slowly, but without hesitation or embarrassment'.[48] The Archbishop of Canterbury immediately moved an amendment which would have had the effect of rejecting the bill. A number of bishops spoke in his support. Several speakers, including Lord Salisbury who had reluctantly seconded the Address in February, said that the lack of adequate securities in the bill would oblige them to oppose it. The Lord Chancellor's speech was said to be '*very* clever and ingenious, impudent to the last degree...'[49] He boldly admitted that he had formerly opposed Catholic emancipation, gave himself full marks for intelligently studying the subject and then changing his mind, and launched a pointless attack on his predecessor, poor old Lord Eldon, who clearly had not much fight left in him.

Although there was nothing new to say, many peers still felt obliged to explain and justify the vote they intended to give, especially if it was against the bill. On the second day, Friday the 3rd, the debate dragged on into the small hours. The ultras demanded an adjournment over the weekend. Wellington agreed to an adjournment, but only until one o'clock that same day; he claimed there was a precedent for a Saturday meeting of the Lords in 1810. The most notable speech on the last day of the debate was made by the Whig leader, Lord Grey. He had decided that Catholic emancipation was too important to be treated in any way as a party question, and his comprehensive survey of the whole issue, ending with a warm tribute to Wellington, made a strong impression on both sides of the House.[50] Even Mrs Arbuthnot, no friend of the Whigs, called it a 'splendid oration'.

When the Lords at last divided, at eleven o'clock that Saturday evening, they gave the Catholic relief bill a second reading by a majority of 105 votes. It was a much bigger majority than anyone had expected, and Wellington was in high spirits when he sat down at midnight to dine with the Arbuthnots.

During the committee stage of the bill the more determined ultra peers continued to fight a hopeless rearguard action. Eldon got involved in a rather fractious dispute with the Bishop of Oxford about the degree of idolatry to be found in the Roman Catholic Church. Other ultras, more relevantly, moved amendments designed to weaken the bill or limit the damage they feared it might cause.

Winchilsea, eccentric as usual, wanted to omit from the new oath the phrase renouncing the opinion that excommunicated princes could be murdered or deposed by their subjects. He said he opposed the principles, not the members of the Roman Catholic Church and he knew several whose feelings were hurt by these words.[51] But the government would allow no tinkering with the bill whatever the motive. All the ultras' amendments were either negatived or withdrawn, and the date of the third reading was set for two days hence, the 10th. When Cumberland heard this he left the chamber, according to Ellenborough, 'like a disappointed fiend'.

By the time of the third reading the ultras had largely accepted defeat and mostly confined themselves to predicting the disastrous consequences of Catholic emancipation. Falmouth described the bill as 'the most fatal, the most infatuated and suicidal measure ever adopted by a British Parliament'. Newcastle dismissed Wellington's justification as 'perfect trumpery' and claimed that the bill 'would effect a thorough revolution in the country'. Cumberland, in a comparatively subdued mood, briefly declared that his opinion was unchanged. But Eldon spent two hours uttering his valedictory thoughts on the subject. They included a sharp attack on Wellington and Lyndhurst which stung the duke, in his winding-up speech, into an equally sharp reply.

At the end of the debate that evening the bill was given a third reading by a majority of 104, including ten bishops. Wellington did not try to conceal his delight. 'Well', he said gaily, turning to the Whig peer, Lord Duncannon, 'I said I would do it, and I have done it handsomely, have I not?'[52]

While the Catholic relief bill was proceeding inexorably through the House of Lords, a few ultra peers deluded themselves with the hope that the King might yet be persuaded not to sign a measure he so frankly and intemperately disliked. Once more Eldon, Newcastle, Falmouth and others made the pilgrimage to Windsor, armed with petitions or simply with their own eloquence. On the 9th Eldon spent nearly three hours with the King, listening to his tale of woe about his cruel treatment at the hands of his tyrannical ministers. By his own account, Eldon did not offer much in the way of sympathy. He agreed that everything was now tending towards revolution, but suggested the King was largely to blame by failing to put his foot down at an early stage, if necessary by sacking his ministers. Whether he would break his coronation oath if he now signed the bill was, declared Eldon, a matter between him, God, and his conscience. This unhelpful, not to say minatory, pronouncement moved the King to declare that if he did sign the bill he would go to Hanover and never come back.[53]

Meanwhile a plan was being laid to hold a meeting in Hyde Park on the 10th – when the Catholic relief bill was due to reach the end of its journey in the House of Lords – and then carry a petition to Windsor to be presented to the King by his brother Cumberland and about twenty other peers and bishops. When wind of this reached the government, precautions were immediately taken, not so much against the bearers of the petition as against the mob that might choose to accompany what the organizers hoped would be a lengthy carriage procession of respectable citizens. On the 9th Wellington wrote twice to the King to warn him and to beg him not to receive any petition except through the regular channel of the Secretary of State.[54] The gates of Hyde Park were locked, and Sir Robert Birnie, the chief magistrate at Bow Street, went down to Windsor with some extra police. Peel prepared to follow him next day. He even considered posting an infantry guard on the bridges at Datchet and Windsor.[55]

But most people had had enough; they realized that the battle against Catholic emancipation was lost. Not more than four carriages trundled down to Windsor on the morning of the 10th; no turbulent 'no-popery' mob cheered them on their way. At Windsor they were told they must present their petition through the Home Secretary; and they meekly dispersed.

But the King was unreconciled and dithered to the bitter end. On Monday, 13 April, his procrastination caused the Cabinet fresh perturbation. His signature to the relief bill (given, he told the Lord Chancellor, with 'pain and regret') arrived only two hours before commissioners were due to give the royal assent to it in the House of Lords.[56] The Commons were summoned at four o'clock to witness the ceremony and hear the clerk of Parliament declare 'le Roi le veut' to the Catholic relief bill.* Decorum prevented them from giving vent to their feelings in the Lords' chamber, but when they got back to their own the cheers were long and loud.

Among those who visited Parliament that day was Thomas Wyse, the Catholic landowner who in the 1826 general election had organized

---

* The royal assent was also given to the Irish franchise bill, which had proceeded uneventfully through the House of Lords, and to nearly forty other bills which had been deliberately kept back in order to force a decision on the relief bill.

the campaign to persuade the 40s. freeholders in County Waterford
to vote for a pro-Catholic candidate. Now that the restrictions against
which he had fought for so long had been lifted at last, he felt an
overwhelming sense of personal liberation. 'I shall regard this day', he
wrote in his journal, 'as the most remarkable day of my life. I feel
another man. I can look my equals in the face...'[57] O'Connell
echoed the same emotion next day when he wrote at the top of a letter
to a friend in Dublin: 'The first day of freedom!' He went on to
describe the relief bill as a 'bloodless revolution more extensive in its
operation than any other political change that could take place'.[58] He
was anxious that nothing should mar their peaceful victory and sent
word to the Catholics of Dublin not to celebrate by illuminating the
city in case it should provoke a disturbance. But he was determined to
claim the fruits of victory without delay and confidently expected to
take his seat in the House of Commons after the Easter recess.

There was a widespread feeling, not only among the Opposition,
that O'Connell ought to be allowed to enter Parliament without
having to be re-elected, although there were doubts, even among the
Whigs, about his strictly legal right to do so. O'Connell, for his part,
believed he could make out a strong legal case, and in spite of Peel's
unhelpful attitude during the debate on the relief bill, he gained the
strong impression – it is not clear how – that the government would
not stand in his way.[59] On Friday, 15 May, he appeared before a
crowded House of Commons. He refused to take the oath of supremacy and in his turn was refused the right to take the new oath.
When he had obeyed the Speaker's command to withdraw, Brougham
argued that O'Connell ought to be allowed to present his own case
before the Commons. Peel at first opposed this, but when the debate
was renewed after the weekend, he relented. O'Connell's speech,
made standing at the bar of the House, was favourably received,
but after a long debate devoted largely to precedents and legal
technicalities, the Commons accepted, by 190 votes to 116, the
Solicitor-General's motion that O'Connell should be excluded unless
he would take the oath of supremacy.*

So the first Catholic Member of Parliament in 1829 was not
O'Connell but the Earl of Surrey, the Duke of Norfolk's son, who was
elected for his father's pocket borough of Horsham. (Norfolk himself
took his seat in the House of Lords five days after the Relief Act had

---

* It was widely rumoured at the time that the King was responsible for O'Connell's
exclusion from Parliament. But there is apparently no hint of this in the letters and
diaries of those who were closely involved.

received the royal assent.) O'Connell was re-elected, unopposed, for County Clare on 30 July, too late to take his seat before the long summer recess. In practical terms the delay was not important. But in more intangible terms it was. The government argued that the Relief Act was not retrospective and therefore O'Connell could not benefit from it. But it failed to explain why it could not have made the law retrospective in the first place. It seemed to be indulging in a petty and futile gesture towards the man who had forced it into a humiliating change of policy. Whether justified or not, this impression was later strengthened by the authorities' refusal to admit O'Connell to the inner Bar when other Irish Catholic barristers of less legal distinction were given silk. But neither individual slights nor the tenacity with which the Protestant Ascendancy clung to profitable public posts – 'Protestantism was still the proper faith for place-hunters'[60] – could diminish the exhilarating sense of liberation, the psychological boost, that the grant of political equality gave to the Irish Catholics, at least to those educated enough to understand what emancipation meant.

Many of the peasants who rejoiced at the news of emancipation by lighting bonfires on the hilltops did not understand. Some thought that wages would be doubled and there would be work for all. Others claimed that they need never work again because O'Connell and Sheil would pour gold into their pockets. Some even saw the approach of the millenium. Disillusion came swiftly. The law might change, but religious, social and racial prejudices did not. Nor did men's determination to pursue their own selfish interests. The eviction of poverty-stricken peasants who could not pay their rent grew worse, not better. The pressure to pay tithes was unrelenting and the resistance to paying them grew stronger and more violent. Less than two years after emancipation, the starving peasants, without work or hope, had plunged the country into a state of near-anarchy. When the leader of an armed gang was reproached by a local priest, he replied that they hae been turned off their land and denied a living wage. 'To whom should we address ourselves? Emancipation has done nothing for us. Mr O'Connell and the rich Catholics go to Parliament. We die of starvation just the same.'[61]

The wretched Irish peasants could not be expected to perceive the significance of what O'Connell has achieved – and, moreover, had achieved peacefully, thanks to the good sense and self-confidence of the Duke of Wellington. By forcing the English government to concede political equality to Roman Catholics, he had made an essential breakthrough without which the Irish could not even hope to modify or remove English rule by peaceful, legal means. The fact that O'Connell had, perhaps inevitably in the circumstances, only limited success in exploiting the breakthrough, does not detract from its importance. In the House of Commons he built up a well-disciplined party which he used to help or hinder the Whig government which took office in 1830. He gave it invaluable support over the Reform bill and he fought it bitterly over the repressive coercion bill with which it tried to restore order in the Irish countryside. After the 1835 general election the Whigs needed the votes of O'Connell's followers to hold office. For six years O'Connell loyally supported them and in return pressed for, among other things, municipal reform and a much more radical reform of the Irish Protestant Church than the Whigs had managed to carry in 1833.* He did not get very much – a moderately satisfactory settlement of the tithes issue and a limited instalment of municipal reform. (Agrarian reforms were not high on O'Connell's agenda until the last years of his life.) In Ireland itself he had more cause for satisfaction. The sympathetic administration installed by the Whigs in Dublin Castle co-operated closely with him in making – for a time – more of a reality of emancipation by appointing Catholics to a wide range of administrative and judicial posts.

But O'Connell's most important aim was always the repeal of the Union. He introduced a motion for repeal in the House of Commons in 1834. It was crushingly defeated, and during his years of co-operation with the Whigs he did not raise it again. But when the Tories returned to office under Peel after the general election of 1841, O'Connell saw nothing further to be gained from restraint or even from regular attendance at Westminster. He embarked on a popular campaign for repeal in Ireland and succeeded in harnessing the peasants to his repeal bandwagon as he had once mobilized them in the cause of Catholic emancipation. The campaign was a failure. The English who had backed him over political equality would not help him to dissolve the Union, and he himself was not a revolutionary, however much his demagogic oratory seemed to suggest that he was.

Catholic emancipation, introduced primarily to pacify the Irish, did not bring them peace, prosperity and an end to sectarian discord. Nor did it prevent the future of Ireland and its institutions from being a perennial source of bitter conflict at Westminster. Even more tragically, the ungracious, reluctant manner in which emancipation

---

* The appropriation of the surplus revenues of the Irish Church for secular purposes, especially education, was the great stumbling block to further reform.

was conceded – as a matter of expediency, not of right – did nothing to heal the ancient antagonism that divided the Irish and English peoples.

In Britain, on the other hand, the consequences of Catholic emancipation were momentous. It did not immediately bring complete political equality – practising Jews were not admitted to Parliament until 1858.* Neither did it, as its opponents had feared, deal a calamitous blow to the British constitution, although it opened the way to the disestablishment of the Irish Protestant Church forty years later. But it removed an obstacle that for thirty years had blocked the path to the reforms that were essential to the country's peaceful political and constitutional evolution. 'This question', wrote the *Edinburgh Review* in March 1829, 'has stood of late years like a Michael Angelo in a gallery, blinding us to everything else.' Emancipation did not create the demand for the great reforms of the 1830s and 1840s – parliamentary, municipal, social and economic – but it, as it were, cleared the decks for them. It showed that the constitution was not sacrosanct, that it could be safely amended. It also contributed to the slow evolution in constitutional practice that was already taking place. The government's victory in its long battle with the King over emancipation pushed forward the change that was gradually taking place in the monarch's relations with his ministers. The capitulation of the Lords, after defying the Commons for years on the Catholic issue, emphasized the gradual shift in the balance of power in Parliament. The Lords' retreat was an important precedent, even though it may have been due to a considerable extent to the state of Ireland at that time.

But although the ultras in Parliament eventually gave way, emancipation was only passed at the cost of a damaging blow to the already shaky morale and cohesion of the old Tory party which had ruled the country almost without a break for more than forty years. Some of the ultras could not forgive Wellington for having, as they felt, '*gulled* and *misled* them'. In November 1830, when his government was in serious trouble, it was their defection that finally brought it down and opened the way for the Whigs to form a government and push through – although without much enthusiasm – a measure of parliamentary reform.

---

* Practising Jews could not take the parliamentary oath which contained the phrase 'on the true faith of a Christian'. From time to time after 1829 Jewish emancipation bills were passed by the House of Commons and then thrown out by the House of Lords. In 1858 both Houses accepted a compromise which allowed each to decide separately on the oath to be taken by its own members.

Paradoxically, emancipation opened the way to further reforms, but was itself passed by an unreformed House of Commons almost certainly against the wishes of a majority of the country. This caused the surprising spectacle of some ultra conservatives, like the Marquess of Blandford, calling for parliamentary reform on the grounds that the government had used its 'corrupt' influence in pocket boroughs to secure a pro-Catholic majority. (Peel's re-election for Westbury was also a blatant use of the old 'corrupt' system.) Most of these ultras eventually changed their minds when they realized the full implications of what they were supporting. But for genuine reformers, like the radical Thomas Attwood, the founder of the Birmingham Political Union, the passage of Catholic emancipation had a different significance. To them it was an inspiration and a model. The Irish Catholics had shown how popular pressure could be brought to bear on governments effectively and without bloodshed. The English radical reformers sought and received O'Connell's support and advice. In May 1829 Attwood told a Birmingham audience that reform was not the work of a day, but the Duke of Wellington had taught them how to command it.

> By union, by organization, by general contribution, by patriotic exertion and by discretion, always keeping within the law and the constitution. These are the elements of Reform. By the peaceful combination of means like these the Irish people have lately obtained a glorious and bloodless victory.[62]

The Reform bill was not passed without serious disorder and some bloodshed, but the violence was primarily due to the extreme economic hardship of those years.

Educated contemporaries undoubtedly attached the greatest importance to the passage of Catholic emancipation, even though at the time they may have only vaguely understood why. As J. S. Mill put it,

> ... the alteration of so important and so old a law as that which excludes Catholics from political privileges, has given a shake to men's minds which has weakened all old prejudices, and will render them far more accessible to new ideas and to rational innovations on all other parts of our institutions.[63]

In the changing world of the early nineteenth century, a 'shake to men's minds' was perhaps the best preparation the English people could have had for the reforms of the next two decades.

Notes

INTRODUCTION

1. Parliamentary Debates, Hansard, new series, vol. XII, col. 793, 28 Feb. 1825.
2. H. Twiss, *Lord Chancellor Eldon*, vol. 3 (1844), p. 39.
3. H. Knatchbull-Hugessen, *Kentish Family* (London, 1960), p. 172.
4. G. Pellew, *Life and Correspondence of the Rt Hon. Henry Addington, First Viscount Sidmouth*, vol. 3 (London, 1847), p. 349, Dr Adam Clarke, Apr. 1821.
5. Twiss, *Eldon*, vol. 2, p. 538, to Rev. Arthur Surtees, Feb. 1825.
6. Hansard, XIII, 743, 17 May 1825.
7. Hansard, XVI, 964, 6 Mar. 1827.
8. Sydney Smith, *Peter Plymley's Letters* (1929 edn.), p. 24.
9. Hansard, XII, 772, 28 Feb. 1825.
10. Parliamentary Papers, 1826–7, vol. IV, pp. 190–3 (Commons Select Committee on elections – expenses of candidates).
11. J. Skinner, *Journal of a Somerset Rector, 1803–1834*, ed. H. and P. Coombs, Bath, 1930 (1971 edn.), pp. 76–7.
12. M. D. R. Leys, *Catholics in England 1559–1829: A Social History* (1961), pp. 204–5.
13. Ibid., p. 212.
14. Jerningham, *Letters, 1780–1843*, vol. 2 (1896), p. 21.
15. R. B. Sheridan, *Letters*, ed. C. Price, vol. 3 (Oxford, 1966), p. 136, to Sir Oswald Mosley, 29 Nov. 18 [11].
16. Jerningham, *Letters*, vol. 2, pp. 23–4.
17. R. Meredith, 'The Eyres of Hassop', *Recusant History*, 9 (1968), p. 272.
18. W. Scott, *Journal 1825–1832*, ed. W. E. K. Anderson (Oxford, 1972), p. 1.
19. T. Creevey, *The Creevey Papers*, vol. 2 (1903), pp. 175–6, to Miss Ord, 5 Oct. 1828.
20. G. Carnall, *Robert Southey and his Age* (Oxford, 1960), p. 80.
21. Smith, *Peter Plymley's Letters*, pp. 9–10.
22. Parliamentary Papers, 1825, vol. VII, p. 134 (Lords Select Committee 1824, on disturbances in Ireland).

23. Hansard, XVI, 871, 5 Mar. 1827.
24. Lord Broughton, *Recollections of a Long Life*, vol. 3 (1910), p. 94.
25. Creevey, *Papers*, vol.2, p. 183.
26. D. O'Connell, *Correspondence*, vol. 3 (1974), p. 176, 18 May 1825.
27. Parliamentary Papers, 1825, vol. VII, p. 263 (Commons Select Committee 1824, on disturbances in Ireland).
28. O. MacDonagh, *The Hereditary Bondsman: Daniel O'Connell, 1775–1829* (1988), p. 218.
29. O'Connell, *Correspondence*, vol. 3, p. 340, to his wife, 9 Aug. 1827.

CHAPTER 1   TRIALS OF A SOLDIER TURNED POLITICIAN

1. British Library (BL), Additional Manuscripts, 38754.
2. Wellington, Arthur, Duke of, *Despatches, Correspondence and Memoranda*, new series, 1819–1832 (hereafter WDNS), vol. 4, p. 185, to Eldon, 10 Jan. 1828.
3. G. Peel (ed.), *Private Letters of Sir Robert Peel* (1920), pp. 103–4, to his wife, [10] Jan. 1828.
4. A. Aspinall, 'The Last of the Canningites', *English Historical Review*, 50 (1935), p. 640.
5. Ibid., pp. 639–40.
6. N. Gash, *Mr Secretary Peel* (1961), p. 453.
7. W. Huskisson, *The Huskisson Papers* (1931), p. 235, to Granville, 31 Aug. 1827.
8. BL Add. MSS 38754, to Granville, 11 Jan. 1828.
9. Hansard, XVII, 460–1, 2 May 1827.
10. A. Aspinall, *The Formation of Canning's Ministry, February–August 1827*, No. 227, to Aberdeen, 27 Apr. 1827.
11. BL Add. MSS 38754, Huskisson to Peel, 14, 15, 17 Jan. 1828; Huskisson to Dudley, 16 Jan.; Peel to Huskisson, 14, 15 Jan.
12. K. Bourne, *Palmerston: The Early Years 1784–1841* (1982), p. 274.
13. BL Add. MSS 38754, 17 Jan. 1828.
14. C. Arbuthnot, *Correspondence*, No. 100.
15. Bourne, *Palmerston*, p. 275.
16. P. Ziegler, *Melbourne* (1976), p. 97.
17. Anglesey, Marquess of, *One-Leg: The Life and Letters of Henry William Paget, First Marquess of Anglesey* (1961), p. 183.
18. Granville, Countess Harriet, *Letters*, vol. 2 (London, 1894), pp. 5 and 7–8, 18 and 28 Jan. 1828.
19. BL Add. MSS 38754, 25 Jan. 1828.
20. C. Arbuthnot, *Correspondence*, No. 99, to Mrs Arbuthnot, 18 Jan. [1828].
21. J. W. Croker, *Correspondence and Diaries*, vol. 1 (1884), p. 404, to Lord Hertford, 21 Jan. 1828.
22. Arbuthnot, *Correspondence*, No. 101, 22 Jan. 1828.
23. WDNS, vol. 4, pp. 257–8, 4 Feb. 1828.

24. Aspinall, 'The Last of the Canningites', pp. 644–5.
25. Croker, *Correspondence*, vol. 1, p. 404, Croker to Lord Hertford, 24 Jan. 1828.
26. BL Add. MSS 38754, to Seaford, 25 Jan. 1828.
27. C. S. Parker, *Sir Robert Peel*, from his private papers, vol. 2 (1899), p. 30, to the Bishop of Oxford, 15 Jan. 1828.
28. Ibid., pp. 30–1.
29. Lord Ellenborough, *A Political Diary 1828–30*, vol. 1 (1881), p. 3.
30. Hansard, XVIII, 287,11 Feb. 1828.
31. BL Add. MSS 38755, 5 Feb. 1828.
32. Ibid., to Planta, 12 Feb. 1828.
33. Hansard, XVIII, 477–81, 18 Feb. 1828.
34. Ibid., XVIII, 290–1, 11 Feb. 1828.
35. Ibid., XVIII, 641–8, 25 Feb. 1828.
36. See footnote, Ch. 6, p. 161.
37. Hansard, XVIII, 769, 26 Feb. 1828.
38. R. W. Davis, *Dissent in Politics 1780–1830* (1971), p. 215.
39. Ibid., p. 223.
40. London Record Society, Committees for Repeal of the Test and Corporation Acts, Minutes 1786–90, 1827–8 (1978), p. 67.
41. B. L. Manning, *The Protestant Dissenting Deputies* (1952), p. 223.
42. R. Peel, *Memoirs*, vol. 1 (1856), pp. 66–7, to Bishop Lloyd, 19 Feb. 1828.
43. Hansard, XVIII, 728–9.
44. Ibid., XVIII, 742–3.
45. Ibid., XVIII, 778–81.
46. Ibid., XVIII, 756–7.
47. Ibid., XVIII, 741–2.
48. E. Longford, *Wellington: Pillar of State* (1972), p. 157.
49. Ellenborough, *Diary*, vol. 1, p. 42.
50. London Record Society, p. 95.
51. Hansard, XVIII, 1194, 18 Mar. 1828.
52. Lord John Russell, *Early Correspondence*, vol. 1 (London, 1913), p. 272, to Thomas Moore, 31 Mar. 1828.
53. London Record Society, p. 97.
54. Twiss, *Eldon*, vol. 3, p. 37, to his daughter, [Apr.] 1828.
55. Lord John Russell, *Early Correspondence*, vol. 1, pp. 273–4.
56. London Record Society, p. 98.
57. Lord Ilchester (ed.), *Elizabeth, Lady Holland, to her Son, 1821–1845* (London, 1946), p. 80.
58. Hansard, XIX, 43, 24 Apr. 1828.
59. Ibid., XIX, 115, 25 Apr. 1828.
60. WDNS, vol. 4, pp. 405–6.
61. Ellenborough, *Diary*, vol. 1, pp. 89–90.
62. WDNS, vol. 4, p. 410.
63. Ibid., p. 412, 30 Apr. 1828.
64. BL Add. MSS 38755, 27 Apr. 1828.

65. Ibid.
66. H. L. Bulwer, *Life of Henry John Temple, Viscount Palmerston*, vol. 1 (1870), pp., 245–6 (Journal).
67. Mrs Arbuthnot, *Journal*, vol. 2 (1950), p. 179.
68. Bulwer, *Palmerston*, vol. 1, p. 246 (Journal).
69. Ibid., p. 250.
70. Ellenborough, *Diary*, vol. 1, p. 76.
71. Hansard, XIX, 1538, 27 June 1828.
72. Ibid., XVII, 1202, 11 June 1827.
73. Ibid., XVII, 683, 8 May 1827.
74. Ibid., XIX, 803–4, 19 May 1828.
75. Bulwer, *Palmerston*, vol. 1, pp. 256–7 (Journal).
76. WDNS, vol. 4, p. 449.
77. Bulwer, *Palmerston*, vol. 1, pp. 258–69 (Journal).
78. BL Add. MSS 38756, Memorandum, 23 May 1828.
79. Ibid., to Anglesey, 26 May 1828.
80. Ibid., to Granville, 23 May 1828.
81. Ibid., to Huskisson, 26 May 1828.
82. Ibid., to Anglesey, 26 May 1828.

CHAPTER 2   THE TURNING POINT

1. *The Times*, 23 Jan. 1828.
2. J. A. Reynolds, *The Catholic Emancipation Crisis in Ireland, 1823–1829* (1954), p. 28.
3. *The Times*, 29 Jan. 1828.
4. O. MacDonagh, *The Hereditary Bondsman*, p. 240.
5. T. Wyse, *Historical Sketch of the late Catholic Association of Ireland*, vol. 1 (1829), pp. 339–40.
6. Lady Palmerston, *Letters* (London, 1957), p. 173, 10 Aug. [1827].
7. Anglesey, *One-Leg*, p. 182.
8. Ibid., p. 178.
9. BL Add. MSS 38754, 9 Jan. 1828.
10. Anglesey, *One-Leg*, p. 182.
11. WDNS, vol. 4, p. 208.
12. BL Add. MSS 40325, 26 Jan. 1828.
13. Anglesey, *One-Leg*, p. 184.
14. Ibid., p. 186.
15. BL Add. MSS 40395, to Peel, 2 Feb. 1828.
16. Public Record Office (PRO), HO 100 / 224, to Lamb, 19 Feb. 1828.
17. R. B. McDowell, *The Irish Administration 1801–1914* (London, 1964), p. 63, n. 4.
18. Melbourne, *Lord Melbourne's Papers*, ed. L. C. Sanders (London, 1889), p. 106.
19. Anglesey, *One-Leg*, pp. 191–2.

20. Ibid., p. 371, n. f.
21. Pückler-Muskau, Prince, *Tour of England, Ireland and France, 1828 and 1829*, vol. 2 (1832), p. 83.
22. R. Peel, *Memoirs*, vol. 1, p. 38.
23. PRO, HO 100 / 22, 2 May 1828.
24. Anglesey, *One-Leg*, p. 190, 27 Apr. 1828.
25. PRO, HO 100 / 222, 18 May 1828.
26. BL Add. MSS 40325, 20 May 1828.
27. PRO, HO 100 / 222, 2 June 1828.
28. R. Peel, *Memoirs*, vol. 1, pp. 166–77.
29. PRO, HO 100 / 224, 14 Aug. 1828.
30. Anglesey, *One-Leg*, pp. 194–5, Lamb to Anglesey, 24 Mar. 1828.
31. R. Peel, *Memoirs*, vol. 1, p. 24, to Lamb, 20 Mar. 1828.
32. Ibid., p. 44, memorandum, 12 Apr. 1828.
33. Ibid., p. 56.
34. PRO, HO 100 / 224, to Lamb, 8 May 1828.
35. Croker, *Correspondence*, vol. 1, pp. 418–19, 9 May 1828.
36. PRO, Northern Ireland, D619 / 27A / 16, to Anglesey, 13 May 1828.
37. R. W. Davis, 'The Tories, the Whigs and Catholic Emancipation 1827–9', *English Historical Review*, 97 (1982), p. 96.
38. E. Ashley, *Life and Correspondence of Henry John Temple, Viscount Palmerston*, vol. 1 (1879), p. 163, to William Temple, 8 June 1828.
39. PRO, HO 100 / 222, 2 June 1828.
40. A. Paget (ed.), *The Paget Papers*, vol. 2 (1896), p. 390, 2 June 1828.
41. PRO, Northern Ireland, D619 / 26C(p. 48), 28 May 1828.
42. PRO, HO 100 / 222.
43. BL Add. MSS 40325, 5 June 1828.
44. Aspinall, 'The Last of the Canningites', p. 655.
45. BL Add. MSS 40325, 12 and 13 June 1828.
46. Paget, *Papers*, vol. 2, p. 392, to Sir Arthur Paget, 20 June 1828.
47. BL Add. MSS 40325, to Peel, 13 June 1828; Paget, *Papers*, vol. 2, p. 392.
48. Anglesey, *One-Leg*, p. 198, 21 June 1828.
49. R. Peel, *Memoirs*, vol. 1, p. 223, 23 Sept. 1828.
50. Paget, *Papers*, vol. 2, p. 391, to Sir Arthur Paget, 2 June 1828.
51. BL Add. MSS 40307, to Peel, 17 May 1828.
52. Hansard, XIX, 1292.
53. Ashley, *Palmerston*, vol. 1, p. 164, to William Temple, 27 June 1828.
54. Hansard, XIX, 1292.
55. Broughton, *Recollections*, vol. 3, p. 279.
56. O'Connell, *Correspondence*, vol. 3, p. 383, 19 June 1828.
57. C. Greville, *Memoirs* (1888 edn.), vol. 1, pp. 136–7, 18 June 1828.
58. O'Connell, *Correspondence*, vol. 3, p. 382, to R. Newton Bennett, 27 May 1828.
59. Paget, *Papers*, vol. 2, p. 393, to Sir Arthur Paget, 20 June 1828.
60. *Dublin Evening Post*, 17 June 1828.
61. BL Add. MSS 40322, 28 May 1828.

62. *Dublin Evening Post*, 19 June 1828.
63. Ibid., 24 June 1828.
64. R. L. Sheil, *Sketches, Legal and Political*, vol. 2 (1855), p. 109.
65. Paget, *Papers*, vol. 2, p. 395, to Sir Charles Paget, 23 June 1828.
66. W. J. Fitzpatrick (ed.), *Correspondence of Daniel O'Connell*, vol. 1 (London, 1888), p. 161.
67. O. MacDonagh, *Hereditary Bondsman*, p. 250.
68. F. O'Ferrall, *Catholic Emancipation: Daniel O'Connell and the Birth of Irish Democracy* (1985), p. 192.
69. R. Peel, *Memoirs*, vol. 1, p. 107, to Peel, 17 June 1828.
70. Ibid., p. 111, to Peel, 29 June 1828.
71. BL Add. MSS 40325, 30 June 1828.
72. Ibid., Anglesey to Gregory, 27 June 1828.
73. R. Peel, *Memoirs*, vol. 1, p. 135, 30 June 1828.
74. Anglesey, *One-Leg*, p. 199.
75. Ibid., p. 199.
76. Sheil, *Sketches*, vol. 2, p. 136.
77. M. MacDonagh, *Life of Daniel O'Connell* (1903), p. 162.
78. Ibid., p. 161.
79. Sheil, *Sketches*, vol. 2, p. 138.
80. *The Patriot*, 28 July 1828.
81. *Dublin Evening Post*, 5 July 1828.
82. Anglesey, *One-Leg*, p. 199.
83. PRO, Northern Ireland, D619 / 32A, 4 July 1828.
84. R. Peel, *Memoirs*, vol. 1, pp. 114–15, 5 July 1828.
85. *Dublin Evening Post*, 10 July 1828.
86. M. MacDonagh, *O'Connell*, p. 165.
87. R. Peel, *Memoirs*, vol. 1, p.106.

CHAPTER 3   SEARCH FOR A SOLUTION

1. Twiss, *Eldon*, vol. 3, p. 54.
2. WDNS, vol. 4, p. 509, Peel to Wellington, 4 July 1828.
3. Ellenborough, *Diary*, vol. 1, pp. 162–3.
4. Paget, *Papers*, vol. 2, p. 396.
5. BL Add. MSS 40334, to Peel.
6. Paget, *Papers*, vol. 2, p. 396, to Sir Arthur Paget, 8 July 1828.
7. O. MacDonagh, *Hereditary Bondsman*, pp. 261–2.
8. J. Belchem, *'Orator' Hunt* (1985), p. 191.
9. R. Peel, *Memoirs*, vol. 1, p. 117.
10. Ibid., pp. 155–6, Peel to Anglesey, 16 July 1828; pp. 159–60, Opinion of Joy and Doherty, 19 July; p. 157, Anglesey to Peel, 20 July.
11. BL Add. MSS 40307, Wellington to Peel, 19 July 1828; R. Peel, *Memoirs*, vol. 1, pp. 160–1, Peel to Anglesey, 23 July.
12. R. Peel, *Memoirs*, vol. 1, p. 162, 23 July 1828.

13. Paget, *Papers*, vol. 2, pp. 395–6, to Sir Arthur Paget, 8 July 1828.
14. R. Peel, *Memoirs*, vol. 1, pp. 146–9.
15. Ibid., p. 154.
16. Ibid., p. 165, 26 July 1828.
17. Paget, *Papers*, vol. 2, pp. 397–8, 27 July 1828.
18. BI Add. MSS 40307, 31 July 1828.
19. R. Peel, *Memoirs*, vol. 1, p. 163, 26 July 1828.
20. BL Add. MSS 40325, 27 July 1828.
21. PRO, Nothern Ireland, D619 / 26C (p. 101), 24 Aug. 1828.
22. Ibid., D619 / 26C (p. 94), 4 Aug. 1828.
23. Parker, *Peel*, vol. 2, p. 66, 25 July 1828.
24. WDNS, vol. 4, p. 575, Wellington to Peel, 6 Aug. 1828.
25. Ibid., pp. 577–8, Peel to Wellington, 7 Aug. 1828.
26. Ellenborough, *Diary*, vol. 1, p. 143.
27. Mrs Arbuthnot, *Journal*, vol. 2, p. 201.
28. Ibid., p. 198.
29. Greville, *Memoirs*, vol. 1, p. 222.
30. Wellington, seventh Duke of (ed.), *Wellington and his Friends* (London, 1965), p. 70, 28 Sept. 1826.
31. Princess Lieven, *The Letters of Dorothea, Princess Lieven during her Residence in London 1812–34*, ed. L. G. Robinson (London, 1902), p. 152.
32. R. Fulford, *George IV* (1949 edn.), p. 212.
33. G. M. Willis, *Ernest Augustus, Duke of Cumberland and King of Hanover* (1954), p. 170.
34. A. Bird, *The Damnable Duke of Cumberland* (1966), p. 170.
35. Princess Lieven, *Correspondence of Princess Lieven and Earl Grey*, ed. Guy Le Strange (London, 1890), p. 126, 13 Aug. 1828.
36. *Dublin Evening Post*, 12 Aug. 1828.
37. G. I. T. Machin, *Catholic Emancipation in English Politics, 1820–1830* (1964), pp. 133–4.
38. Newcastle, fourth Duke of, *Thoughts in Times Past Tested by Subsequent Events* (1837), pp. 70–80.
39. *The Times*, 18 Sept. 1828.
40. J. Prest, *Lord John Russell* (1972), p. 35; Lord John Russell, *Early Correspondence*, vol. 1, pp. 283–4, Althorp to Russell, 22 Oct. 1828.
41. Twiss, *Eldon*, vol. 3, p. 59, to Lord Howe [Oct. 1828]; p. 61, to Lord Stowell [28 Nov. 1828].
42. Lady Shelley, *The Diary of Frances, Lady Shelley, 1818–1873*, vol. 2, ed. R. Edgcumbe (London, 1913), p. 183, Rutland to Lady Shelley, 25 Sept. 1828.
43. Davis, 'The Tories, the Whigs and Catholic Emancipation', p. 97.
44. BL Add. MSS 40336, Peel to Leveson-Gower, 17 Jan. 1829.
45. W. Hinde, *George Canning* (London, 1973), p. 438.
46. WDNS, vol. 4, pp. 565–70, 1 Aug. 1828.
47. Ibid., pp. 564–5, 1 Aug. 1828.
48. Ibid., p. 573, 3 Aug. 1828.

49. Sir Robert Heron, *Notes* (Grantham, 1850), p. 164.
50. Greville, *Memoirs*, vol. 1, pp. 138–9.
51. Wellington, *Wellington and his Friends*, pp. 83–4, to C. Arbuthnot, 10 Aug. 1828.
52. R. Peel, *Memoirs*, vol. 1, pp. 189–200.
53. WDNS, vol. 4, p. 617, Wellington to Peel, 16 Aug. 1828.
54. Bathurst MSS, ed. F. Bickley, Historical Manuscripts Commission (London, 1923), p. 656, C. Arbuthnot to Bathurst, 17 Aug. 1828.
55. WDNS, vol. 4, pp. 604–10.
56. Greville, *Memoirs*, vol. 1, p. 166.
57. BL Add. MSS 40334, 26 Aug. 1828.
58. WDNS, vol. 4, p. 664, 25 Aug. 1828.
59. Ibid., p. 643, to R. Wilmot Horton, 20 Aug. 1828.

CHAPTER 4   IRELAND ON THE BRINK

1. BL Add. MSS 40334, 26 Aug. 1828.
2. Wyse, *Historical Sketch*, vol. 1, p. 413.
3. A. de Tocqueville, *Journeys to England and Ireland* (London, 1958 edn.), p. 138, 23 and 24 July 1835.
4. *Dublin Evening Post*, 14 Aug. 1828.
5. G. Broeker, *Rural Disorder and Police Reform in Ireland 1812–1836* (1970), p. 183.
6. PRO, HO 100 / 222, to Gregory, 2 Sept. 1828.
7. Ibid., Major Drought to Anglesey, 2 Sept. 1828.
8. BL Add. MSS 40334, 12 Aug. 1828.
9. *Spectator*, 30 Aug. 1828.
10. PRO, Northern Ireland, D619 / 26C (p. 101), to Holland, 24 Aug. 1828.
11. Wyse, *Historical Sketch*, vol. 1, p. 415.
12. Pückler-Muskau, *Tour of England*, vol. 2, pp. 118–19.
13. O'Connell, *Correspondence*, vol. 3, p. 141, 17 Mar. 1825.
14. Paget, *Papers*, vol. 2, p. 399, to Sir Charles Paget, 17 Aug. 1828.
15. BL Add. MSS 40326, to Peel, 16 Aug. 1828.
16. *Spectator*, 13 Sept. 1828.
17. Lady Gregory (ed.), *Mr Gregory's Letter-Box 1813–1830* (1898), p. 237.
18. Lord Cloncurry, *Personal Recollections* (1849), p. 332.
19. BL Add. MSS 40335, 20 Aug. 1828.
20. Ibid., 22 and 25 Aug. 1828.
21. BL Add. MSS 40326, 26 and 30 Aug. 1828.
22. WDNS, vol. 4, p. 666, 26 Aug. 1828.
23. R. Peel, *Memoirs*, vol. 1, pp. 203–4, 14 Aug. 1828.
24. Parker, *Peel*, vol. 2, p. 68, 18 Sept. 1828.
25. Anglesey, *One-Leg*, pp. 209–10.
26. WDNS, vol. 5, pp. 92–3, 28 Sept. 1828.
27. BL Add. MSS 40335, 15 Sept. 1828.

28. Ibid., Leveson-Gower to Peel, 18 and 19 Sept. 1828.
29. R. Peel, *Memoirs*, vol. 1, pp. 218–22.
30. PRO, HO 100 / 223, to Leveson-Gower, 22 Sept. 1828.
31. BL Add. MSS 40335, Thornton to Leveson-Gower, 23 Sept. 1828.
32. PRO, HO 100 / 223, to Peel, 24 Sept. 1828.
33. Ibid., Evelyn Shirley (Carrickmacross) to Leveson-Gower, 28 Sept. 1828.
34. R. Peel, *Memoirs*, vol. 1, pp. 210–18, 22 Sept. 1828.
35. Ibid., pp. 223–5 and 230, Peel to Anglesey, 26 and 27 Sept. 1828.
36. Ellenborough, *Diary*, vol. 1, p. 226.
37. BL Add. MSS 40326, 22 Sept. 1828.
38. WDNS, vol. 5, pp. 86–7, 27 Sept. 1828.
39. Ibid., pp. 91–2, to Anglesey, 28 Sept. 1828.
40. O'Ferrall, *Catholic Emancipation*, pp. 228–9.
41. BL Add. MSS 40326, Anglesey to Peel, 28 Sept. 1828.
42. BL Add. MSS 40336, Leveson-Gower to Peel, 1 Oct. 1828, enclosing Thornton's letter of 29 Sept. 1828.
43. WDNS, vol. 5, p. 62, 18 Sept. 1828.
44. R. Peel, *Memoirs*, vol. 1, p. 233, to Peel, 2 Oct. 1828.
45. Anglesey, *One-Leg*, p. 208.
46. WDNS, vol. 5, pp. 106–7, Peel to Leveson-Gower, 2 Oct. 1828; Parker, *Peel*, vol. 2, p. 69, Peel to Wellington, 2 Oct. 1828.
47. Bulwer, *Palmerston*, vol. 1, pp. 309–10 (Journal).
48. BL Add. MSS 40336, 13 Oct. 1828.
49. Ibid., 20 Nov. 1828.
50. WDNS, vol. 5, pp. 218–19, to Peel, 6 Nov. 1828.
51. BL Add. MSS 40308, Wellington to Peel, 8 Nov. 1828; 40336, Peel to Leveson-Gower, 8 Nov. 1828.
52. WDNS, vol. 5, p. 246, Anglesey to Wellington, 14 Nov. 1828.
53. Henry Brougham, Lord Brougham and Vaux, *Life and Times*, vol. 2 (Edinburgh, 1871), p. 499, to Grey, 4 Oct. 1828.
54. Pückler-Muskau, *Tour of England*, vol. 2, pp. 27–8.
55. Reynolds, *Catholic Emancipation Crisis*, p. 29.
56. PRO, HO 100 / 224, Thomas Williams to Major Warburton, 20 Oct. 1828.
57. WDNS, vol. 5, pp. 133–6, 14 Oct. 1828.
58. Ibid., p. 214, to Peel, 5 Nov. 1828.
59. R. Peel, *Memoirs*, vol. 1, pp. 243–6, Peel to Anglesey, 23 Oct. 1828.
60. Ibid., pp. 247–52 and 255–61.
61. Pückler-Muskau, *Tour of England*, vol. 2, p. 117.
62. O'Connell, *Correspondence*, vol. 3, p. 408, to Pierce Mahoney, 17 Sept. 1828.
63. *Spectator*, 11 Oct. 1828.
64. Ibid., 8 Nov. 1828.
65. BL Add. MSS 40308, 25 Nov. 1828.
66. Lord Colchester (Charles Abbot), *Diary and Correspondence*, vol. 3 (London, 1861), p. 590, 3 Dec. 1828.

67. BL Add. MSS 40308, 27 Nov. 1828.
68. WDNS, vol. 5, p. 142, 16 Oct. 1828.
69. *Spectator*, 25 Oct. 1828; Sheil, *Sketches*, vol. 2, pp. 201–16.
70. O'Connell, *Correspondence*, vol. 3, p. 421, to O'Connell [25 Oct. 1828].
71. Machin, *Catholic Emancipation*, p. 142.
72. Ibid., pp. 143 and 144.
73. *Catholic Miscellany*, vol. 7 (1827), pp. 60–1.
74. B. Ward, *The Eve of Catholic Emancipation*, vol. 3 (1912), pp. 243–4.
75. WDNS, vol. 5, pp. 240–1, 11 Nov. 1828.
76. Ibid., pp. 244–8, 14 Nov. 1828.
77. Ibid., p. 270, to Anglesey, 19 Nov. 1828.
78. Ibid., pp. 278–9, to Wellington, 23 Nov. 1828.
79. PRO, Northern Ireland, D.619 / 32E (p. 66), to Holland, 13 Jan. 1829.
80. WDNS, vol. 5, pp. 240–1, 11 Nov. 1828.
81. Ibid., p. 246, 14 Nov. 1828.
82. Ibid., p. 280, to Bathurst, 24 Nov. 1828.
83. Ibid., p. 289, 26 Nov. 1828.
84. BL Add. MSS 40336, Leveson-Gower to Peel, 17 Nov. 1828; Peel to Leveson-Gower, 19 Nov. 1828.
85. WDNS, vol. 5, p. 242, 11 Nov. 1828.
86. Ibid., pp. 254–68, memorandum; pp. 252–4, Wellington to King, 16 Nov. 1828; p. 268, King to Wellington, 17 Nov.
87. Ibid., p. 314, to Rutland, 8 Dec. 1828.
88. Ibid., pp. 366–7, 28 Dec. 1828.
89. BL Add. MSS 38757, Anglesey to Huskisson, 3 Jan. 1829.
90. WDNS, vol. 5, pp. 308–9, 4 Dec. 1828.
91. Ibid., p. 326, 11 Dec. 1828.
92. Anglesey, *One-Leg*, pp. 214–15, 23 Dec. 1828.
93. PRO, Northern Ireland, D619 / 32E (p. 40), to Holland, 6 Jan. 1829.
94. Anglesey, *One-Leg*, p. 215.
95. Ibid., p. 217.
96. Ibid., p. 217.

CHAPTER 5   PROTESTANT PROTESTS

1. Croker, *Correspondence*, vol. 2, p. 6, 11 Jan. 1829.
2. WDNS, vol. 5, p. 457, J. F. Kiernan, 20 Jan. 1829.
3. BL Add. MSS 40334, to Peel, 20 Jan. 1829.
4. Greville, *Memoirs*, vol. 1, p. 157 (Lord Mount Charles).
5. Croker, *Correspondence*, vol. 2, p. 5, 11 Jan. 1829.
6. Longford, *Wellington*, p. 176.
7. R. Peel, *Memoirs*, vol. 1, pp. 282–94.
8. Ibid., pp. 294–5.
9. Gash, *Peel*, p. 547.
10. BL Add. MSS 40334, 1 Feb. 1829.

11. Greville, *Memoirs*, vol. 1, p. 164, 25 Jan. 1829.
12. WDNS, vol. 5, pp. 453–4, 18 Jan. 1829.
13. Ibid., p. 455, Wellington to Northumberland, 18 Jan. 1829; pp. 456–7, to Leveson-Gower, 19 Jan. 1829.
14. Ellenborough, *Diary*, vol. 1, p. 305.
15. Ibid., p. 325.
16. Hansard, XX, 29–30, 5 Feb. 1829.
17. Ibid., XX, 35.
18. Mrs Arbuthnot, *Journal*, vol. 2, pp. 237–8.
19. Hansard, XX, 72–87.
20. Broughton, *Recollections*, vol. 3, p. 302.
21. WDNS, vol. 5, p. 492, 7 Feb. 1829.
22. Greville, *Memoirs*, vol. 1, p. 176.
23. WDNS, vol. 5, p. 488, to Lord Camden, 6 Feb. 1829.
24. Ibid., pp. 489–92, 7 Feb. 1829.
25. Ibid., pp. 493–4, 8 Feb. 1829.
26. Ibid., pp. 494–5, 8 Feb. 1829.
27. Ellenborough, *Diary*, vol. 1, p. 338.
28. O'Ferrall, *Catholic Emancipation*, p. 241.
29. *John Bull*, 15 Feb. 1829.
30. *Spectator*, 21 Feb. 1829.
31. G. O. Trevelyan, *Life and Letters of Lord Macaulay* (London, 1876), 1908 edn., p. 106.
32. *The Times*, 23 Feb. 1829.
33. *Bristol Mercury*, 16 Feb. 1829; Hansard, XX, 394–5, 19 Feb. 1829.
34. Hansard, XX, 610, 27 Feb. 1829; XX, 572 and 579, 26 Feb. 1829.
35. Ibid., XX, 655, 2 Mar. 1829.
36. Ibid., XX, 150–1, 9 Feb. 1829.
37. *Spectator*, 28 Feb. 1829; Hansard, XX, 422, 19 Feb. 1829.
38. Hansard, XX, 525, 24 Feb. 1829.
39. Ibid., XX, 803, 6 Mar. 1829.
40. Ibid., XX, 1315, 19 Mar. 1829.
41. *West Briton and Cornish Advertiser*, 3 Mar. 1829.
42. Hansard, XX, 704, 4 Mar. 1829.
43. Ibid., XX, 672, 3 Mar. 1829.
44. PRO, HO 100 / 226, George Drought, 13 Feb. 1829.
45. *Dublin Evening Post*, 12 Feb. 1829.
46. Lady Morgan, *Memoirs*, vol. 2, ed. W. H. Dixon (London, 1863), pp. 275–6, 13 and 15 Feb. 1829.
47. Hansard, XX, 235, 10 Feb. 1829.
48. Croker, *Correspondence*, vol. 2, p. 7.
49. Ellenborough, *Diary*, vol. 1, p. 341.
50. R. Peel, *Memoirs*, vol. 1, p. 327, 11 Feb. 1829.
51. J. H. Newman, *Letters and Correspondence*, vol. 1, ed. Anne Mozley (London, 1891), p. 200, to his sister, 17 Feb. 1829.
52. Broughton, *Recollections*, vol. 3, p. 302.

53. BL Add. MSS 40343, 11 Feb. 1829.
54. Ibid., Lloyd to Peel, 14 Feb. 1829.
55. Gash, *Peel*, p. 563.
56. *The Times*, 27 Feb. 1829.
57. BL Add. MSS 40398, [26 Feb. 1829].
58. Machin, *Catholic Emancipation*, p. 153.
59. E. M. Forster, *Marianne Thornton* (London, 1956), p. 89.
60. BL Add. MSS 40398, 1 Mar. 1829.
61. Newman, *Letters and Correspondence*, vol. 1, pp. 202–3, to his mother, 1 Mar. 1829.
62. W. G. Hoskins and H. P. R. Finberg, *Devonshire Studies* (London, 1952), pp. 413–18, for the following account of Lopes and the Westbury election.
63. BL Add. MSS 40399, to Planta, 2 Mar. 1829.
64. George IV, *Letters 1812–1830*, vol. 3 (1938), pp. 451–2.
65. WDNS, vol. 5, pp. 442–3.
66. George, Prince of Wales, *Correspondence 1770–1812*, vol. 8, ed. A. Aspinall (Cambridge, 1971), p. 479; WDNS, vol. 5, pp. 482–3, Wellington to Cumberland, 2 Feb. 1829.
67. Willis, *Cumberland*, p. 174.
68. Ibid., p. 175.
69. Ibid., p. 179.
70. Ibid., p. 178.
71. Hansard, XX, 398, 19 Feb. 1829.
72. Ellenborough, *Diary*, vol. 1, p. 352.
73. Hansard, XX, 472–8, 23 Feb. 1829.
74. Greville, *Memoirs*, vol. 1, p. 181.
75. WDNS, vol. 5, p. 509, 25 Feb. 1829.
76. George IV, *Letters*, vol. 3, pp. 454–5.
77. Mrs Arbuthnot, *Journal*, vol. 2, pp. 245–6.
78. Willis, *Cumberland*, p. 186.
79. George, Prince of Wales, *Correspondence*, vol. 8, pp. 480–1, 1 Mar. 1829.
80. Ellenborough, *Diary*, vol. 1, pp. 371–4.
81. WDNS, vol. 5, pp. 515–16, 2 Mar. 1829.
82. Ibid., p. 517, 3 Mar. 1829.
83. R. Peel, *Memoirs*, vol. 1, pp. 343–7.
84. Ellenborough, *Diary*, vol. 1, pp. 376–7.
85. Mrs Arbuthnot, *Journal*, vol. 2, p. 248.
86. WDNS, vol. 5, p. 518, 4 Mar. 1829 (8 p.m.).
87. Ibid., p. 518, 5 Mar. 1829 (7.15 a.m.).

CHAPTER 6 'LE ROI LE VEUT'

1. Greville, *Memoirs*, vol. 1, pp. 186–7.
2. Hansard, XX, 760–1, 5 Mar. 1829.
3. PRO, Northern Ireland, D.619 / 26Cii (p. 48), to Holland, 1 July 1828.

4. BL Add. MSS 40343, Feb. 1829.
5. Ellenborough, *Diary*, vol. 1, p. 323.
6. BL Add. MSS 40323, to Vesey Fitzgerald, 27 Jan. 1829.
7. Ellenborough, *Diary*, vol. 1, p. 350.
8. Hansard, XX, 729–80, 5 Mar. 1829.
9. Greville, *Memoirs*, vol. 1, p. 188.
10. Broughton, *Recollections*, vol. 3, pp. 308–9.
11. Austin Mitchell, *The Whigs in Opposition 1815–1830* (Oxford, 1967), p. 215; Mrs Arbuthnot, *Journal*, vol. 2, p. 250.
12. Georgiana Blakiston, *Lord William Russell and his Wife 1815–1846* (London, 1972), p. 188, 10 Mar. 1829.
13. O'Connell, *Correspondence*, vol. 4, p. 20, 6 Mar. 1829.
14. Ibid., p. 16, 3 Mar. 1829.
15. Ibid., p. 27, O'Connell to E. Dwyer, 10 Mar. 1829.
16. BL Add. MSS 40399, to Curran, 28 Mar. 1829.
17. Hansard, XX, 1406, 23 Mar. 1829.
18. Mrs Arbuthnot, *Journal*, vol. 2, p. 251.
19. J. Golby, 'A Great Electioneer and his Motives: The Fourth Duke of Newcastle', *Historical Journal*, 8 (1965), p. 204.
20. *West Briton and Cornish Advertiser*, 13 Mar. 1829.
21. Mrs Arbuthnot, *Journal*, vol. 2, p. 251.
22. George IV, *Letters*, vol. 3, pp. 455–6, 9 Mar. 1829.
23. Mrs Arbuthnot, *Journal*, vol. 2, p. 252.
24. Ibid., p. 252.
25. Ellenborough, *Diary*, vol. 1, p. 387.
26. Ibid., p. 398.
27. Mrs Arbuthnot, *Journal*, vol. 2, p. 254.
28. W. Wordsworth, *Letters of William and Dorothy Wordsworth. The Later Years*, vol. 1, ed. E. de Selincourt (Oxford, 1939), pp. 356–67, 3 Mar. 1829.
29. H. Cockburn, *Memorials of his Time* (Chicago edn., 1974), pp. 427–8; *Edinburgh Evening Courant*, 16 Mar. 1829.
30. W. Scott, *Letters*, vol. 11, ed. H. C. Grierson (London, 1936), p. 154, to Croker, 21 Mar. 1829.
31. Trevelyan, *Macaulay*, p. 109, to his father, 14 Mar. 1829.
32. Hansard, XX, 1151–4, 17 Mar. 1829.
33. Ibid., XX, 1263, 18 Mar. 1829.
34. WDNS, vol. 5, pp. 547–8.
35. Ibid., pp. 526–7.
36. Ibid., pp. 539–45, J. R. Hume to Duchess of Wellington, 21 Mar. 1829; Ellenborough, *Diary*, vol. 1, p. 403; Greville, *Memoirs*, vol. 1, pp. 196–8.
37. Ellenborough, *Diary*, vol. 1, p. 404.
38. WDNS, vol. 5, pp. 546–7, 22 Mar. 1829.
39. Hansard, XX, 1356–63, 19 Mar. 1829.
40. Lady Gregory, *William Gregory's Letter-Box*, p. 310, 1 Apr. 1829.
41. Machin, *Catholic Emancipation*, p. 176, n. 2.
42. Colchester, *Diary*, vol. 3, p. 607, 14 Mar. 1829.

43. Greville, *Memoirs*, vol. 1, pp. 201–2.
44. Mrs Arbuthnot, *Journal*, vol. 2, p. 261.
45. Ibid., pp. 262–3.
46. Bulwer, *Palmerston*, vol. 1, p. 328, to William Temple, 30 Mar. 1829.
47. Greville, *Memoirs*, vol. 1, p. 203.
48. Broughton, *Recollections*, vol. 3, p. 315.
49. Mrs Arbuthnot, *Journal*, vol. 2, p. 264.
50. Hansard, XXI, 319–48, 4 Apr. 1829.
51. Ibid., XXI, 521–2, 7 Apr. 1829.
52. Broughton, *Recollections*, vol. 3, p. 318.
53. Twiss, *Eldon*, vol. 3, pp. 86–7, memorandum.
54. WDNS, vol. 5, pp. 577–8.
55. BL Add. MSS 40399, Peel to Hobhouse, 7 Apr. 1829.
56. WDNS, vol. 5, p. 580, 13 Apr. 1829 (10 a.m.).
57. J. J. Auchmuty, *Sir Thomas Wyse (1741–1862)* (1939), p. 118.
58. O'Connell, *Correspondence*, vol. 4, p. 45, to E. Dwyer, 14 Apr. 1829.
59. Ibid., pp. 57–8, to J. Sugrue, 13 May 1829.
60. Cloncurry, *Personal Recollections*, p. 342.
61. De Tocqueville, *Journeys to England and Ireland*, p. 132.
62. Reynolds, *Catholic Emancipation*, p. 174.
63. J. S. Mill, *Collected Works*, vol. 12, ed. F. E. Mineka (Toronto, 1963), p. 28, to Gustave d'Eichtal, 11 Mar. 1829.

Select Bibliography

Manuscript Sources

British Library (BL) Additional Manuscripts: Huskisson, Peel MSS.
Public Record Office (PRO): Home Office, Ireland.
Public Record Office (PRO), Northern Ireland: Anglesey MSS.
Thesis: G. F. A. Best, 'Church and State in English Politics' (Cambridge University Ph.D. thesis, 1955.)

Published Sources

(This is not intended to be a comprehensive list of either the works of modern authorities or contemporary biographies, memoirs and journals.)

Anglesey, Marquess of, *One-Leg: The Life and Letters of Henry William Paget, First Marquess of Anglesey, KG, 1768–1854*, London, 1961.
Arbuthnot, C., *Correspondence 1808–1850*, ed. A. Aspinall, Royal Historical Society, Camden, 3rd series, vol. 65 (1941).
Arbuthnot, Mrs, *Journal*, vol. 2, ed. Francis Bamford and Duke of Wellington, London, 1950.
Ashley, E., *Life and Correspondence of Henry John Temple, Viscount Palmerston*, vol. 1, London, 1879.
Aspinall, A., 'The Last of the Canningites', *English Historical Review*, 50 (1935), pp. 639 ff.
Aspinall, A., *The Formation of Canning's Ministry, February–August 1827*, Royal Historical Society, Camden, 3rd series, vol. 59 (1937).
Auchmuty, J. J., *Sir Thomas Wyse (1741–1862)*, London, 1939.
Aveling, J. C. H., *The Handle and the Axe: The Catholic Recusants in England from Reformation to Emancipation*, London, 1976.
Belchem, J., *'Orator' Hunt: Henry Hunt and English Working-Class Radicalism*, Oxford, 1985.
Best, G. F. A., 'The Protestant Constitution and its Supporters 1820–29',

Transactions of Royal Historical Society, 5th series, vol. 8 (1958), pp. 105 ff.

Best, G. F. A., 'The Constitutional Revolution, 1828–32, and its Consequences for the Established Church', *Theology*, 62 (1959), pp. 226 ff.

Bird, A., *The Damnable Duke of Cumberland*, London, 1966.

Bossy, J., *The English Catholic Community 1570–1850*, London, 1975.

Bourne, K., *Palmerston: The Early Years 1784–1841*, London, 1982.

Brock, M., *The Great Reform Act*, London, 1973.

Broeker, G., *Rural Disorder and Police Reform in Ireland 1812–36*, London, 1970.

Brose, O. J., *Church and Parliament: The Reshaping of the Church of England 1828–1860*, Stanford / London, 1959.

Broughton, Lord (John Cam Hobhouse), *Recollections of a Long Life*, vol. 3, London, 1910.

Brown, T. N., 'Nationalism and the Irish Peasant 1800–1848', *Review of Politics*, 15 (1953), pp. 403 ff.

Bulwer, H. L. (Lord Dalling), *Life of Henry John Temple, Viscount Palmerston*, vol. 1, London, 1870.

Chadwick, O., *The Victorian Church*, vol. 1, London, 1966.

Cloncurry, Lord, *Personal Recollections*, Dublin, 1849.

Creevey, T., *The Creevey Papers*, vol. 2, ed. Sir H. Maxwell, London, 1903.

Croker, J. W., *Correspondence and Diaries*, vols 1 and 2, ed. L. J. Jennings, London, 1884.

Davis, R. W., *Dissent in Politics 1780–1830: The Political Life of William Smith MP*, London, 1971.

Davis, R. W., 'The Tories, the Whigs and Catholic Emancipation 1827–1829', *English Historical Review*, 97 (1982), pp. 89 ff.

Ellenborough, Lord, *A Political Diary 1828–30*, 2 vols, London, 1881.

Fulford, R., *George IV*, London, 1935 (2nd edn. 1949).

Gash, N., *Mr Secretary Peel: The Life of Mr Robert Peel to 1830*, London, 1961.

George IV, *Letters 1812–1830*, vol. 3, ed. A. Aspinall, Cambridge, 1938.

Golby, J., 'A Great Electioneer and his Motives: The Fourth Duke of Newcastle', *Historical Journal*, 8 (1965), pp. 201 ff.

Gregory, Lady (ed.), *Mr Gregory's Letter-Box 1813–1830*, London, 1898.

Greville, C., *Memoirs*, vol. 1, ed. H. Reeve, London, 1888.

Gwynn, D., *The Struggle for Catholic Emancipation (1750–1829)*, London, 1928.

Henriques, U., *Religious Toleration in England 1787–1833*, London, 1961.

Hexter, J. H., 'The Protestant Revival and the Catholic Question in England, 1778–1829', *Journal of Modern History*, 8 (1936), pp. 297 ff.

Hibbert, C., *George IV: Regent and King 1811–1830*, London, 1973.

Huskisson, W., *The Huskisson Papers*, ed. L. Melville, London, 1931.

Jerningham, *Letters*, vol. 2, ed. Egerton Castle, London, 1896.

Leys, M. D. R., *Catholics in England 1559–1829: A Social History*, London, 1961.

Linker, R. W., 'The English Roman Catholics and Emancipation: The Politics of Persuasion', *Journal of Ecclesiastical History*, 27 (1976), pp. 151 ff.

London Record Society, *Committees for Repeal of the Test and Corporation Acts. Minutes 1786–90, 1827–28*, ed. T. W. Davis, London, 1978.

Longford, E., *Wellington: Pillar of State*, London, 1972.

McCullagh, W. Torrens, *Memoirs of Richard Lalor Sheil*, 2 vols, London, 1855.

MacDonagh, M., *The Life of Daniel O'Connell*, London, 1903.

MacDonagh, O., *The Hereditary Bondsman: Daniel O'Connell, 1775–1829*, London, 1988.

McDowell, R. B., *Public Opinion and Government Policy in Ireland 1801–1846*, London, 1952.

Machin, G. I. T., 'The Duke of Wellington and Catholic Emancipation', *Journal of Ecclesiastical History*, 14 (1963), pp. 190 ff.

Machin, G. I. T., 'The No-Popery Movement in Britain in 1828–9', *Historical Journal*, 6 (1963), pp. 193 ff.

Machin, G. I. T., *Catholic Emancipation in English Politics, 1820–1830*, Oxford, 1964.

Machin, G. I. T., 'Resistance to Repeal of the Test and Corporation Acts, 1828', *Historical Journal*, 22 (1979), pp. 115 ff.

Macintyre, A., *The Liberator: Daniel O'Connell and the Irish Party 1830–1847*, London, 1965.

Manning, B. L., *The Protestant Dissenting Deputies*, Cambridge, 1952.

Newcastle, Duke of, *Thoughts in Times Past Tested by Subsequent Events*, London, 1837.

Nowlan, K. B. and O'Connell, M. R. (eds), *Daniel O'Connell: Portrait of a Radical*, Belfast, 1984.

O'Connell, D., *Correspondence*, vols 3 and 4, ed. M. R. O'Connell, Dublin, 1974 and 1977.

O'Farrell, P., *Ireland's English Question: Anglo–Irish Relations 1534–1970*, London, 1971.

O'Ferrall, F., *Catholic Emancipation: Daniel O'Connell and the Birth of Irish Democracy, 1820–1830*, Dublin, 1985.

Paget, A. (ed.), *The Paget Papers*, vol. 2, London, 1896.

Parker, C. S., *Sir Robert Peel, from his private papers*, vol. 2, London, 1899.

Parliamentary Debates, Hansard, new series.

Parliamentary Papers, Select Committee Reports:
  1825, VII (Lords), Disturbances in Ireland.
  1825, VII (Commons), Disturbances in Ireland.
  1826–7, IV (Commons), Elections – Expenses of Candidates.

Peel, G., *Private Letters of Sir Robert Peel*, London, 1920.

Peel, R., *Memoirs*, vol. 1, *The Roman Catholic Question, 1828–9*, London, 1856.

Prest, J., *Lord John Russell*, London, 1972.

Pückler-Muskau, Prince, *Tour of England, Ireland and France, 1828 and 1829, by a German Prince*, trans. by S. Austin, 4 vols, London, 1832.

Reynolds, J. A., *The Catholic Emancipation Crisis in Ireland, 1823–1829*, Yale, 1954.

Sheil, R. L., *Sketches, Legal and Political*, 2 vols, ed. M. W. Savage, London, 1855.

Smith, S., *Peter Plymley's Letters with Selected Writings*, London, 1929.

Thompson, N., *Wellington after Waterloo*, London, 1986.

Trench, C. C., *The Great Dan, A Biography of Daniel O'Connell*, London, 1984.

Twiss, H., *Lord Chancellor Eldon*, vols 2 and 3, London, 1844.

Ward, B., *The Eve of Catholic Emancipation*, vol. 3, London, 1912.

Wellington, Arthur, Duke of, *Despatches, Correspondence and Memoranda*, new series, 1819–1832, 8 vols, London, 1867–80.

Western, J. R., 'Roman Catholics Holding Military Commissions in 1798', *English Historical Review*, 70 (1955), pp. 428 ff.

Willis, G. M., *Ernest Augustus, Duke of Cumberland and King of Hanover*, London, 1954.

Wyse, T., *Historical Sketch of the late Catholic Association of Ireland*, 2 vols, London, 1829.

Ziegler, P., *Melbourne, A Biography of William Lamb, 2nd Viscount Melbourne*, London, 1976.

Index